THE PASSION
OF BEING WOMAN

THE PASSION
OF BEING
WOMAN

A LOVE STORY FROM THE PAST
FOR THE
TWENTY-FIRST CENTURY

MARY HUGH SCOTT

MacMurray & Beck Communications
Aspen, Colorado

Copyright © 1991 by Mary Hugh Scott
Published by:
MacMurray & Beck Communications
P.O. Box 4257
Aspen, CO 81612

Printed and Bound in the United States of America

Designed by Pam Wilson
Cover Art: Gustav Klimt, *Love*
Kunsthistorisches Museum, Vienna
Bridgeman/Art Resource, NY

Library of Congress Catalog Card Number: 91-62265

Publisher's Cataloging in Publication
(Prepared by Quality Books Inc.)

Scott, Mary Hugh, 1933-
    The passion of being woman : a love story from the past for the
21st century / by Mary Hugh Scott. --
    p. cm.
    Includes bibliographical references and index.
    ISBN 1-878448-50-1 (cloth)
    ISBN 1-878448-51-X (pbk.)
    1. Patriarchy.   2. Feminism--Philosophy.   3. Mythology, Greek.
I. Title.

HQ1399   305.3
                                    QBI91-1296
                                    MARC

CONTENTS

DEDICATION

This book is dedicated to the glory of Christ
and in memory of
my mother, Agnes Louise Cullen Arnold;
my sister, Wilhelmina Ann Arnold Barnhart;
my grandmothers, Elizabeth MacMurray Arnold
and Lilly Cranz Cullen;
my great grandmothers, Agnes Kessler Cranz
and Louise Beck (Cullen);
and the legacy of their loving passionately and
their thinking independently.

ACKNOWLEDGMENTS

First and foremost I wish to acknowledge that without Dr. Richard Corriere I could not have written this book. With all my heart I thank him for his steadfast friendship, astute coaching, years of patient editing, and always his staunch encouragement. His loyalty and loving guidance are indeed beyond the limits of what we think of as dedication.

I wish to acknowledge with a grateful heart all my friends, including my Houston and Aspen prayer groups. These women have taught me so much about the beauty and dignity, the laughter and great courage, in being woman that they rank above even the greatest teachers of all the saints. I also wish to thank my Aspen reading group. They have so patiently listened to the seemingly endless versions of this manuscript that surely it has won them their sainthood!

With pleasure I acknowledge Lorelei Bosserman who over two years did the final editing. I want to thank her for her competence and precision. But I want to thank her most of all for her camaraderie and sense of humor that allowed us to work together so compatibly that the results were often much more than the sum of the parts.

I want to acknowledge and thank my husband, Russell, for his teaching the little girl I was how to become a grown-up lady, conscious of her self, her world, and her erotic love; and my grandson, Andrew, for his boundless enthusiasm and wealth of ideas. And I want to thank them both most particularly for their patience and for allowing Psyche and Eros to become part of our family.

And finally I want to acknowledge the Holy Spirit Who has guided and guarded me for over half a century and Who has inspired whatever insights I may have gleaned through living the life It has given me. With humble heart and joyful spirit I give thanks for my creation, preservation, and all the blessings of this life.

PREVIEW

Everyman and everywoman knows what it feels like to be unhappy. Yet the "solutions" that they think will make them happy seldom do. What few women (and fewer men) realize is that there are four tasks that women must accomplish in order to end their unhappiness. And what almost no one knows is that men need women who have completed these tasks. Only such a woman can challenge and encourage a man to develop fully his masculinity (which will end his unhappiness).

This book looks at the ache in women's hearts and the emptiness in men's from a different perspective—the perspective of myths and symbols. Symbols represent, express, or identify those aspects of our lives that are invisible and intangible. We use them all the time. Symbols have the ability to arouse feelings as well as express them.

Myths and symbols profoundly influence the way people think and feel. By learning to listen to them, we can change their power to influence into the power to teach. Myths are like dreams, they tell us a whole lot about ourselves but we have to figure out what they mean. Every culture contains the seeds of its destruction and the seeds of its redemption. So myths can often show us, in the same manner that dreams do, what the problem is and how to overcome it. But myths, like dreams, need to be interpreted in order to help us. This book is the author's interpretation of what the myth of Psyche and Eros has to say to us men and women as we face the twenty-first century.

About 2500 years ago in what we call "Western culture" a myth evolved because, like today, people were unhappy. Both men and women were having trouble being as sexual and as spiritual as they could be. This myth was about a woman named Psyche, and the god of love, Eros, who fell in love with her. But in order to love Psyche, Eros had to become a man: he had to assume human flesh.

Psyche and Eros were super beautiful, super wonderful, and super smart. Yet they were caught in the same trap in which we everyday people are ensnared, the trap which makes both sexes so unhappy. The problem was not that they needed to be more understanding or more self-sufficient or more able to relate to others. Being super anything was not the solution. What Eros and Psyche needed was a different way of thinking and feeling, being and doing, loving and living.

The love story of Psyche and Eros is the story of a woman who, by her courage to love passionately and sexually, found a different approach to the problem of being human. Because she refused to give her self up, renege on her impassioned love and return to respectability, a new reality unfolded for both Psyche and Eros—a reality they experienced as passionate love, as freedom, as fulfillment, and as joy. And this new reality can produce happiness for everywoman and everyman who want to enter it. But the price is high! And worth it.

In the myth Eros fell madly in love with Psyche. After he had courted her—wooed her with his masculine passion— she fell madly in love with him. Their love, like all erotic love, was intense and glorious. But their relationship began to deteriorate for reasons which neither of them understood. This was not acceptable to Psyche. She did not like feeling unhappy, afraid, and unfulfilled. Psyche had to face the fact that she was living her life as only a part of the spiritual and sexual person she could be. And the consequence of living this way would be the death of her soul.

To claim her divinely given right to know her self, her man, and the meaning of love, and to become who she could be and enjoy her erotic love, Psyche had to disobey what she and Eros had been taught was right and good and true. She had to experience panic and bear the wrath of the culture that condemned her. In order to develop the self she had found and regain her erotic love, Psyche gambled and undertook four high-risk tasks. And so must every woman who wants to be happy.

The first task helps a woman learn how to differentiate who she is and what she needs and wants from what everyone else tells her she should be. This task is called sorting the seeds.

The second task shows a woman where to find her self-worth and power—and how to obtain it without killing her femininity. In this process she learns to use her feminine strengths and virtues as well as her masculine ones. This task is called gathering the golden fleece.

The third task teaches a woman how to reclaim her feminine spirit from all of the causes and people to whom she has given it. She learns how to forget consciously everything that stops her growth and diminishes her happiness. This task is called filling the crystal vessel with the water from the fountain of forgetfulness.

The fourth task shows a woman how to get in touch with her deepest feminine self in order to transform her mistakes and painful memories into creative adventures. This last task, the most demanding and dangerous of all, is called the descent into hell.

Because Psyche chose the way of erotic love, risking her life in order to sustain it, she changed the rules. She rediscovered an ancient but long hidden way of thinking and feeling, being and doing, loving and living—a way which frees both men and women from their unhappiness so they can become the persons they were created to be. But Psyche had to go beyond her accomplished tasks in order to claim her wholehearted and whole-souled womanhood. She had to be willing to fail, to lose everything for the sake of her love—even her heart's dearest desire, the man she wanted.

Only such a woman can reestablish the worth of the Feminine, bringing into her life the combined joys of sexuality and spirituality. Only she who has dared to descend into the depths and bring into consciousness the immortal beauty of being woman can restore to men the power of their masculinity. Only she who has risked her life and her heart's dearest desire can reinstate the authority of erotic love, the love that draws the opposites together, connecting heart to heart and body to body.

As you follow Psyche's story you will go with her from her initial hopelessness and despair to an ending that surprised everyone. And you will go with Eros from his initial sense of betrayal and fury, his pain and denial of his inadequacies as a man, to his full and abundant love for his masculinity. Such exuberant masculinity can only be discovered when man consciously and passionately values the Feminine as much as he does his own life. Fully man, Eros expressed his love for his own masculinity in his passionate desire for the woman he loved. And in the myth's surprising ending we can catch a glimpse of the joys of a new reality (one which was foreshadowed in an ancient reality)—the reality of men and women living a shared humanity in ever-increasing erotic love.

Psyche and Eros were up against the same obstacles to happiness that men and women are today. What plagued Psyche's and Eros's happiness was a way of thinking and feeling, of being and doing, that was radically opposed to their erotic love and honor for each other. And the same thing plagues us. It is called patriarchy.

Patriarchy is the rule of others by a domineering male—the "father" of the family, the "father" of the country, or the "father" who rules from heaven. It means that society is organized around the indoctrination and the enforcement of the presumed supremacy of men. Only upon the elimination of the worth of the Feminine and the desecration of the holiness of erotic love can patriarchy gain the power it needs to rule and to perpetuate itself.

The patriarchal value system exalts armed might, control, and subjugation. It uses violence and its own twisted system of "justice" (might makes right). It values power *over* others instead of power *for* others. It spends the wealth of the community on the production of increasingly sophisticated means of murder and destruction (in modern times called the military budget or defense spending). It does not view power as the means to make life better for each individual. Indeed, the patriarchal way does not tolerate individuals. It destroys personal independence and communal interdependence—person-to-person and sex-to-sex relationships. But most of all it destroys the worth of the Feminine and the holiness of erotic love.

By deliberate design—by the laws of its states, the commandments of its religions, and the structure of its societies—the patriarchal belief system and its mind-sets destroy the holiness of erotic love and murder the feminine soul. In an attitude of overwhelming arrogance, patriarchal man designates woman as the source of evil. She is the cause of man's infidelity to the Spirit. She causes his betrayal of his own assumed superiority. At the same time he debases the Feminine, patriarchal man elevates himself, and anything masculine, to the role of redeemer. This is the patriarchal pattern, no matter how disguised or scaled down in everyday living: man presents himself as the "good one" and depicts woman as the "bad one." Not only is man the capable one and woman the incapable one, he is the redeemer of her incapacity!

Patriarchal authority simultaneously eliminates the worth of the Feminine and destroys the holiness of erotic love. And this it must do because the values that erotic love promotes are diametrically opposed to patriarchal ones. Exalting armed might and the power of destruction automatically makes the male—the more physically powerful—more valued than the female. Exalting erotic love and all the creative aspects of life automatically makes both sexes valuable and honors human sexuality.

In order to kill the Feminine and destroy the holiness of erotic love, patriarchy debases human sexuality: it makes human sexuality something bad, something opposed to spirituality. To use sexual desire to give and receive pleasure, even to express love and enhance personal relationships, is considered sinful. The "flesh" is considered antagonistic to the "spirit." And according to patriarchal beliefs it is the cultivation of the "spirit" and the denial of the "flesh" that ensures life.

But what Psyche discovered was that human sexual desire is good and erotic love is holy. It is the primary means by which human beings are touched by some Extraordinary Power. Erotic love is that mysterious internal happening which floods the heart with gladness, drawing people together and causing them to connect with each other and to care passionately about one another. Specifically, it is the power that unites the sexes *without* destroying the identity of either individual. But erotic love can develop only between equals.

Erotic love creates tremendous energy. It makes women and men feel alive and strong, joyful and enthusiastic. Simultaneously, it makes them feel good about themselves and confident in their ability to achieve and to love. While it draws people together it also makes them independent persons.

Erotic love is Spirit and it touches people where and when it will. It is irrational, unexplainable, and unreasonable. It is also uncontrollable. No one can make this kind of love happen. But all people, by the way they think, feel, and act, can be open to it. People cannot make themselves fall in or out of love, but they can kill it and its possibility. A person can kill it directly, by enough cruelty, or indirectly, by retreating from the hard task of expanding his or her consciousness.

By its very nature erotic love must be continually evolving and increasing. When a person does not have enough of an expanding consciousness to contain it, erotic love dwindles away or blows up. But when two people who are in love and who each honor the worth of the other are expanding their individual awarenesses, then *nothing* can destroy their love.

Erotic love is conscious; it is not blind. It requires an intimate knowledge of the goodness of human sexuality and the holiness of imperfect human love. It makes people aware of themselves as adults with all the afflictions human beings are heir to. Therefore, it is compassionate.

Erotic love is paradoxical. It includes all people—it cannot exclude anyone—but at the same time it is not a "blanket" love. It is not some vague sentiment for all humanity; it is love for an individual. Erotic love has as its object an unrepeatable human being, a particular personality for whom it is *impossible* to substitute another person. Erotic love cannot be "taken" from one person and "given" to another. Erotic love is individualized love. Therefore, people can love as many individuals as their hearts can hold. No one has less love or more love than another, because each one is loved for the unrepeatable person she or he is.

While erotic love contains sexual desire, it is more than that. Sexual desire is the primary way of opening us to the possibility of erotic love. But it is not the only way.

Because sexual desire is the primary way of opening people to loving the *otherness* of their earthly opposites (and receiving love from them), it opens them to receiving love from the Divine, which is the complete *Other* of the human. And it inspires them to love an Infinite Supreme Being, the *Total Other* of a finite human being. (See Appendix B for definitions of *other* and *otherness*.)

And so patriarchal belief systems, which debase human sexuality, degrade human sexual desires, and desecrate the holiness of erotic love, effectively cut men and women off from any personal experience of the Divine Spirit. And people need to personally experience the Divine in order to become wholeheartedly human.

Having deprived people of any firsthand, personal experience of the Divine, patriarchal authorities can tell them who "God" is and what is Divine. They can tell them what is good and what is evil. They can tell them how to avoid what patriarchy designates as sinful and strive for what it designates as redemptive.

Patriarchy perverts the goodness of being human, claiming that human nature is basically bad. Men and women are taught to fear each other and to fear the divinely given attraction between the sexes. Only patriarchal marriage (or some modern equivalent) can ameliorate such carnal need. For it is only by obedience to some "higher" (patriarchal) authority that people can be saved.

What Psyche and every woman is up against is that the patriarchal distortion of what it means to be a man has left her bereft of the passionate masculine love for the Feminine she needs in order to grow into the fullness of her womanhood.

In the process of destroying the Feminine, patriarchy has also corrupted and distorted the Masculine. While patriarchy glorifies man and anything male, it seeks to kill the spirit of the Masculine, casting out any man who dares to love the Feminine and be loved by woman. The patriarchal mentality, which promotes male superiority and armed might, perverts the spirit of man. It turns the goodness of man—which naturally desires love, reveres life, and reaches out to others—into a demonic mentality, a mentality bent on control, destruction, and meanness, greedy for earth's treasures and envious of the wealth of others, desiring war and lusting for sex, mesmerized by cruelty, brutality, and pornography.

In the face of such perversion, conscious of it or not, woman experiences her sexual desire with abhorrence and shame. And patriarchal culture (regardless of how many "sexual revolutions" there have been) tells her this is the proper attitude. It is therefore imperative that women remember the innate goodness of man.

What Eros and every man is up against is the patriarchal mentality that has driven the worth of the Feminine Principle out of the hearts and minds of men, women, and the culture. The patriarchal mentality men face does not hesitate to use force, brutality, or imprisonment to drive the worth of the Feminine underground. And in that underground cave of darkness, patriarchy turns the love and goodness of the Feminine into a diabolical horror. Without the real masculine love she needs, the mother becomes the witch and the lover the seductress.

What real man would want to love such inferiority, such evil? So, conscious of it or not, patriarchal man experiences his sexual desire for someone so inferior to him as humiliating and disgusting, even horrifying. And so Eros, like every man caught in the patriarchal web, was bereft of the passionate, sexual love of the Feminine for the Masculine that he needed in order to become a whole man.

Thus do patriarchal values, which consider all of human sexuality (but especially female sexuality) "dirty," make people afraid of sexual desire. No longer is sexual desire considered a good, as it once was—a good that makes life exciting and happy, that enhances relationships and enriches life, and that leads to erotic love and the intimate knowledge of Divine Love.

When a culture denies the worth of the Feminine, restricts the development of the Masculine, and debases human sexuality, terrible things happen between men and women. And because man and woman together form the basic unit of all societies, terrible things happen in the world.

What Psyche and Eros were up against, and what we are up against today, is living without erotic love from the opposite sex. So we are deprived not only of human erotic love but also of Divine Love. This makes us feel ugly about ourselves, mean and irritable, and critical and belligerent towards others. Men and women accuse each other, blaming each other with a malice only love turned to hatred can create. This enmity is reflected in our world as one nation (or ethnic group or religion or race) accuses another, blaming and killing without mercy. Without erotic love the sexes are at war; they are disunited, and all humanity is disunited with them.

Without consciousness of the worth of the Feminine, man cannot be man, and without consciousness of the worth of the Masculine, woman cannot be woman. To be doomed to live life as only a part of the person one can be creates a sorrow so deep and a longing so great that it is impossible in patriarchy to love ourselves and connect passionately and consciously with others.

We find ourselves at the mercy of uncontrollable jealousy, resentment, and rage. A vengeance beyond our control compels us to hurt others, disregarding the effect upon them and even the effect upon ourselves. Our personalities, instead of connecting with others, turn inward and downward until we lose consciousness of love. We become the hollow people, empty, left with a terrible loneliness that nothing in our patriarchal culture can fill.

The myth of Psyche and Eros evolved out of the tragedy patriarchy inflicts on us, to tell us that there is a way for men and women to regain their loves and their happiness. There is a way to right the relationship between man and woman.

And when this happens wonderful things happen both to individuals and in the culture as a whole. People become people who love and care because they feel loved and cared for by the most important *others* adults can have—their sexual opposites. And when there is healthy sex people find within themselves the human spirit that can commune with Divine Spirit, because sexual love and Spirit are inseparable. When the primary unit of society—man and woman—is rebalanced, rooted, and grounded in the truth of erotic love, civilization can also be righted and the evolution of true human nature can proceed.

Unlike any other revolution, the transition from the patriarchal way to a way that reestablishes the worth of the Feminine, the goodness of the Masculine, and the holiness of Erotic Love begins not in bloodshed but with a woman who was willing to discover and fight for her erotic love, cost what it may!

To speak of "following the way of Psyche" is paradoxical, because every individual is the destination of her own journey. Psyche leaves us no road maps, but she gives us an example of how to do what must be done in every life in order to transcend patriarchy and achieve the abundant happiness and love we humans were meant to have. All individuals must find their own ways, taking their own risks, blazing their own trails.

Following the example of Psyche takes the utmost courage—the courage of a heroine and the courage of a hero, the courage of a magnanimous heart, and the courage of a creative soul.

THE MYTH
OF PSYCHE AND EROS

The principal characters in this Greek myth are Psyche, Aphrodite, Eros, and Zeus.

Psyche was the daughter of a king and queen who were good, god-fearing people. She was incredibly beautiful, and her name is the Greek word for "soul." She was a good daughter—kind and true and obedient. However, she encountered a terrible fate. But the god of love rescued her and she overcame her predicament by accomplishing four do-or-die tasks that were assigned to her by Aphrodite. Though she failed at the end, her failure became the means to her success, which turned out to be more than she (or anyone else) had expected. Psyche is both the hero and the heroine of this myth.

Aphrodite is the Greek name for the Great Goddess. The Goddess was not only the oldest of all gods; She was the Mother of all deities. In words inscribed upon Her shrine at Athens She was described as the First Mother, the Essence of Love, the Essence of Motherhood, Oldest of Fates. Her full name, Aphrodite Urania, means "Aphrodite, Queen of Heaven." The ocean, as well, was Her dominion. This is symbolized by Aphrodite's birth from the sea. She arose from the depths, full-grown, borne upon a seashell. In the depths of the ocean—in preconscious chaos, irrationality, and absurdity—She held court, just as She ruled in crystal conscious-ness from the highest ether of heaven. As Queen of Earth She was the Goddess of beauty and sexual love, the Goddess of femininity and genesis, who had ruled since the beginning. She was extremely powerful, for She reigned from a primor-dial, unformed, wordless, ever-evolving time. She appeared before time itself, before memory, and She appears in the deepest hearts of all humans, for She loves all of Her creation and embraces an open acceptance of human sexuality. Men and women adored Her as the Giver of all good gifts. One of Her most treasured gifts to humanity was consciousness of the pleasure of sexual desire as something sacred and good; it opened the door to adulthood and kept women and men lusty and healthy and happy even into old age. She is the catalyst for action in this myth.

Eros was the god of love. Although he became a god later in time he was very influential and powerful; he had the power to change the course of people's lives. He was the son of Zeus, the king of the Greek gods, and Aphrodite, the God-dess of love and beauty. He was the most beautiful of all the gods and ultimately the most powerful, for not even Zeus was exempt from the power of one of Eros's arrows. The golden-pointed arrows of Eros had the power to cause both mortals and gods to fall in love. Eros became Psyche's husband.

Zeus was the king of the gods and goddesses of Mount Olympus. He was called father, but not so much in the sense of creating; rather, in the sense of the *pater familias,* the head of the family of the gods and goddesses and the ruler and protector of the human family. As such, he encouraged hos-pitality for guest-friends and respect for suppliants. He was also considered the god of justice. He was not nearly as old a god as Aphrodite was a Goddess. When he was born he had to be hidden in a cave so Kronos, king of the Titan gods, would not swallow him up. Later Zeus dethroned Kronos, and together with the other Olympian gods he fought the Titans (the previous gods) and won. The sun, lightning, and thunder were his signs, and the eagle was his bird. He held court atop Mount Olympus, and he ruled in a conscious, direct, and logical (though often erratic) fashion. He was the father of Eros.

THE STORY

Once upon a time there lived a king and a queen who had three lovely daughters. The two oldest were beautiful and charming and their father had no trouble finding good, handsome princes for them to marry. But the third daughter was beautiful and charming and something more. She had an unworldliness about her, a magnificence of sexuality and a purity of spirit, some extraordinary quality of bearing, and an almost unapproachable femininity that men seemed to worship and adore but not to love. So Psyche was sadly without lovers to marry.

Instead, a cult of worship began to spring up about her. When this young princess went into the temple (where all virgins came to sacrifice to the Queen of Heaven before accepting the love of a man), men began to say, "Here is the new Aphrodite." They offered her the garlands of flowers they had brought for the Goddess.

While the ashes on the altars of Aphrodite began to grow cold, Aphrodite began to grow hot with anger. Her anger punished Psyche, though the poor girl was in no way to blame. Finally Aphrodite decided to put a stop to the whole business, and in Her ocean queendom of unknown and unclaimed primordial femininity She plotted the girl's death.

By this time Psyche's father was desperate to find a husband for her. Suspecting that her state of affairs might be caused by the displeasure of the Goddess, he went to the oracle of Aphrodite, for She was the arranger of marriages in heaven above and on earth below. He asked what he should do, and the answer he received allowed no further doubt about the wrath of the gods. Aphrodite's oracle proclaimed a terrible fate for Psyche: "Dress thy daughter like a bride; lead her up the mountainside. There an unknown winged foe, feared by all who dwell below, and even by the gods above, will claim her as the hawk the dove."

Psyche was to be married to the ugliest, the most terrifying, the most devouring of all monsters: the monster whose name was Death. Unlike the other gods, the dark-robed lord, Thanatos, had no temples of worship. He hated gifts. Even the other gods feared him.

Psyche's parents were devastated, but they had no recourse. Oracles were the final word; there was no higher court. Psyche was to be taken, in all her wedding finery, to the top of a mountain. There she was to be chained to a rock and left for the monster.

So on the appointed night Psyche's bridesmaids and her maid of honor dressed her in her wedding gown. The people of her parents' court formed a wedding procession which was also a funeral cortege. Her father led the weeping bride to the rock where he chained her. Then all the torches were extinguished and Psyche was left alone in the dark.

In the meantime Aphrodite had called in Her son, Eros, the handsome god of love. He was the bane of everyone's existence, including the great gods of Mount Olympus, for not even the most powerful were exempt from the potency of an arrow of Eros. She ordered him to go and shoot Psyche with one of his golden-pointed arrows to ensure her falling in love with Death. He was delighted to shoot anyone.

So Eros, borne upon his mighty wings and needing no instruments of earth, soared by. But seeing the object of his aim, he was smitten by Psyche's beauty. Flinging control aside, he abandoned himself to the joy of his sexual desire. In his passion, Eros accidentally pricked himself on one of his own arrows, and looking at Psyche again, fell madly in love with her. Without further thought or ado, he decided to claim her for his own. He called his good friend, Zephyrus, the god of the west wind, and asked him to lift Psyche gently from the rock and blow her down into his valley of paradise.

After the last sound of human footsteps had died away, the lovely bride sat weeping in fear and trembling. But instead of teeth and claws and rape, she felt the soft, cool breath and downy wings of Zephyrus, who did his friend's bidding. Puffing out his cheeks, he blew her down into a beautiful green valley and laid her softly on a bank of violets.

The sweetness and peace of the moonlit valley eased Psyche's fears for the moment and she fell asleep.

Fears in the human heart, however, are hard to erase, and in the morning when she awakened, there they were. The sight of a beautiful grove of tall trees took her mind off of her troubles, though. In the midst of the trees she saw a most wonderful palace. The great arches of the roof were supported by golden columns, the walls were covered with silver carvings, and the floors were mosaics of precious stones.

Timidly Psyche entered. She could see no one, but she heard low voices as if fairies were talking. She came upon a room of unearthly beauty where a table was laid for a feast. Evidently only one person was expected, for she could see only one chair and one place setting. Psyche, half afraid, sat down, whereupon she was waited on by invisible nymphs. There was a chorus of singing, and then she heard a single voice singing to her, accompanied by the lyre.

As darkness came to the waiting twilight Psyche began to tremble, for she feared that the owner of this place would prove to be the dreaded monster of the oracle. Then she heard footsteps coming lightly and quickly to where she was sitting. Her flesh froze in breathless fear. But the voice that spoke to her was softly musical and excitingly masculine. The touch she felt was gentle and enamoring.

"Beautiful Psyche, do not be afraid. This palace and all it holds are yours if you will consent to live here and be my bride. The voices you have heard are the voices of your handmaids, who will obey your every command. Every night I will spend here with you, but before dawn can light the sky I must fly away. Do not ask to see my face or to know who I am. Only trust me; I ask nothing more." So, though Psyche could not be sure that this was not the voice of the monster, her fears were allayed enough and she consented.

Then Eros made love to her. It was the most beautiful thing that had ever happened to Psyche. With his arms around her, Eros told Psyche how beautiful it was. So, although Psyche could not see Eros, his loving her confirmed the magnificence of her sexuality and assured her that masculine sexuality was good, not something to be feared.

Eros came to Psyche every night. He called her by her name, and her heart pounded new life through every particle of her body. He touched her, and she felt the earth quake. He made love to her, and volcanoes erupted fire, pouring hot lava even into the soles of her feet. Until this time Psyche had never known she had a body; now she knew beyond rhyme and reason. "I don't know who you are," she told him, "but I love you passionately, as I love life." As their bodies vibrated pleasure, so their hearts were filled with joy.

Most of the time Psyche looked forward to Eros's coming with delight, but there were times when the sound of his wings filled her with terror.

One day, when she was gathering roses within sight of the rock to which she had been chained, she saw her two sisters weeping and crying out in mourning for their dear, dead sister. Psyche believed that in spite of their unkindness in the past they really loved her, and she was moved to pity. So that night, when Eros came to her, she asked him if she could see her sisters to let them know she was alive and happy. Reluctantly, Eros gave his consent.

The next day Zephyrus blew the sisters down into Psyche's garden. They seemed more surprised to see her good fortune than glad to see her. But Psyche, in her joy, did not notice their jealousy. She did not know that each sister was miserable in her "good marriage." One sister was married to an old man who treated her with a condescending tolerance. The other was married to an invalid boy who made her responsible for his welfare. They asked her a good many questions, particularly about her husband. Psyche only told them he was away hunting. Then Zephyrus, thinking the sisters were getting too inquisitive, blew them away. Thus ended the first visit.

Psyche reported all of this to Eros, who warned her that she was in great danger. He told her that if she continued to see her sisters there would be a disaster. If she tried to find out who he was, he would take her out of paradise, fly away, and leave her all alone. He declared that their child, who was now on the way, would be born mortal instead of divine if she disobeyed him. Psyche felt a little quakey.

Though her sisters' questions agitated Psyche about who her husband really was and Eros's lecture intimidated her, she decided she wanted to see them again. She had grown tired of being alone, waiting for Eros to come home. She was bored with picking roses. After again warning Psyche, Eros gave his consent. So Zephyrus blew the eager sisters once more into the valley.

These envious, malicious women had been brooding over their sister's superior good fortune and had concocted a plan to destroy her happiness. They told Psyche that her husband was actually a horrible winged serpent, the loathsome monster of the oracle. The people of the valley had reported seeing him coming into the valley every evening at dusk. Psyche must not be deceived by his seeming kindness, for when her baby was born he planned to devour both her and her baby.

Poor Psyche was now much more than agitated; she was frantic. Her sisters now had her where they wanted her. Oozing kindness, they told her to listen to them; they were older and wiser and wanted to help her. They had a plan. "Take a knife and whet it to fine sharpness. While your pretended lover sleeps light a lamp you have readied with oil. Then look at him. If our words prove true, you can strike off his head and save yourself and your child from an awful death." With this her sisters departed.

After they left, Psyche could not rid her mind of the fears that she had kept at bay and that her sisters had now raised. If all were well, why was her lover so anxious to keep her hidden? And why did he come to her only at night, under cover of darkness? Why did he fear her sisters' visits? And, thought Psyche, with panic rising in her throat, why did he have wings?

Finally Psyche decided she must find out who he was, and an energy called courage began to rise in her heart. She would disobey her husband. She had chosen to see him.

Eros came as usual after dark and fell asleep beside Psyche. Quietly she got up and, trembling with fear, lit her lamp. Taking the knife in one hand and the lamp in the other, she went to the couch where Eros lay. The light of the lamp fell full on his face—and in stunned amazement, Psyche saw no horrible monster or dark-hooded lord of death. She saw Eros, Love himself, the most beautiful of all the gods. Thick curls fell back from his wonderful face; his red lips were slightly parted in the sweet smile of sleep; his snow-white wings were folded, the down on them as delicate as the wings of a butterfly. His strong male body lay stretched out in relaxed trust. At his feet lay his bow and arrows. In her bewilderment and consternation Psyche dropped the knife and, trying to pick it up, accidentally pricked herself on the golden point of one of his arrows. Holding high her lamp, she turned to look at Eros again. Then, beholding him in all the glory of his manhood, she fell overwhelmingly in love with him. Gazing at him in ecstasy, she bent down to kiss him. But her hand trembled and a drop of hot oil from the lamp fell on the god's shoulder. Burned, he awakened in pain and saw what had happened. With a reproachful look, he flew away to the house of his mother, Aphrodite, where he sulked, tending his minor burn.

The beautiful palace disappeared, and Psyche found herself all alone on a deserted plain. Eros had taken away everything. What was she to do? She did not want to go back to her parents' house. She had known love, and she was no longer daughter but wife.

Panic exploded in her mind. Since she was now her own person Psyche decided she would go to the river and throw herself in. But at the riverside she met the cloven-footed god, Pan, sitting by the river playing his magical flute. He saw that Psyche was about to drown herself, and he came and played for her. His music dissuaded her. He then told her she must pray.

So, praying, Psyche went from one deity to another, but no one would help her because they all feared Aphrodite's wrath. Finally Psyche decided to go to Aphrodite Herself, thinking that the mother of Love might be kind to her for Love's sake. But Aphrodite was very angry. She had learned all that had happened. A sea gull, Her own bird of the ocean, had flown to Her and told Her everything. Aphrodite blamed Psyche for all that had passed.

Aphrodite gave a bitter, tyrannical speech. Psyche was reduced to nothing. She was told that she was a good-for-nothing slut, that even the job of a scullery maid was too good for her. But Psyche bore the Goddess's wrath. She stood there and took it.

At last Aphrodite relented, but only so far as to prescribe several nearly impossible tasks for Psyche to do in order to earn her deliverance from death and the return of Eros. These were do-or-die tasks; either Psyche would succeed or she would die. And Aphrodite planned for her to die.

On the morning of the first task the Goddess pointed to a great heap of seeds: the food of the doves that drew Her chariot and of the little blue birds that accompanied Her on Her journeys. The heap was composed of wheat, barley, millet, and other kinds of seeds all mixed together carelessly. "Take these," said Aphrodite, "and separate them grain by grain. Place each kind by itself, and finish the task by nightfall." And off She went in grandeur, Her sapphire chariot pulled by Her white doves.

Poor Psyche, all of her brave determination gone, just sat with drooping head and folded hands. Then a little ant ran out from under a rock and, seeing Psyche's plight, called the whole army of ant people. They came for love's sweet sake and quickly separated the seeds, laying each kind by itself in neat piles. The ant people filled Psyche's heart with hope once more.

At the close of day Aphrodite came, garbed in the brilliant colors of sunset. She saw that Psyche had finished her task and, in haughty annoyance, threw her a crust of bread. She said She would return in the morning and set Psyche a much more difficult and dangerous task. Exhausted, Psyche fell asleep on the ground.

In the morning she woke up yearning for her lost love. Aphrodite came in beauty adorned, and arrogantly pointed to the river. On the opposite shore grazed the sun rams, whose wool was golden fleece. "Bring me some of that wool," She demanded.

Once again Psyche went into a panic, knowing the rams would kill her. She made for the river to drown herself for sure this time. But the reeds that grew by the river's edge whispered encouragingly to Psyche to be still. "Do not go near the rams, for they are fiercest in the noonday heat." They told her to wait until the evening, when the day had cooled and the river song had lulled the rams to sleep. Then she could cross the river and pick all the wool she liked from the bushes, where the sheep had left it clinging. So Psyche waited until the sun was low and the day had cooled. Then she crossed the river to pick the golden fleece, unnoticed by the rams, and returned with her arms full of the golden wool.

When Aphrodite came and saw that Psyche had collected the golden fleece, Her anger knew no bounds. Furious, She gave the instructions for the third task: "Take this crystal vessel and fill it with the waters from the Fountain of Forgetfulness."

This fountain—with its twin, the Fountain of Remembrance—was at the top of a very high mountain, higher than any man could climb. The two fountains gushed forth from two huge rocks and joined in the valley below to form the River of Life. On either side of the rushing waters was a cave, and in these two caves dwelled two deadly monsters.

When Psyche climbed to the top of the mountain and saw all of this, she was so horrified she could not move or speak. Even the rushing waters yelled at Psyche to flee, so deadly were the monsters.

In the meantime, however, Zeus had gotten tired of Aphrodite's jealousy and rage. He was now willing to come openly to Eros's aid. As Psyche stood paralyzed by fear and hopelessness, Zeus sent his eagle to help her. The eagle was his chief agent, for the eagle was stronger and could fly higher than any other bird. When the eagle had landed, he told Psyche to come and spread her arms out over his wings and lay her head upon his neck. So, with her heart in her mouth, Psyche knelt down behind the great bird and did as she was told.

Then he bore her up on his eagle wings and soared her to the Fountain of Forgetfulness. With powerful grace, he dipped his wing over the gushing fountain. There he hovered while Psyche reached out with the hand that once had held the knife, and filled the crystal vessel with the gushing waters. Then he bore her back safe and sound and set her down on the mountainside, where Psyche stood up with the crystal vessel filled with the healing waters.

In joyful radiance, Psyche skipped down the mountain that was higher than any man could climb, which in the dawn's light she had labored up.

Psyche went happily to Aphrodite with the crystal vessel full of the water from the Fountain of Forgetfulness, just knowing the Goddess would be pleased.

But Aphrodite was not pleased. She was angrier than ever and determined to destroy the hated woman once and for all. The fourth task She devised was almost foolproof. She gave Psyche a small pot with a tight-fitting lid and told her that she must descend into the dark underworld. There she must obtain from the hand of Persephone some of her immortal beauty ointment and deliver it to Aphrodite unopened.

When Psyche heard this, she knew beyond doubt that Aphrodite meant her utter destruction. Thinking that it was of no use to struggle any longer against the will of the Goddess, and despairing of ever seeing Eros again, she climbed to the top of a tower to throw herself off.

But the very stones of the tower cried out to her: "Psyche, Psyche! Stop. Listen. From yonder dark chasm, choked with thorns, a path leads down into the underworld. Put two coins in your mouth and take two pieces of barley bread in your hands, then follow this rough path. Refuse to help a lame donkey driver who will ask you to pick up some kindling wood. When you come to the river Styx, Charon will ferry you over for one of your coins. Refuse the groping hand of a dying man as he reaches up out of the water begging you to save him. Pass by and do not assist three women weaving the threads of fate and fantasy. Toss one of your pieces of barley bread to Cerberus, the three-headed dog, who stands guard at the entrance to hell. While the three heads are fighting over the one piece of bread, enter the palace of Hades where Persephone is queen. She will give you a portion of her immortal beauty ointment, shutting it into the pot with a tight-fitting lid. Then repeat the whole process in reverse on the way back up. And remember, you must deliver the pot unopened."

Psyche was thankful indeed for this advice. Hope arose anew in her heart; she might see Eros again. So she willingly descended into the world of the dead for the sake of her love. Putting the two coins in her mouth and taking one piece of barley bread in each hand, she made for the dark chasm that led into the world of the dead. Psyche followed the advice in detail. She knew that if she made one little slip she would die, for she was in the realm of death.

At last Psyche was safely back on earth. All she had to do was deliver the pot of immortal beauty ointment unopened to Aphrodite, and Aphrodite would have to deliver Eros back to her and let her live. But her sufferings had been so great and her longing for her love so intense that she knew her beauty was nearly gone. So she opened the pot to use just a bit of the immortal beauty ointment for herself—to be beautiful for Eros.

But alas and alack, a strange, invisible vapor rushed from the opened pot. Overpowered, Psyche fell into a sleep so deep that she dropped to the ground as if dead. She might never have awakened again if Eros, healed of his wounds and walking about, had not heard the thud of her fall.

He flew to her and, dropping to his knees, felt the soft current of her breath on his face. Eros took Psyche by the shoulders and shook her awake. "Psyche, Psyche! Wake up. I love you and in love there are no endings, only beginnings."

Psyche blinked her eyes open and saw the face of her beloved. Her joy exploded! In rapture, they beheld each other, their love overflowing. And the love that moves the universe knew no boundaries in their bodies; spirit joined with spirit in high rejoicing; two bodies united, yet two wholes remained. So gladness came to be her handmaiden and mirth her companion.

Afterwards, Eros wiped the beauty ointment off Psyche's face and slipped it back into the pot, slapping the lid on tight. He gave it to Psyche and told her to take it to his mother; She would never know the difference. Then he flew to Mount Olympus to plead Psyche's case for immortality before his father, Zeus.

Of course, there was no case to plead, for the king of the gods readily agreed. He sent Hermes to bring Psyche immediately up to Mount Olympus. In the meantime, all the goddesses and gods assembled for a great feast. Then, with all gathered together, Zeus himself handed to this mortal woman the cup of nectar that imparted immortality.

Psyche reached out and took the cup from Zeus's hand. But before she drank she turned and looked at Aphrodite. There stood the most radiant Goddess of all, smiling at her with tears like diamonds on her cheeks. And Psyche knew. She comprehended that what was almighty was the everlasting strength of the Goddess's love. With human tears wet upon her face, she smiled back at Aphrodite. Then she drank, and straightaway two beautiful butterfly wings sprang from her shoulders. Though she became immortal like the gods, Psyche remained forever human.

Then Psyche and Eros were united in a new wedding. Apollo sang; and Aphrodite, her wrath and jealousy forgotten, danced at their wedding.

Out of their love a daughter was born; out of their love a new reality was given. And Psyche and Eros named her Pleasure. She was both human and divine.

WORSHIPED
AND
ADORED

Once upon a time there lived a king and a queen who had three lovely daughters. The two oldest were beautiful and charming and their father had no trouble finding good, handsome princes for them to marry. But the third daughter was beautiful and charming and something more. She had an unworldliness about her, a magnificence of sexuality and a purity of spirit, some extraordinary quality of bearing, and an almost unapproachable perfection that men seemed to worship and adore but not to love. So Psyche was sadly without lovers to marry.

Instead, a cult of worship began to spring up about her. When this young princess went into the temple (where all virgins came to sacrifice to the Queen of Heaven before accepting the love of a man), men began to say, "Here is the new Aphrodite." They offered her the garlands of flowers they had brought for the Goddess.

Psyche's father had no trouble finding husbands for his two oldest daughters because they struck no terror into the hearts of men. They believed the patriarchal promise like the sun rising: be lovely, kind, and true (meaning obedient) and you will find a good, committed husband who will reward your obedient service. He will give you his name (your identity), take care of you, provide all the material goods you deserve, and make you a goddess (i.e., a mother) to ensure your "immortality."

Psyche's sisters believed the patriarchal lie that promised them the ultimate security (immortality) for their obedience. They, like a lot of women today, paid no attention to the unconscious fear of dying that made them want to be worshiped and adored as goddesses. "Goddesses do not have to die." Psyche's sisters paid no attention to their fear of being unacceptable; they made themselves conform. Not knowing what they were doing, they willingly obeyed the patriarchal demand that a woman remain unravished (physically unawakened and psychologically unconscious) and function as a man's adoring servant, a virgin mother forever pure and unaware, in whatever "palace" he provided. They willingly denied their own love/spirit, sacrificed their womanhood, and gave up finding their own identities.

Most women think they want lovers to marry, but in reality they do not. They have not claimed responsibility for their own lives and their own sexual desires. They are afraid of erotic love; they are afraid of the urgency of their sexual desires and the single-mindedness of masculine sexual passion. Thus they are content to marry "good" men who will adore them and provide the security they think they need. And they pretend—to themselves and to the world—that they are in love.

But the king was having trouble finding a husband for Psyche. Unlike her sisters, Psyche did strike terror into the hearts of men. Her body radiated the powerful feminine energy that is generated by the irrational combination of sex and spirit. Every woman is born with beauty, charm, and a delightful sex appeal—regardless of her physical features. Also innate in every woman are passionate sexual desires and a powerful feminine spirit that brings joy to the otherwise ordinary process of daily living.

What differentiated Psyche from her sisters was that she instinctively refused to relinquish either the magnificence of her sexuality or the purity of her spirit to masculine control. Though she did not know how to protect herself, she knew she was not willing to deny her love/spirit. She did not want to marry a bully or a man who worshiped her. The thought of remaining the unravished bride of a play-it-safe passionless man was horrifying to her. She was Psyche: soul in feminine sexuality! She wanted to marry a lover!

This gave Psyche a quality of bearing men found unapproachable. Her feminine energy challenged their rational control by demanding a passionate (irrational) response from them. By claiming both her spirituality and her sexuality Psyche was demanding a lover to marry, thereby opposing patriarchal rational control of her inherent irrational femininity.

Men found it easier and safer to worship and adore Psyche than to try to meet her demand for a passionate response. They were afraid to risk losing their sense of control. But in order to love and cherish a woman and be loved and embraced by her, a man must live life on a higher level; he cannot be obsessed with controlling his lover or his passions. He has to enter the realm of irrationality, which is not controllable by rational means.

Psyche was too irrational for any patriarchal, play-it-safe man. And so is every woman who intuitively expresses the magnificence of her sexuality through her spirit and the purity of her spirit through her body. Patriarchal man is incapable of comprehending the union of a magnificence of sexuality and a purity of spirit. There is nothing in the patriarchal value system that teaches him how to reconcile, much less unify, these two different ways of being. The patriarchal belief system has taught man that sex and spirit are two separate, opposing forces that are irreconcilable. If a person is sensual and sexual, then he or she cannot be pure and spiritual (and vice versa). The "rationality" of patriarchal man dictates that everything has to be either-or: either sex or spirit, either goddess or whore, either man or alien. People cannot be both, especially at the same time!

In patriarchal man's rational thinking, there is an irrevocable split between mind and body, between spirit/love and flesh. Patriarchal man elevates the mind and spirit to the realm of the holy while he debases the body and relegates flesh to the devil. In the patriarchal mentality, rationality has to deny irrationality, especially the irrationality of joining the sexual and the spiritual into one united whole. Patriarchal authority demands that woman capitulate to the "rational" dichotomy between flesh and spirit.

But woman knows that her spirit/love is in her body; that is what makes her flesh so sweet. In the irrationality of the Feminine there is no split between sex and spirit. New life, the spirit incarnated, comes out of a woman's body! Magnificence of flesh and purity of spirit go together. A woman's sexuality is not expressed in bared bosoms or sexy poses but in her spirit—that wonderful spirit that administers healing grace, that changes water into wine, and that gives meaning to our daily bread. And the purity of a woman's spirit is expressed not in pious prayer or self-righteous good works but in her sexuality, in her human nature to yield to love and to her erotic desires. Only through her erotic desires can a woman be awakened from the sleep of her girlhood and enter into a consciousness of her adult womanhood, where she finds that love is her supreme value.

The passion of being woman requires erotic love to awaken it and to fuel and refuel the fires of its feminine spirit/love with masculine, sexual passion for the Feminine. Such love does not have to be genitally expressed. Erotic love finds many ways to express its message, sometimes even over great separations by distance or time. Therefore, the way in which a woman develops her femininity—becomes conscious of her passionate sexual self and awakens to the power of her spirit—is by allowing herself to become aware of being ravished by man's erotic, irrational love for her.

Psyche's love/spirit dwelt in her body, so her body needed to be penetrated by the impassioned love of man in order to awaken her consciousness of her love/spirit. But it is not necessarily physical penetration that awakens a woman's consciousness of her love/spirit. Indeed, there are many women who have been married for years but still have not experienced being penetrated by a man's passionate sexual love for them. What is necessary is that a woman's heart be penetrated by the full force of masculine erotic love for her, which communicates to her the passionate love in the Masculine Principle for the Feminine.

Only through the experience of erotic love can a woman's self-love become fully realized and creative. It is her experience of impassioned masculine love that gives birth to her consciousness of the Masculine dwelling within her. When a woman becomes conscious of her inner man she will have forever the masculine love she needs living within her. This inner masculine love is what will fuel the fires of her spirit and encourage her to develop her full femininity. When she is in contact with her deepest, innermost femininity, a Psyche can develop her unique self. This self then becomes the center of her personality, transformed by the power of the Feminine and loved by the Masculine.

In his heart man longs for a woman's spirit as well as her body. In order to experience the power in the passion of being man, a man needs a woman's spirit to embrace his sexual desires, and a woman's sexuality to respond to his irrational spirit.

To accomplish the tasks of becoming the man he has not yet become requires that he value the Feminine as much as he values the Masculine. To develop his masculinity, a man must love and value a woman as much as he does his own self. To experience the full power of his masculinity, he needs to recognize that what he wants is to have the woman he desires desire him and love him erotically.

Through consciousness of his erotic love for a woman, man learns to yield to the power of being loved by the female. He learns to value the Feminine and, consequently, to integrate it into his personality. As a woman's arms encircle a man and pull him close when making love, so the Feminine encircles him and pulls him closer to his own soul. In that experience a man becomes conscious of his inner woman. Then he will have forever the feminine love he needs living in him. It will free him from his patriarchal bondage, connect him to his soul, and give meaning to his life.

But patriarchal man has despised the value of woman's spirit and refused to incorporate the Feminine into his own nature. Instead, he has sought control. He must control power: his own masculine power, the power of the written word, the power of symbol making, the power of nature, the power of making money, the power of other nations, and, above all, the power of the feminine. Without these controls he could not control himself.

Man is thus faced with a world in which control has the highest value. But he has a kind of control that must banish erotic love from his life, because erotic love is uncontrollable. He must banish the worth of the Feminine because man's natural love for woman threatens his sense of control. His nature urges him to love the Feminine, his intellect urges him to respect the Feminine, and his spirit urges him to honor the Feminine. Therefore, he must destroy the value of the Feminine and degrade women. How can he love, respect, and honor what has no value?

But man's passion is so powerful that it frightens him. So he has established the ethic of obedience to outside authorities to protect himself from the passion of being a man. His authorities then enforce the taboo against erotic love, and ensure the devaluation of the Feminine. Through obligatory obedience to them he tries to control the irrational. He tries to defuse the power of feminine energy, which demands the development of his own masculinity, and he tries to rob erotic love of its holiness, which demands human consciousness. By establishing outside authorities that demand obedience—such as religion and courts of law—patriarchal man institutionalizes his control. With justification from his religious commandments, rationale from his codes of law, and the legalized force of police, unevolved man has little trouble enforcing his taboo against erotic love and continuing his devaluation of the Feminine.

Today, as in the past, man maintains self-control by painting woman as a goddess or a whore. He convinces himself that woman is only an adjunct of the male, created to serve him. By seeing woman as a deformed human who lacks the body parts of the (superior) male, or as a goddess he should not touch, man vindicates his refusal to develop the Feminine in himself.

But without the Feminine there is nothing that can connect him to the full power of his own masculine spirit and passion, nothing that can connect him to the meaning of his life. Thus, by extinguishing the value of the Feminine and forbidding erotic passion, patriarchal man sacrifices the power of his individual masculinity.

Trapped in the culture he created, a patriarchal man cannot love a Psyche. He is terrified of her. He is afraid he may corrupt her pure spirit, knock her off her pedestal with his hot desire, or make her immoral (as if he could). He is also afraid that if he tries to satisfy her erotic desires he will fail. Before the power of the erotic Feminine, a man stands stripped of his excuses for not developing his self. So he either worships or ridicules woman's spirituality; he either adores or scorns her body. He either worships her as a goddess or debases her as a whore. But these are two sides of the same coin: unconscious woman. In either case patriarchal man refuses to let women be anything but unconscious icons.

Man's control—and all of his outside authorities—is threatened most by that which he desires most. He fears that he and his control will be corrupted by loving woman and honoring the Feminine. Ironically, he is right! The illuminating power of the irrational, which lives in the Feminine Principle, is the same power that can annihilate patriarchy. The Feminine, including the mysterious inner woman within each man, has the power to destroy the patriarchal family, the patriarchal state, the patriarchal religion, and (most terrifying of all) man's patriarchal self. But the death of his patriarchal Self is also the birth of his true masculinity.

So patriarchal man replaces the erotic love he has forbidden with commitment to a goddess who is passionless, or he tries to make up for its absence by fucking a whore who is powerless. What he is left with is *passionless commitment* and *powerless sex*. In neither can he find the feminine energy he needs to free himself from his man-made prison. Passionless commitment is a lousy substitute for erotic love. And powerless sex is like throwing dust to the wind.

Like Psyche, most women want passion, not commitment; they want erotic love, not powerless sex. No woman wants to be worshiped and adored. She wants a man who will love her, just as she wants a man she can love. *Being worshiped* is the same terrifying and lonely experience as *being repudiated,* cast out of the land of the living, scorned and ignored. A man who is stuck in patriarchy draws back when a woman becomes warm and soft, erotic and yielding—the very things that he indicated he wanted. He becomes a worshiping wimp or a self-righteous bully. It terrifies him to acknowledge that she has the same desires he has—desires over which he has so little control.

When a man evokes a woman's passionate response and then pulls away from her she feels embarrassed by her own erotic nature. She is baffled. What did she do wrong? A strange and unjustified guilt haunts her. She feels abandoned, forsaken, and very alone. When there is no passionate masculine response, a Psyche feels humiliated and violated. She is tempted to capitulate to patriarchy and accept worship and adoration as her only connection to the Masculine. But by doing so she cuts herself off from her deep, life-giving, transforming feminine nature. She is divorced from the passion of being woman!

When worship and adoration are substituted for love, woman is not only denied expression of her sexuality but also rendered unaware that her sexual desires are good and her spirit is holy. She becomes an object rather than a living woman. She is reduced to hero-worshiping or monster-fearing. In a patriarchy a woman can have either a wimp who worships her or a monster who violates her.

Either way she is obsessed by the externals of life, especially her appearance. Would a hero ever desire some flat-chested, scrawny-legged woman? Or would a budding young doctor ever desire someone with untoned muscles? The energy she spends worrying about her figure, her face, and her hair is mind-boggling. Yet if the hero doesn't claim her, the monster will get her! So both the hero worshiper and the monster fearer are obsessed with adhering to all the right do's and don'ts.

In order to make the subjugation of women easier for men, patriarchal culture goes to great lengths to persuade a woman that she does not really want a passionate response, that what she wants is security and commitment. Sex is only the icing on the cake, she is told. And being economically dependent on men, patriarchal woman *must* desire what she needs: security and commitment. And so she goes without the passion and sexual desires that could ignite her spirit.

To further ensure her subjugation, undeveloped man must prevent woman from finding out that her sexuality belongs to herself. Therefore, patriarchal values and systems of belief convince men and women that woman is created to serve man! He must convince her that both her body and her soul belong to him. She must go from being her father's daughter to being her husband's wife; only within the framework of this possessive paternalism, which has been enlarged a bit but not abolished, is she allowed to find her identity. She must have no mind except his mind, no spirit except his spirit, no personality except what he allows. If she does not question this, she is rewarded by being considered good. And in a patriarchy "good" means remaining unconscious of her self and committed to the service of men: an asexual, spiritless being devoid of her humanity.

Furthermore, patriarchal man must not allow himself or woman to become aware that erotic love is what reveals Divine Love. He tells her her body is unclean and her spirit is earthbound. Her erotic desires are sinful and must be purified by some kind of baptism: patriarchal marriage vows, motherhood, and service to others. He hides the truth that woman's spirit is majestic; that the passion of woman's love is representative of the all-inclusive Divine Love for each individual. He denies the truth that her spirit/love inhabits her body; that both her spirit and her body are infused with the Divine, making all her erotic desires holy. Patriarchal man *must* devalue the priceless worth of the Feminine and debase women (or worship them out of existence) so he can keep himself ignorant of the holiness of erotic love.

If man cannot convince her of these things, patriarchy brainwashes her by using economic, political, and social coercion or enough violence to make the threat of violence real. Ridiculing and criticizing her, however, is a much safer, much nicer way to dishonor and debase her than having to use outright violence. And such thinly veiled violence is usually enough to keep a woman in her place. But worshiping and adoring her is still the easiest and least strenuous way to convince woman of men's superiority and their right to subjugate her.

Psyche stood in the temple of the Goddess of Love, unloved. Not knowing the cause, she thought something was wrong with her. She felt an isolation that broke her heart, as well as an unwarranted guilt about her sexual nature which crippled her spirit. Psyche's isolation and crippled spirit were not imaginary, and neither are those of modern women. They were the reality of her existence.

If a woman refuses to relinquish to man and his authority the magnificence of her sexuality and the purity of her spirit, she becomes too great a threat to patriarchy. Man must divorce himself from her and make her an outcast. But in doing so he forbids himself and his culture the power of the Feminine. And a naked loneliness he cannot identify consumes his empty heart.

A culture that restricts men to the choice between goddess and whore dooms women to an existence of semiconsciousness, at best. A woman's life is then full of cold platitudes that try to disguise the cruel reality of her condemnation. And such a culture dooms men to a horrible self-loathing. The women men want they cannot have, and the women men have they do not want. Without consciousness of the value of the Feminine, neither men nor women can fall erotically in love. Erotic love can only happen between two equally valued human beings. Thus, in a patriarchy, not only men but also women are stripped of the compassion and comfort, the benevolence and joy, that live in the Feminine, and so they are devoid of the energy generated by erotic love.

Neither man nor woman can come alive as adults without the power of erotic love. Nor can either grow in self-awareness without consciousness of the value of the other. They cannot enter the fullness of adulthood without being conscious of their opposite sexuality dwelling within them. If not loved erotically, both men and women distort their *others* (that is, each one's personal perception of the opposite sex). Thus, they distort their own identities. And their spirits suffer in a hell of mutual antagonism.

If a woman internalizes a man's worship, reasonable love, and commitment, or his hate and violence, then she becomes narcissistic, able to see herself only as an object to worship or to hate. Patriarchy has successfully blocked her path to her spiritual and sexual self-understanding. *Limited to a patriarchal understanding of her self, she has lost access to true self-love and her own power to be.* And where there is no love, there is no spirit; her self disappears.

When all a woman knows is worship and adoration or ridicule and scorn, then all she can offer her man is her reflection of a distorted masculinity and a narcissistic version of her own disowned femininity. What he then internalizes is an unintegrated, narcissistic femininity that allows an unintegrated, half-developed male.

Not only does the woman worshipped as a goddess cease to exist as a living woman, but the man who worships her (or violates her) exists only as an unintegrated, partially realized man.

ANGER AND PUNISHMENT

While the ashes on the altars of Aphrodite began to grow cold, Aphrodite began to grow hot with anger. Her anger punished Psyche, though the poor girl was in no way to blame. Finally Aphrodite decided to put a stop to the whole business, and in Her ocean queendom of unknown and unclaimed primordial femininity She plotted the girl's death.

The traditional (patriarchal) interpretation of this myth pits a petty, jealous Aphrodite against an ineffectual, panicky Psyche. It depicts the incarnation of Eros, the potent god of love, as an immature Cupid rather than an adult, virile man. However, the older interpretations knew Eros as the personification of the powerful Masculine Principle, representing the life-force of penetrating love, born of Aphrodite. They recognized Aphrodite as the great, all-powerful Goddess, Creator of all, and Psyche, Her child, as the soul expressed in human sexuality.

What clues us in about the truth of the Goddess's anger is the statement "the ashes on the altars of Aphrodite began to grow cold." That was what was happening: men were ceasing to worship the Great Goddess. Instead, they were dressing themselves up in Her royal robes; they preferred to rule and exercise power over others rather than love the

Feminine and use power for others. (Ministers, priests, and judges still wear the robes of the Goddess! And they still mistake power as power over others. And they still betray the love and wisdom of the Great Goddess.)

Yes, Aphrodite grew hot with anger. Man had betrayed Her love and desecrated Her gifts. She knew that if men stopped worshiping Her, the One who loved all Her creation passionately, and started worshiping a male god who despised the Feminine, abhorred sexual desire, and called erotic relationships evil, they would no longer know how to give or receive love. She knew that when man stopped valuing the Feminine he stopped loving his own masculinity, and the less man loved his own human sexuality the less he could love woman. The heart of the Goddess was rent in two when She thought of Her daughters and sons having to submit to loveless lives.

Aphrodite knew that without the goodness of the love that can exist only between equal opposites—between man and woman, who together constitute the fundamental unit upon which all societies are built—the whole world is condemned to live in darkness. The split between male and female, which the patriarchal devaluation of the Feminine fosters, is the split that is reflected in all the wars, disharmonies, divorces, civil strife, religious contentions, and family dissensions that erupt on the face of the earth like death-boils on a human body.

Yes, Aphrodite was jealous—but not of Psyche. She was jealous for Her power. Instead of worshiping Her and honoring female sexuality, patriarchal man was making a male god supreme in heaven to endorse his superiority on earth. And he was depreciating the priceless worth of the Feminine to nothing! Obeying the orders of his almighty god, man was destroying worship of the Goddess, offering no burnt sacrifices on Her altars, and debasing Her idols. She was no longer Goddess but captive consort to a father-ruler god until he could dispose of Her altogether and reign alone. Aphrodite foresaw the thousands of years of darkness that would ensue with devaluation of the Feminine. She knew that, deprived of consciousness of Her power, neither man nor woman could become a whole human being.

The Feminine Principle cannot be simply added or subtracted at whim. Man cannot subtract the Feminine either from his own being or from the culture without diminishing the Masculine and distorting his own self. Nor can patriarchy be cured by simply adding the Feminine to it. The Feminine is one of two necessary ways of being human. It cannot be ignored or devalued if men and women are to be whole—they need both the Masculine and the Feminine Principles. Without a valued Feminine and an undistorted Masculine, man and woman are incapable of sustaining erotic love, which is the basis of human evolution and the basis of personal development. If one half of being human is murdered, the other half becomes the walking dead!

The Goddess knew that to try to add the Feminine to a system of male dominance was futile. Something had to happen that would enable people to transcend patriarchy, leave behind what they had been taught, and take humankind into a healing unknown. So Aphrodite had to devise a plan that would restore the value of the Feminine, return the spirit of man, and reestablish the goodness of sexual gratification and the holiness of erotic love.

As it is from a woman's body that new life is born, so it had to be from the Feminine that a new reality was given. Thus Aphrodite decided to take a chance on Psyche. She would do everything in Her power—including using Her anger—to see that Psyche became the mother of a new reality by becoming a whole-souled, fully sexual adult woman. (But note: Aphrodite never ever let Her anger control Her; She controlled it. Always behind the anger of the Goddess is Her love.)

Though patriarchy tried to destroy the power of the Goddess, it could never completely succeed. Aphrodite continues to reign, but from the unconscious. Pushed underground, the power of the Feminine will torture men and punish women until they wake up, grow up, and love erotically.

The Goddess of Love was gravely displeased that patriarchal man could do no more than worship and adore the one whom he was created to love and to passionately penetrate with his masculine erotic passion. She knew that Psyche could not find her personal identity as an adult woman without a passionately loving sexual response from the Masculine. (This masculine response does not have to be found only in a person-to-person relationship with a man; it can also be encountered in a culture or a religion that has the undistorted Masculine in it.) Aphrodite was offended that Psyche was accepting worship and adoration rather than love and respect. And so is a woman's deep, inner feminine self offended.

Without passionate masculine love, and honor for the Feminine powerfully penetrating her, a woman cannot bring forth her adult self. The Goddess was furious that Psyche had been cheated out of participation in the fullness of life by a truncated masculinity that denied her her erotic love and forbade her consciousness of self. By worshiping her, patriarchal man and his culture debased the magnificence of Psyche's sexuality to whore (only whores are sexual) and mocked her purity of spirit by an empty goddesshood. A woman worshiped as goddess is the other side of the coin of unconscious femininity: a whore fucked. The worship given to Psyche forced her to sacrifice her spirit to patriarchal values and her sexuality to the service of a distorted masculine ego as surely as did the devaluation of the Feminine and the subjugation of woman.

Aphrodite was furious, but not just at the men who could only worship and adore, she was also furious at Psyche. She was angry with a womankind that was obedient to patriarchal authority, that had squelched the anger needed to stand up for the Feminine and that allowed women to be worshipped and adored, dishonored and debased.

Aphrodite's blood boiled while Psyche stood in the temple unfeeling, sweetly smiling, accepting men's garlands of praise, cool and composed but helpless and hopeless. The girl was unconscious of the horror happening to her; she was therefore powerless to get herself out of the temple of worshiping wimps. But Psyche's ignorance and passive acquiescence were unacceptable to the Goddess! Like Aphrodite, woman's deep unconscious self boils with anger when she lets men worship and adore her as much as when they dishonor and debase her.

By placing Psyche on a pedestal, man immobilized her: the only way she could remain there was to be still—the still unravished bride of patriarchy, whose masculine authority she must obey. This authority is still sanctified by his religions, codified into his laws, and interpreted by his own fancy. Man must keep a woman on that pedestal so that he does not have to see a real, live woman. Truly seeing her might cause him to encounter her femininity, and her femininity has the power to arouse his erotic desires. Man avoids having to really see woman by worshiping and adoring her (as much as he does by debasing and scorning her). Placed on a pedestal woman becomes invisible. And how nice—how humble—that makes man look.

If man does not have to "see" woman, then he can control his sexual desires more easily and avoid facing his underdevelopment, which is caused by the lack of value placed on the Feminine in his male-centered society. He "sees" only his idealized conception of a goddess he thinks promises him immortality. Or he "sees" a whore whose body he can use. He does not see a real live woman who can love him, but whose love would demand an erotic response from him.

Under patriarchal subjugation, a woman suffers as a mindless body, a whore, or as a bodiless spirit, a goddess. How humiliating it is to a woman when she tries to make herself so mindless that she drifts into nothingness until she fails to exist. But mindless, she does not have to suffer as severely from paternalistic man's destructive anger and hate, his accusations and criticisms. Mindless, she does not have to suffer as much from the knowledge that she has capitulated to a system that requires her subordination to man.

At the same time, a woman in a patriarchal society has to learn how to become bodiless. An invisible body does not take up any space, nor does a bodiless spirit have to feel death. If she can live outside of her body in her mind—if she can cut her feelings off at the head—then she cannot be ruled through her body. She cannot feel the hurt masculine debasement of her body causes nor the horror of masculine invasion of her space. But she cannot feel love either, because human expression of love requires bodies with which to feel, and minds in which to register feeling.

To make herself mindless and bodiless takes tremendous physical effort. Such effort is stressful to the body. And what takes even more of a woman's effort is to know when to be mindless and when to be bodiless. This stress on a woman's body is compounded when nothing she does seems to do her any good; when all her actions are met with only more controlling responses by the men in her life and by the masculine forces in the culture, which caused her pain in the first place. Prolonged periods of stress place such strain on the human body that they can lead to long-term health problems. Patriarchal mind-sets and value systems destroy a woman's health: they deplete her body and sap the vitality of her spirit.

Without a body with which to love and be loved, without a mind in which to register love, Psyche was cut off from her spirit. In the Feminine way of being, spirit is love and love is spirit and they need her body in which to dwell, and they need her mind in which to function. Patriarchal values lock woman's spirit/love in her head where all the energy just spins around, confusing her and everyone around her. Without her body every woman is effectively cut off from her spirit, and without her spirit she is effectively cut off from the meaning of her life.

In a patriarchy women suffer profound debasement. Their womanhood is not accepted as a personhood. A woman's life has no meaning in and of itself. The value of her personal female sexuality—the very basis of her self-identity—is dishonored and debased. The value of her personal feminine spirituality—the very basis of her integrity—is worshiped out of existence or ridiculed and scorned. Any meaning to their lives women are allowed depends upon the males to whom they belong or the people they serve in patriarchal institutions (including the patriarchal institution of motherhood). A modern Psyche is valuable only as she makes herself conform to a man's picture of a virgin goddess (an obedient daughter, a good wife, a subservient secretary, a productive worker, and a perfect mother, for instance). Her worth is dependent on man's approval; his reactions to her determine her value and her meaning. It is difficult for a woman to find an identity in a culture that denies the value of the Feminine!

The literature of our culture supports the patriarchal system. The Bible validates the subjugation of women, starting with the second chapter of Genesis and continuing through the Old Testament and into the New. Aristotle, too, expressed his definitive views on the superiority of the male and the inferiority of the female. These are the two major sources of the theological and philosophical psychodynamics that have formed our modern patriarchal culture. These motivational forces are still active today, though most people have forgotten their sources.

Every woman in a patriarchy is in a no-win situation. If she succeeds in fitting herself into the patriarchal picture, she loses her sense of self. But if she tries to maintain her sense of self, she loses her value in a patriarchal society because she is not being an obedient woman. Either way, she faces an overwhelming sense of not being there—of not accounting for anything, not existing. Any time woman tries to become alive, aware, and responsive to her self and her life, she is oppressed. The terrible temptation to non-be—just to fade out—in the face of worship and adoration, or contempt and condemnation always hovers around her like a polluted cloud. Her oppression is the smog she must breathe every day.

Contrary to popular psychology, it is real, live men who oppress her, not some unresolved oedipal complex. It is not some unconscious projection of a father figure that holds authority over her; it is real, live men, who occupy positions of real power within a real socio-political and economic system who hold authority over her! She is not neurotically imagining that men have power over her.

This is the reality of most women's lives. A woman may be free to divorce her husband or resign from her job, and this is certainly better than being held prisoner in a miserable situation. But she is not free from the patriarchal consequences. She may be "free" as an individual to search for another job, just as she is "free" to search for another husband. But in doing so she only exchanges one master for another. Even if she were to find the perfect husband and the perfect boss, she would not escape from the system that sanctions her subjugation. It is the patriarchal system—regardless of how innocently it is rationalized—that deprives her of access to her own power: the right to decide for herself, the right to make money for herself, the right to participate in symbol-making, and the right to write history.

Murderous rage is the only sane response to a masculinity that dishonors the Feminine, that degrades her virtues and discounts her strengths, that rapes a woman rather than charms and delights her with passionate masculine love. Without masculine love and honor, patriarchy cheats women out of participation in life—a life most men are afraid to live. The deeply buried but still living Feminine in every Psyche is in passionate revolt against the stifling effects of patriarchal values and belief system that murder the Feminine and make the Masculine impotent. Where can a woman find the passion necessary to ignite and fuel her spirit in a spiritless, rational, sexless, male-dominated society that has outlawed erotic love?

The patriarchal belief system has coercively indoctrinated society into believing that women are "naturally" dependent, helpless creatures. But dependency is not an attribute inherent in the Feminine. Women are incredibly imaginative and resourceful human beings, about as dependent as a tigress.

The fury of Aphrodite is the fury of every woman's unconscious self at being subjugated by a male-dominated culture that makes her dependent. Such a culture forces her to surrender her autonomy; she must give up her sexuality to man's control, and exchange her reproductive capacities and her unpaid domestic services for whatever economic support he cares to give. She must give up the right to her spirit and worship a male god (in some form or other) who abominates women and degrades the Feminine in exchange for his social protection (according to his whims). Every woman's spirit rebels at being forced to live the lie of such demoralizing dependency. And every woman's body rebels at being forced to live the lie that this is masculine love!

What is inherent in the Feminine is the knowledge that all creatures are interdependent and the sociability needed to express interdependence. Sociability is the wonderful quality of being able to focus on people. It is found in the Feminine Principle and is realizable in both men and women. It is the ability to see everyone as an individual—listening and responding, laughing and smiling, weeping and caring. But patriarchy cannot survive with interdependent people who are also independent. It needs dependent men as well as dependent women in order to maintain its control over society.

Patriarchy blocks man from becoming independent and powerfully masculine by preventing the birth of his consciousness of his inner woman. If man despises (or worships) women and abhors the Feminine, then he certainly will not want to find his own feminine self. Patriarchy blocks woman from becoming independent and powerfully feminine by preventing the birth of her consciousness of her inner man. If she is never ravished by masculine erotic love, how can she find a loving inner man-self?

When individuals are blocked from what they need, want, or desire, they become angry. Patriarchal societies are very angry ones. So in order to tone anger down, patriarchy has had to indoctrinate people into believing that anger, like sexual pleasure, is a sin. Like erotic love, anger has the power to arouse disobedience. Therefore, in a paternalistic culture anger is decried as a vulgar, ugly emotion. Nice people don't have it—especially respectable, *feminine* women.

The exception is masculine authorities—from the father of the family (the husband of his wife) on up through the Papa, the Pope, and all other heads of state. They have the right to get angry and punish anyone who displeases them. Their anger is the policing force that keeps subordinates in line.

Patriarchy cannot tolerate feminine anger because once a woman can get really angry at what patriarchal values do to her it becomes impossible for her to remain entrapped in submissive behavior. She can see what daylong tension and nightlong agonizing does to her. Such anger ignites her courage to question the counterfacts of patriarchy and stand up for herself. She challenges the assumption that male development is the norm and female development is only a deviation.

Most men cannot imagine what it is like to live life as a deviation. Many women cannot face the horror either, and instead of the hard work of becoming aware they choose to remain as unconscious as possible. Enslaved in the system, they will change lovers, jobs, houses and environments, anything but themselves. (And men are no different; they hate to change themselves even more than women do.) But no sane woman wants to remain a slave to the system—no matter how privileged a man might make her—or become a stand-in for a man, a substitute deputy for patriarchal authority. She wants to express the power of her femininity.

Yes indeed, Aphrodite—the symbol of deep, unconscious feminine love—grew hot with anger. She was boiling mad at Psyche's capitulation to male domination. The Goddess could not tolerate Psyche making herself a nonbeing to please play-it-safe men. She detested the stench of corruption arising from a culture that had killed the Feminine and left it rotting, while glorifying the Masculine and exalting patriarchal values.

Aphrodite was sick and tired of worshiping wimps and play-it-safe, self-righteous bullies—males who refused the hard work of becoming men. She abhorred males who used their power to abuse the women in their lives but who were powerless to imbue them with virile, ardent love. She wanted passionate, sexual men who could love a powerhouse like Psyche, and passionately penetrate her with the single-mindedness of masculine sexual love until she knew what a man's love for the Feminine felt like. Aphrodite wanted developed men and developed women to meet in a passionate, sexual love that transformed them both.

She was furious that impotent men and sexless women had bought patriarchal love substitutes: worship and adoration, reasonable love and commitment, goddesshood and motherhood. She knew that Psyche must not be seduced into thinking that the way to become independent was to be a supermother, a superwife, or a superwoman—that the way to become loved was to be obedient, kind, and true and never angry. Nor must Psyche be deceived into thinking that the way out of patriarchal subjugation was through the masculine approach of directed consciousness and logical thinking because man would always win at his own game of rationalizing. Trying to think, act, and feel like a man would not release her from patriarchal bondage any more than being the ideal feminine woman would. However, rebelling against patriarchy was no more a way out than compliance was.

The truth is that there is *no* patriarchal step a woman can take to free herself. And the same is true for man: there is no patriarchal step he can take to free himself from being the unconscious tool of the system he operates, which denies him his full, conscious manhood. The tragic paradox is that even as man abhors the Feminine and despises every trace of it in himself, he is woman's prisoner, and woman, denied the worth of the Feminine, at the same time she is cast out of the masculine world that subjugates her, is man's prisoner. In a patriarchy men and women end up each other's jail keepers (not a relationship very conducive to love).

The terrible price of patriarchal culture is the murder of the Feminine. For both men and women alike it is the loss of the Feminine that causes them their inner self-loathing. And being unconscious of self, they project their self-loathing onto the opposite sex, creating a hell for which each blames the other.

Since there was no way in patriarchy for Psyche to free herself, Aphrodite knew She had to force her out of Her temple. Only the anger of the Goddess could make Psyche find an effective way out of subjugation and into freedom. So sooner or later the anger of her deep feminine self, represented by Aphrodite, was going to punish Psyche even though, as the myth says, the poor girl was in no way to blame. No, the girl was not to blame; but the would-be woman was.

Like Psyche in the temple, many a modern woman hopes to avoid responsibility for her plight. It is difficult for her to face the anger she feels towards her own cowardice. It is painful for her to admit that she has capitulated to her underdeveloped, puny, tyrannical inner Masculine. It is easier to project this anger onto the men in her life, blaming them for all her woes.

But men do not cause all her woes. What was punishing Psyche was her own repressed, unconscious anger at her refusal to see the evil of the patriarchal system and her refusal to stand up for herself and fight for her freedom. The more anger a woman pushes out of her conscious awareness, the more anxiety-producing it becomes. Patriarchal values make anger a frightening emotion for most women. It feels as if she were ever to get angry she would explode! She has borne not only the pain inflicted on her but the pain inflicted on her mother and sisters and on her friends, and worst of all, the pain inflicted on her children. She can barely stand it. She grinds her teeth in her sleep until her head aches; she frowns her forehead into wrinkles trying to cope with a system that denies her and every individual in it.

It takes a tremendous physical effort for a woman to not recognize her anger at her own capitulation to the patriarchal system. The physical effort it takes to keep herself in the system and to deal with her patriarchal devaluation as if it did not exist is what causes her fatigue, her feelings of lifelessness, her feeling that she does not count for anything of value, and always that inescapable sense of being invisible.

And man, unconsciously hating himself because he does not have the courage to love the Feminine or the courage to passionately penetrate the woman he desires with his powerful masculine sexuality, projects his anger onto the women in his life. He blames them for his miseries as a child and his failures as an adult. But it is the anger of the devalued and despised Feminine in a man that punishes him for capitulating to a rational system—a system that robs him of his full, potent, and abundant masculinity. It is this unrecognized anger which causes man his ulcers and depressions, his heart attacks and strokes.

It is the fury of an Aphrodite that punishes women and men alike. (And that is the purpose of anger: to inflict enough pain on the targeted person to compel change.) The unconscious power of the Feminine in both men and women is furious at women who refuse to become conscious, who refuse the arduous task of the individuation of their selves. These women accept worship and adoration, commitment and obligation as qualified substitutes for erotic love and personal growth. They accept moral and legal subjugation instead of the freedom to be. How can men ever grow up if women do not take a stand against man's anger and hate, his tyranny and control? And how can they be healthy, whole-souled, wholehearted women if they don't take a stand?

We live in a logical, passionless society where there is paltry masculine passion and little left of the Feminine to experience it. Men, as well as women, need the anger of the Goddess to clear away the buying and selling of love substi-tutes. Aphrodite had to punish Psyche. Otherwise she would still be standing in the temple, outside of erotic love which leads to real life. Without passionate masculine love to awaken her from the sleep of her girlhood, Psyche needed Aphrodite's anger because it was fiercely akin to passionate love. Both ignite the fires of her spirit.

The liberating anger of the Feminine does not use the destructive, clobbering, brutal methods that masculine anger does. It uses the intuitive: Feminine cunning, wiles, guiles, and "guerrilla" tactics. In order to circumvent the masculine rationalization that denies feminine irrationality, Aphrodite wove a plot so irrational that it approached the absurd. *"In her ocean kingdom of unknown and unclaimed primordial Femininity, she plotted the girl's death."*

And of course Psyche would have to die. Only the death of her girlhood allows the birth of a woman's adulthood. The second birth is produced by the awakening of adult sexual desire out of the sleep of childhood. And only the death of Psyche's obedience to patriarchal values would allow the birth of her full, passionate womanhood.

Even though Psyche could not hear now, the Goddess spoke as She speaks to all women who want passionate love in their lives. "O.K. Psyche, if you, a beautiful, powerful princess, cannot get yourself out of the temple and into life, then I am going to kick you out and chain you to the rock of female obedience on top of the masculine garbage heap man calls a mountain. If you cannot get yourself out of the patriarchal picture that damns you, then I am going to make you live it and be subject to the obedience masculine authority tells you is so good and rewarding that it leads straight to heaven. I will show you where obedience leads."

Aphrodite saw that if Psyche would not stand up to her subjugators then Her only option was to make Psyche marry the monster of patriarchal subjugation: Death. Aphrodite had to push Psyche to the edge. Psyche was so blinded by the counterfacts of patriarchy that she could not see that it was not any "deviation" in herself that had caused her plight but the fact that there were no patriarchal men worthy of her. Therefore, Aphrodite was going to make Psyche marry the death of patriarchal union. In fact, She was going to make Psyche fall in love with the Death she had to marry.

What could be worse than to love the thing you hate, to love what oppresses you and denies you your existence? That is what patriarchy requires of women! And the horror is that many an oppressed woman would sell out for it. If only a woman could have reasonable, safe "love" and forget about experiencing the love of an exuberant masculine erotic passion, if only she could love being man's adoring servant, content—even grateful—for his passionless commitment, if only she could love the death she has to marry in patriarchy—then she could love being subordinate to man.

So Aphrodite, the full power of the creative Feminine Principle, had to invent a plot so irrational that it could expose the rationalization of patriarchy's illogical counterfacts. The anger of the Goddess was the only energy that could force Psyche to find a way into freedom and life and out of patriarchal death. Only by becoming wholly Psyche—the one who embodies the full power of Feminine love consciously individuated in her self, but that is still connected to the chaotic, primordial Feminine energy in her unconscious— could she free both women and men from the prison of patriarchy. Only then could she restore the transforming power of the Feminine and reestablish the royal authority of Love, not only for herself and for her man, but also for all humanity. Then in freedom would man and woman be able to connect in passionate erotic love—that love which allows humankind to resume evolution.

Though patriarchy has driven the knowledge of the love and judgment, the goodness and creativity of the Goddess out of our conscious minds, it cannot drive the Feminine Principle out of the unconscious. Aphrodite, Goddess of Love, still reigns deep in the heart of everyman and everywoman. It may take centuries, as indeed it has, for woman to free herself and men but the anger of the Goddess will not relent until she does.

OBEDIENCE: DEATH

By this time Psyche's father was desperate to find a husband for her. Suspecting that her state of affairs might be caused by the displeasure of the Goddess, he went to the oracle of Aphrodite, for She was the arranger of marriages in heaven above and on earth below. He asked what he should do, and the answer he received allowed no further doubt about the wrath of the gods.

Having reached the limits of rationality, Psyche's father was at the end of his rope. He could not deal with the feminine power Psyche represented. She wanted a lover to marry. He wanted someone "suitable" for her to marry.

Unattached, Psyche was unacceptable in a patriarchal society. She was of age, and her female sexuality was acceptable only when she was safely designated as the private property of one specific man. Then she could perpetuate the patriarchal family, benefit the patriarchal state, and promote patriarchal religion. Psyche's father had to get her back in line, or he was not king.

He reacted to Psyche not as a man or as a father but as the obedient and virtuous executive of patriarchal values. He had to punish any woman who refused to belong to a man. With the outrage of patriarchal society pressing on him, all he could do was carry out the laws, customs, and commandments of his system. To do anything else was unthinkable. Psyche's father could not think of any other way. His male-centered culture had cut him off from his source of alternatives: his irrational consciousness of the wisdom in his unconscious.

Like Psyche's father, patriarchal man is terrified of stepping into the realm of irrationality. That is why the Feminine is so frightening to him, why he likens the Feminine to a witch. But the realm of irrationality is where his major alternative-producing faculty lies. The irrational truth is that in order to become fully conscious, every individual must become more and more aware of the contents of the unconscious. If a man cannot contact his inner Feminine, which connects him to his unconscious, then he cannot tap his major alternative-producing faculty. By devaluing the Feminine, man forfeits his consciousness of his inner feminine self. So he remains in the dark, essentially unconscious, in spite of his use of logical analysis, reason, or any other thinking tool. Patriarchal man does not know how to handle anything that is not reasonable, scientific, or logical. He has not faced the limits of his rationality; he can go no further than his reason allows. He has no idea of how to deal with and use irrationality. Instead, he has created outside authorities to control the frightening power of the unconscious and to rationalize the irrational.

But obedience to these authorities has stripped man of the necessity of learning how to use the irrational power that dwells in his inner Feminine. So Psyche's father was forced to go to the oracle of Aphrodite. The oracle, once the voice of the Goddess, had become the vessel in which man could safely contain the power of the Feminine, which he had driven into the unconscious. It was a "safe" expression of the Feminine, because it contained no Masculine! To spare himself the struggle of decision making, Psyche's father simply did what his unconscious, symbolic "mother" told him to do.

Unconscious, he could not hear the oracle's words as irrational wisdom. Instead, Psyche's father tried to fit what he heard into his patriarchal belief system. If he had responded consciously rather than logically to the oracle, the myth could have ended there. He could have said, "Oh, I see. Forcing my daughter into marriage is like making her marry death. No, I won't do that. It is not my daughter's fault that there are no men who are powerful enough to marry her." But instead he logically obeyed his man-made authority.

Since the highest value in his society had been placed on obedience, and control (the pressure to conform) was considered the greatest good, the greatest evil was disobedience and the greatest danger was anything uncontrollable, such as the Feminine and erotic love. Psyche—unmarried and of no value to her father, to another man, or to society— represented man's uncontrollable, undominated, passionate, sexual *other*. Patriarchal man is terrified of women. His sexual *other* is what "makes" him betray his patriarchal, masculine values. Therefore woman is evil and dangerous, and erotic love is sinful. So man must get her married—under his dominance—to make her good (i.e., to control her). And he must destroy uncontrollable erotic love. Perhaps more threatening to a man than the fear of war is the fear of the uncontrollability of the Feminine, and the irrationality of erotic love.

Contrary to patriarchal beliefs, erotic love is not chaotic. It is considered messy only because patriarchy has created false boundaries for human sexuality and false limits for human spirituality. Without man's laws and his god's commandments, erotic love is anything but messy. It is self-regulated, because it is not unconscious or all-engulfing. It is not blind, and it is not self-consumed. Rather it is consciously directed to specific individuals, whose happiness and welfare are paramount to the lover. Patriarchal man fears erotic love because it is not subject to his control. His laws and logic cannot contain it because no human being or human institution can manufacture or generate or calculate it. Erotic love is a gift from the realm of irrationality. It is a gift from Divine Love. So patriarchy has invented contractual marriage to squelch it.

Erotic love draws together all the pairs of *others*, but it does not destroy the identity of each. Without it the two halves of being human are bereft of what they need for self-identification. Each half needs some means of establishing a passionate, conscious connection with its *other.* Erotic love encourages men and women to recognize and value the feminine and masculine parts of being human. It lets them like being who they are.

In an erotic society adults become responsible for themselves and responsive to the consequences of their behavior. They also become responsive to the value of other individuals and to the welfare of their environment. When erotic love between man and woman is allowed to flourish, other friendships also flourish (friendships between men and friendships between women and friendships between men and women). There is passionate caring for all humankind and for the earth upon which they live.

Erotic love is like an atom bomb to patriarchal values: it blows up the need for obedience and control. Since erotic love gives people the means of knowing and liking who they really are, they do not need any authority to dictate who they should be and what they should do. They would laugh at a commandment to love God. How could anybody not love Divine Love—a power who had given them human sexuality, sexual desire, consciousness of self, and an intelligence comparable to the goddesses and gods themselves?

The social order of an erotic community is based on love rather than control. It is this love that has the power to draw together all different types of human beings into a caring community. It is not some fear of a common enemy that makes people want to support each other. Love emphasizes the integrity and growth of the self, rather than obedience to a system. Therefore the transformation of self from good to better, from a fraction to a whole, from happy to happier, and from productive to creative becomes the goal of personal life. Paradoxically it is this emphasis on individual growth that produces a strong communal life. The enrichment of each individual and the enhancement of the whole living environment become the goals of society.

The fruit of a society based on erotic love is harmony. People who are satisfied sexually are just plain happy. And people who are in love are vibrantly happy. Emotions always precede behavior. This does not mean that people do not feel tired and cross, grumpy and irritable, or sad and discouraged from time to time. On this earth there will always be earthquakes, fire and flood, disease and pestilence, imperfection and the struggle for perfection. But in an erotic community people are encouraged to experience the pleasure of their Divinely given, ontological sexuality. Through the erotic love between a man and a woman people can find the wholeness of being human and the everlastingness of Divine Love.

Without wholeness and happiness, people seek security. They seek to appear good. To avoid the risk of being "wrong" and the hard work of obtaining freedom, people want to be told what to do. They would rather obey than tackle the tasks necessary to grow up. So individuals in a patriarchal society allow invented authorities to tell them how to think, what to do, how to feel, what to love, even how to be saved.

In refusing to take responsibility for themselves, men and women give others the authority that should belong only to their own inner selves. The problem most people have with following their inner voice is that only they can hear it. And of course they have been taught not to trust themselves. There is no way they can prove their inner authority is the best thing for them prior to acting on it. Therefore, unwilling to trust this inner voice, people willingly give away their own authority and make others responsible for their welfare and happiness.

Thus patriarchal authorities have formed "reasonable"-sounding clichés to replace thinking: Don't change horses in the middle of the stream. The early bird gets the worm. Always be obedient, kind, and true. Etc. And to replace feeling, they have formed rigid beliefs about "safe" and "unsafe" emotions: A nice lady is never angry. Big boys don't cry. Married women are always content. Brave men never feel afraid. Etc. Otherwise people would see and feel reality— the reality that life without the passion and depth of erotic love, without the joy and charm of the Feminine, is not worth living!

Obeying is easier and safer than thinking and feeling and acting according to one's personal values. Only by recognizing and prizing the power-loaded Feminine and accepting uncontrollable, unpredictable erotic love can a person's own values emerge. Since such values are very different from what people have been taught, they can cause very frightening thoughts and feelings. The patriarchal prison of unconsciousness feels warm and safe and secure, even if it is only the security of hell.

Unconscious and afraid, people believe the lie that "reasonable love" is better than impassioned love; it lasts longer and is more reliable. They forget what the difference between commitment and devotion feels like. They forget the difference between self-control and self-development, between obligation and the mutual give-and-take of intense erotic love. Being obedient, committed, and obligated really feels like being trapped. It feels as if someone is always following, watching, and judging. Being devoted, being inspired by giving and receiving intense pleasure, and being challenged by the excitement of growing feels much different; it feels like pure joy, enthusiastic anticipation, and passionate work, even though it may feel frightening at times.

People accept the kind of "committed love" that patriarchal marriages (and live-in arrangements) exact ("You do this and I'll do that"). This kind of "love" is really only obedience to a contract! People believe that the mutual suffering imposed by such "committed love" is not only normal but character-building as well. They do not know that there can be both growth of self and concern for others. They do not know what it is like to live in a society based on the joy that the mutual respect and attraction between male and female and the sacrament of sexual love brings. *Patriarchy has systematically debased the union of man and woman that is based on the holiness of erotic love, joy, and the delight of sexual desire.*

By despising the Feminine and glorifying the Masculine patriarchy destroys the equal worth of each person, and the equal worth of Masculine and Feminine values. The codified laws of patriarchal dominance (such as Athenian Law, Hebrew Law, the Middle Assyrian Law, and the Code of Hammurabi that are reflected in our laws today) are in marked contrast to Etruscan Law and Spartan Law, which still honored the holiness of sexual desire, the sacredness of the union between man and woman, and the freedom of women.

To enforce its ideal of committed love, the patriarchal mentality sets up the only acceptable standards by which all people shall be judged. These standards permeate all the media that influence people—movies, T.V., magazines, novels, and even nonfiction. Duty is presented as a higher virtue than pleasure, and obligation as a more noble motive than love. But guilt is the real force that drives men and women to obey. They are afraid to not obey laws and afraid to not fulfill obligations, even though those laws and obligations prevent the growth of their personal selves and prevent them from having real concern for others.

Thus patriarchal man in his infinite wisdom has written the judgment scene! Guilt and the fear of retribution are the directors of the play that patriarchy writes. And by establishing changeable models of "correct" behavior, man sets himself up to be judged. Since he wants judgment so he can consider himself good for obeying Someone Else's standards, that is what he gets. And the judgment of that Someone Else is that man, born in "original sin," *deserves to die*; only obedience to a "higher" authority can save him.

Therefore obedience is not only easier and safer than being free to struggle and decide for one's self, it is also the way to salvation. Both man and woman are seduced by the patriarchal belief that obedience promises them the ultimate security: immortality. "Obey and you will be saved! You won't die alone! In fact, you won't die at all! Just obey—pay your taxes, go to church, go to war, go to school, go to work, go play—and you will be saved; you will be taken care of forever and ever."

The fact that obedience fails to make man feel good escapes his thinking. He does not realize that his guilt-ridden anxiety, his often hostile feelings of resentment, his jealousies, his accusatory suspicions, and his easy condemnation are caused by his having to obey, having to say no to himself, and having to live in fear of breaking some unknown law. And woman, born "inferior" in a patriarchy, always knows she is guilty of some unknown crime. Fear, obedience, and guilt do not make for happy, creative people who are ready to understand the humanity of each and the fallibility of all and who are glad to live in harmony.

Patriarchal man believes that by obeying he can escape the consequences of having sold out his right to become conscious. With false impunity he has driven the Feminine and the power of the irrational underground, and all that energy lies suppressed in the unconscious. Man has made his man-made authority into a god whom he obeys as supreme. But true Deities do not tolerate idolatry! All the unconscious forces man denies gather energy, not only within himself but also within his culture, waiting like a dormant volcano to erupt.

The history of modern patriarchy is the history of the furious outbursts of unconscious forces unleashed upon a mankind whose highest value is control, whose highest virtue is obedience. Patriarchal men have refused to become conscious of who they are; they have debased the holiness of erotic love, and they have destroyed consciousness of the value of the Feminine Principle. But they can never avoid the forces that rebel against being shoved into the unconscious.

The answer Psyche's father received from his man-made authority "allowed no further doubt about the wrath of the gods." However, in his patriarchal blindness he could not see that he encountered the wrath of the gods precisely because he had obeyed the authority he had set up as supreme. He was deaf to his own inner voice. Instead of taking responsibility for himself, the king blamed Psyche for the impotent state he claimed she put him in.

Like Psyche's father, modern man has abdicated his freedom to decide; he has chosen dutiful, empty obligation. He prefers the safe ethic of obedience to the challenging ethic of creativity, which requires the courage to be. He prefers to be a play-it-safe, do-gooding, worshiping wimp. He has abdicated his right to the dignity of consciousness, choosing instead to remain unconscious and half-developed, a crippled and crippling mortal. If his do-gooding does not work, he will just as soon settle for the violence it takes to keep him in control. Psyche's father and all of patriarchy—men, women, and the culture itself—encounter the wrath of the gods at every point of their obedience. *And no man-made authority, no set of laws, no belief system, no almighty father in heaven* can protect them from the consequences of their obedience; no matter how much power they invest in the authorities they obey.

Aphrodite speaks. Would the king could hear.

"Listen, great king, you exemplar of 'godly' behavior and mindless obedience: You have turned my oracle into the voice of your man-made authority, and now I'm going to shove it down your throat. The worship you offer me is worthless. You have dishonored the feminine values that alone can make your life worth living. You have not loved femaleness with your whole heart, and you have not loved yourself and your masculinity as I do. By worshiping and adoring someone you should love and cherish, you have committed idolatry.

"You think you are godly because you obey your laws. But your godliness is a fraud. You have profaned sexual desire and desecrated the holiness of erotic love. You have refused to accomplish the tasks that would make you a man, and you have placed on women the burden of your undeveloped masculinity, conning them out of being ravished by wholehearted, irrational masculine passion for the Feminine. You have cheated women out of the life you are afraid to live.

"You want judgment? Well I will give it to you. In your ethic of obedience, you, you self-exalted king, are damned! You think you can live without the Feminine? Well, that is what you are going to do. You want obedience? That is just what you are going to get. And you are going to taste, swallow, and digest the fruit of your obedience: death."

Thus Aphrodite pronounced sentence on men who demand obedience to a patriarchal authority that they have invented for their own benefit; who subjugate women, destroying the value and passion of being woman; and who outlaw erotic love, destroying the value and passion of being human, the incarnation of the Divine. Her sentence also falls on every woman who ignores the anger of the Goddess and mindlessly obeys the oppressors of the Feminine. The myth shows us in vivid images what happens when we deny our inner authority and look to outer authorities to give us permission to live and love and be: we encounter the wrath of the Great Goddess and all lesser gods. The power of the unconscious will not be denied.

Aphrodite had her oracle proclaim a terrible sentence for Psyche.

"Dress thy daughter like a bride; lead her up the mountainside. There an unknown winged foe, feared by all who dwell below, and even by the gods above, will claim her as the hawk the dove."

Psyche was to be married to the ugliest, the most terrifying, the most devouring of all monsters: the monster whose name was Death. Unlike the other gods, the dark-robed lord, Thanatos, had no temples of worship. He hated gifts. Even the other gods feared him.

Psyche's parents were devastated, but they had no recourse. Oracles were the final word; there was no higher court. Psyche was to be taken, in all her wedding finery, to the top of a mountain. There she was to be chained to a rock and left for the monster.

Psyche's parents were devastated. But they had no recourse. According to the ethic of obedience, rational man must obey the authority he has established. In a patriarchy there can be no higher court than that which man has made. The oracle of his authority exacts his obedience (be it his church, his state, his government, his history, or his principles).

Though Psyche's father was devastated, he obeyed. He dressed his daughter like a bride and led her up the mountainside. Weeping, the still unravished bride obeyed her father. Psyche's father obeyed his highest man-made authority, that he called God, and his daughter obeyed her father, the earthly representative of her father's god. In the most vivid images possible this myth of Psyche and Eros shows us that, regardless of how we dress it up, obedience to anything other than the authority of self leads to death.

And it is no different today. In a patriarchy the ethic of obedience rules the wills of unconscious men and women, who think they know what they are doing. Men and women submit to Someone Else's concepts of right and wrong, good and bad. They are cowards, afraid of taking risks, of venturing into the unknown. They deny their inner voice, believing they are doing "God's will."

But obedience is death. It obliterates consciousness and murders creativity. It renders powerless the energy that only conscious activity and passionate awareness generate. It annihilates our humanity, making robots out of men, women, and children. The destructive offspring of obedience are possessiveness, bigotry, hatred, envy, and resentment. Obedience massacres all of our relationships, including the relationship of the personality to the self. Obedience requires that the fear-motivated ego be the center of the personality; it ignores the authority of the self. And it ultimately kills our relationship to the Giver of Life.

How could Psyche's father obey such a sentence? He did what was "rational." He followed the rules that patriarchy first concocted and then called godly. And so does modern man. Following the rules relieves him of the responsibility of being a man. At the same time it allows him to convince himself that he is doing the right thing. But what man is doing is practicing human sacrifice. He is killing his beloved—the Feminine—in order to avoid the arduous tasks of being a man. And in the process he kills the exuberance of his own masculinity. He sacrifices his own soul alongside his beloved's upon the altar of his man-made god, obeying, thinking he is godly!

Thus man hardens his heart; for if he can be cruel to what he is created to love most, he can be cruel to anyone. And his cruelty to himself causes such a wound that nothing in a patriarchy can ever totally deaden the pain.

By condemning Psyche, Aphrodite exploded the illusion of patriarchal power. She demonstrated that man, in his power system of control, is powerless to save what he loves most: himself! At the same time, Aphrodite exposed the hypocrisy of patriarchal values. Barbaric, patriarchal man, having suppressed the innate goodness of humanity, will "love" woman only until she violates his rules. And she *will* violate his rules out of the innate goodness of her own heart, the goodness inherent in the Feminine! The moment a woman steps beyond the limits of patriarchy she is sentenced, branded as bad.

By telling the king to enforce Psyche's obedience, to chain her up so she could not exert her own will, Aphrodite exposed the emptiness and evil of patriarchal marriage. It is based on contract and commitment. It legally and morally subjugates women and it legally binds man to a contract designed to destroy his true masculinity.

In an unquestioned, unconscious power system Psyche was chained to the rock of obedience at the top of the mountain of belief in patriarchal values. There she awaited the consummation of her marriage to the most awful of all foes. In our culture of unmitigated, male-ordained authority, when women marry, they marry Death!

But so, too, do men. By destroying any consciousness of the worth of the Feminine, patriarchy prevents men from becoming conscious of their inner Feminine. Patriarchal values deny man one half of his being human, thereby denying women the wholehearted masculine sexuality they need to become conscious of being female. Patriarchy has so murdered any idea of what it means to be fully female that women have only a meager awareness of what whole-souled feminine sexuality is. So man, too, has married death. He has married the dead female whom he has destroyed through his obedience to the authority he has invested in his man-made god. And he calls himself godly.

The only power strong enough to save both man and woman from patriarchal death is erotic love. Eros, the god of love, who is destined to rescue Psyche, is representative of the life-force in erotic love that opposes Thanatos, the god of death. Erotic love is the only power that can overcome the seduction of Thanatos—the attraction of remaining obediently unconscious, cradled forever in everlasting arms. Remaining forever unaware is based on the false promise that someone else can be responsible for your life. But nobody else, not even God, can really be responsible for you.

Both man and woman need erotic love—it is one of the few needs adults have. It is also the only power that draws the sexual opposites together in passionate sexual desire, teaching man and woman to draw all the opposites of life together into one creative union. It is feeling the emotion of such love, and valuing the way life surges through one because of it, that introduces man and woman to the power in their adulthood.

Psyche was in the grip of the unconsciousness that would hold her prisoner to patriarchal death. Only consciousness of her erotic love could one day free her. And only faithfulness to her experience of erotic love could encourage Psyche to accomplish the hard tasks which lay ahead of her. Man, also in the grip of his unconscious living death, must relinquish his control long enough to aggressively assert the value of the Feminine and so become a man. Erotic love is the only power strong enough and sweet enough to enable and entice him to do so.

The only thing that can save man (if he wants to change) from a deadly dependence on his mother (or mother substitutes) and restore his masculinity to him is a woman who is intensely conscious of herself and the world around her. He needs a woman who has freed her self from patriarchal values, so that she is vibrantly alive with the power and the passion of being woman.

Such a woman cherishes the greatness that lies in the Feminine and is keenly responsive to the power of erotic love. This liberated woman is one who values her self and her femininity so much that she is willing to risk her life for the sake of her feminine values. And the supreme value of the Feminine is love. Only such an intensely conscious woman can sustain the erotic passion, awakened by impassioned Masculine love for the Feminine, long enough for a man to become a man (if he so chooses).

To feel the full impact of the powerful gift of erotic love is what it means to be "touched by God," to be transformed from an obedient child to a self-assertive adult, to go from being worried about being good to accepting one's own innate goodness. It is erotic love that awakens people to the power of the Spirit, leaving them feeling loved and warmed and humbled, deeply loving and caring. The reality of the Divine Spirit is love and it is incarnated in both man and woman. On earth it is experienced most accurately in the love between the sexes, regardless of how that love is expressed. From the "highest" palpitations of the spirit to the "lowest" movings of sexual desire, where love is, the Divine Spirit is.

Erotic love always has an unexplainable, "crazy" element that lies outside the bounds of logical knowledge. The fact that being shot by one of Eros's arrows is the symbol for falling in love illustrates two facts: humans cannot make love happen, and falling in love is irrational, the result of being touched by some Extraordinary Power. Thus, the myth shows us that when the Feminine is chained up people lose contact with the irrational they need. They lose contact with the Divine, which includes the rational perception of life but is also above and below and beyond it. The irrational is what gives meaning to the rational; it is our inner life that makes our outer life vital. The voice of the irrational is the voice of the inner authority of the self. It speaks as intuition, insight, perception, and dream.

In each person the inner authority lives in the Feminine Principle, which is the home of irrationality. When the irrational is suppressed, repressed, and ridiculed, people experience life as meaningless, empty, and darkened by depression. Passionless, they wait alone in the night for death to claim them. And in the morning they can hardly move because their spirits lie unfueled by love.

So in order for men and women to marry life, they must unchain the Feminine. The Feminine is the leader of each self. She is the guide, the one who envisions. The Masculine is the penetrator and impregnator, the supporter and the aggressive assertor of the value of the Feminine. She is our true guide and will lead us freely to abundant life, creativity, and full, conscious relationships.

When the Feminine is denied, people repress and suppress the forces of irrationality that lie in the unconscious. These energies then become destructive. But when people can allow awareness of the irrational to rise to consciousness, valuing the Feminine as much as they do the Masculine and acknowledging the "touch of God" in the irrational act of falling in love, then these forces automatically become creative and life-renewing. There is no need for commandments and obedience to them. Only by restoring the value of the Feminine and reclaiming the right to erotic love are men and women able to develop the self. Only then can they start living their own lives instead of letting patriarchal values live them.

THE DARK
OF DARKNESS

*So on the appointed night Psyche's bridesmaids and her maid of
honor dressed her in her wedding gown. The people of her parents'
court formed a wedding procession which was also a funeral cortege.
Her father led the weeping bride to the rock where he chained her.*

The people of Psyche's father's court, the high and low
of patriarchal society, formed a wedding procession that was
at the same time a funeral cortege. All the torches were lit
so that society could witness Psyche's marriage and be assured
that the oracle was obeyed.

Patriarchal marriage is a public affair, ordained by the
patriarchal god. It serves not only to perpetuate the patriarchal
family, but also to perpetuate the patriarchal state and patriarchal religion (which is not dependent on church, temple, or
mosque). Contractual marriage, like other contracts, must
be witnessed as well as signed. So all of these people, from
the king and queen on down, were going to climb the
mountain with Psyche to see that she was bound to the rock,
so that her marriage partner could claim her.

But they did not see the terrible irony in the fact that
Psyche's marriage was her death. Unravished, unsexed, and
undifferentiated as an individual from the rest of society,
Psyche was condemned to the patriarchal fate: *while she was*

still alive she was forbidden to live. Thus, in death she surely would die. Her death could not be a doorway to another life.

The wedding party, like those of today, was simply playing out the patriarchal farce. Unmindful of what they were doing, they celebrated the fact that the contract was kept and the oracle obeyed. No matter that they wept for Psyche; they were willing to sacrifice her to the patriarchal value system. Not one soul took pity on Psyche or stayed to watch with her. No one wanted to know what she was experiencing.

And then the deed was done. *All the torches were extinguished and Psyche was left alone in the dark.* The light of the Feminine was extinguished and both men and women were sentenced to live in darkness. And how dark is that darkness! How alone that aloneness!

Not only did Psyche's father lead her up the mountainside where he chained her to a rock so she could not escape, but the women of her father's court, her personal friends, dressed her in her wedding gown! How terrible was their betrayal. Instead of trying to help her escape, they joined the men in their sanctimonious persecution of a woman who dared to ask for more than patriarchy would allow. All these good women participated as much as the men did in this marriage-death ceremony. None of them knew the difference between a wedding and a funeral!

In the darkness of patriarchy, even women punish those women who want more from life than patriarchy sanctions, thus furthering the masculine domination of all women. Psyche was not only alone against patriarchy, she was alone among other women. No mother, no sisters, no friends, and no Goddess.

The dark of patriarchy is dark indeed. Man has extinguished the very light that alone can illuminate the darkness of his unconscious world: the light of the Feminine. Like the moon, the light of the Feminine can shine in the darkness without dispelling it; the Feminine permits the coexistence of light and darkness. Mankind has no other light than that of the Feminine to light the darkness of his night. The sun shines only during the day, when the darkness of night is completely dispelled.

Though the light of masculine rational consciousness can lighten the load of man, ease his existence, and cure his diseases, it cannot shine in the darkness. It is an external light which cannot elevate life above the material, cannot heal wounds or alleviate despair. It cannot liberate woman from patriarchal condemnation. It cannot save man from his emptiness or from the separation that causes his unbearable loneliness and anxiety.

Only the light of the Feminine can transform his patriarchal culture into a shared humanity. But instead man chooses to live by sexual exploitation of the Feminine and by violence against other men and nature. The reward for man's violence is not the power he seeks but rather the emptiness of his heart. Man cannot escape the consequences of his degradation of the Feminine any more than he can escape the destructiveness of his hand grenades and hydrogen bombs.

In the dark of patriarchy man can never know the heart soothing of the love between a man and a woman. He can never know what it means to be her honey-man and sweeten her. Instead, he perverts her goodness and disgraces her love. But man can never rid himself of his longing for his created nature, which in turn longs for the Feminine. His created nature calls him to honor, dignify, and cherish the Feminine he was born to love. She is the source of his life and the music of his soul. From the Feminine he was born, and it is the Everlasting Feminine who bends down to receive him into more abundant life when he dies. It is She who has prepared for him a rebirth and a new life after death in the universe She created out of Her own substance (even as mortal woman creates new life out of the very substance of her body).

Under the reign of patriarchy no woman can ever know the heart soothing of sexual love either. She cannot know the love of man for woman; she cannot know the fulfillment of having a man receive and value her love. She can never feel the protection of masculine strength or taste the care of male nurturing female. Psyche, like every woman, naturally yearned for masculine physical strength to embrace her. But the reality she had to live with was that there was always masculine strength around to clobber her, masculine intelligence to insult her, and masculine spirit to dishonor her. And it is no different for women today.

Without the light of the Feminine, patriarchy condemns man and his civilization to a way of life that makes a shared existence impossible. The patriarchal mentality can envision only a society of domination: either a patriarchy or a matriarchy. The inescapable results of extinguishing the illuminating warmth of the Feminine are wars and murder, disharmonies and disputes, pollution of the air and rape of the land, slavery and masters, lust and sexual abuse.

Without the light of the Feminine women are deprived of recognizing the power in the Feminine. They are doomed to live abortive lives as man's guilty, sinful, impotent, obedient servants: his goddesses and his whores. Without consciousness of the worth of the Feminine, men are so deprived of erotic love that they cannot know the power of their own masculinity.

The most direct way they can experience any sense of their masculine power is through war or some form of fighting and killing. In primitive patriarchal times, men were not allowed to sleep with their wives, concubines, or slaves for three days prior to entering battle. We forget that a soldier of the United States must still undergo six weeks of boot camp, deprived of the love of a woman, before going into war. Since men are forbidden to love erotically, war often acts as the catalyst for the awakening of their spirit.

Psyche represented all that would overthrow patriarchy. And so does every woman who claims her magnificence of sexuality and her purity of spirit. Therefore, such women have to be controlled. In spite of the so-called sexual revolution of the sixties and seventies, man still maintains his control of woman's sexuality. Though it may have unsettled him a bit, man simply stretched his boundaries so as to enclose woman in a larger field. He has not extended his field of vision to include the worth of the Feminine. He has only extended woman's leash!

Every Psyche in every patriarchy must be excluded from symbol making, philosophy forming, history writing, science, and law making. Otherwise she would expose the counterfeited reality patriarchy keeps on redesigning to fit each generation's visions of a new reality. She would overthrow male-dominated symbols and establish new symbols: symbols to represent all of humankind, to initiate independent action, and to free both men and women from a reality that patriarchal belief systems have turned inside out, ass backwards, and upside down.

Therefore, patriarchal man has to subjugate woman. He has done this by controlling her sexuality. Like Psyche, modern woman is kept in the dark about her sexual power because it is her power to be. Patriarchy systematically destroys her power to be by making her sexuality a commodity that man owns. He can sell it, buy it, make alliances with it, or molest and rape it.

Like Psyche's father and husband-to-be, modern man can do anything he wants because patriarchy makes a woman feel bad about being a woman. Her only claim to her own sexuality is an anonymous motherhood, anonymous because she has no individual identity and no name of her own. Her motherhood is therefore devoid of personal authority but heaped with blame.

Man believes every woman needs a man to redeem her from her "original sin" of being born female. And so do most women. Patriarchal man has convinced himself and his society that women's sexuality must be controlled. He thinks that if women were free to pursue sexual pleasure, all the world would become a bordello and marriage would be unthinkable. He has to control the sexuality he believes she is incapable of controlling.

Through the laws of the state and the commandments of religion, man makes his subjugation of women's sexuality legal and moral. Patriarchy could not survive in a society that did not have laws regulating birth control and abortion any more than it could survive without laws about marriage. Without such laws women would be free—conscious enough—to own their own bodies. And men would be free—conscious enough—to enjoy the Feminine in women as well as the Feminine that lives within them. And both would be free for a very different kind of life!

A woman who discovers her own sexual pleasure and appreciates it has something of value to share with her man. This sharing demonstrates the essential difference between the patriarchal way and the combination of a valued Feminine way. In the patriarchal way, man "takes" his pleasure from a woman. In the way of mutual honor and equal value, woman shares the pleasure man gives her, and man shares with her his delight in her sharing her sexuality with him, thus increasing the enjoyment of each. It is through this enhancement of their mutual pleasure that society is enriched, new life is born, and a new way of living evolves.

In the patriarchal way, sexuality is not something to be shared. It is a vulgar necessity that needs redemption. Only as it is sanctioned by patriarchal authority can human sexuality be approved. And only man's approval of her can redeem a woman's sexuality.

Thus patriarchal man makes woman's respectability and class dependent on his approval. He can then control her economically and politically. By dividing women into "respectable" and "nonrespectable" groups, man pits woman against woman. He effectively prevents women from finding the strength and support of other women. If a woman dares to deviate from the norm, she is declassed—not only by patriarchy, but (equally important to the system) also by other women.

By morally and legally subjugating woman, patriarchal man reduces her reason for living to being man's helpmate. He defines her as an inferior creature who is intended by "God" to be a silent and obedient vessel for the production of his children (his sons) and for the pleasure and convenience of men. Motherhood is the fulfillment of her sexuality, and wifehood (the only relationship with an adult man that is permitted) is the fulfillment of her spirituality. Biology is her destiny. Anatomy is her fate.

But even anatomically woman is destined for more than motherhood and wifehood. Patriarchy tells her that she is a deformed male, deprived of a sex instrument. But her sex organ, her clitoris, was created for the sole purpose of giving her sexual pleasure. Unlike the male sex organ, hers has nothing to do with reproduction or urination. But man has to pee, ejaculate, and experience sexual pleasure through his tri-purposed organ. It is woman, not man, who has an exclusively sexual sex organ!

Man tries to separate woman's sexual pleasure from her reproductive role. He insists that procreation—not creativity or new life and certainly not pleasure—is the sole purpose of sexual intercourse (as far as women are concerned). But the truth is that new life evolves from mutual pleasure. And lovemaking creates love!

Because Psyche was in the dark about her sexuality, she could be kept in the dark about her spirit. Since spirit/love inhabits a woman's body, her spiritual power can be controlled by subjugating her sexuality. If Psyche were allowed to discover that her sexual pleasure was boundless, she would recognize her value. Then her spirit, released from bondage, would burst the bonds of rationality! Functioning freely in both men and women, it would make life boundlessly pleasurable.

But Psyche had no way of knowing that her spirit could charm, heal, and transform. She had no idea that it was her own spirit that could change the plain drinking water of everyday life into wine. She had no way of knowing that love was the thing she should value the most. Psyche did not know that her love/spirit was the most desirable prize in creation. Instead, patriarchy had written off all Psyches as marginal.

Woman is nothing but a deviation of the male, naturally dependent on man. Man must dominate her; it is his god-given duty. He must make her subordinate to his superior masculine virtues in order to make her "better." Likewise, he must subordinate whole nations and other cultures of men in order to make them "better." This he calls *noblesse oblige*: the obligation of the nobility to the deprived. And so he writes his history.

But what Psyche was deprived of was education. She was deprived of a system of schooling that would draw out and enhance her intellect, her spirituality, and her creativity—a system that would instruct her in the power of symbol making, informing her of her place in history and her power in heaven. But like most modern women, Psyche was left in the murky darkness of ignorance.

Today's schooling does little to educate women. Women, like men, are schooled in patriarchy. They are taught about literature written almost exclusively by men, philosophy devised by men, music composed by men, paintings painted mostly by men, science as the inner sanctum of male consciousness, laws made by men, and religion concocted by men. Men write the history and compile the dictionaries in accordance with patriarchal values and virtues. Words describing anything masculine are positive, while feminine attributes are generally considered negative. (Irrational women are called crazy, erotic women are called kinky or debased, vulnerable women are called weak, and dependent women are called such names as underling, freeloader, leech, parasite, sponge, and vine.) In a patriarchy even the most educated of princesses must live in a culture that is unenlightened by the wisdom and grace of the Feminine.

Patriarchal women have unconsciously accepted their second-rate status. They do not question the idea that man is superior. Fear of repudiation, homelessness, nakedness, and starvation prevents them from standing up to patriarchal man and demanding freedom. Women who are educated in a patriarchy look hard to find what women may have done (or may be able to do) that is equal to the great deeds of men. They cannot see the greatness of the Feminine because patriarchy has extinguished her light. They are therefore blind to the value of the Feminine Principle.

Instead, many modern women believe that if only they could have more power within the patriarchal system they could be equal to men. If they could be like men, assuming masculine virtues and strengths, then they would be worthwhile. But the liberation of women is not possible within the patriarchal system. Even men, as well as the Feminine they need, are trapped in a system that does not value personhood.

Women turn against each other in a patriarchy, vying for a place of value. When a woman tries to free herself from that senseless quest, she is seen as evil because she repudiates patriarchal values. She claims her right to live life and to love as many men, women, and children as her heart can hold! A woman who experiences her own sexual pleasure and finds value in being a pleasure giver—a lover!—is seen as worse than evil. She must be condemned and excommunicated, because she exposes the truth that man does not want to face: life without the Feminine, without passionate sexual desire, and without erotic love is meaningless, pleasureless, gray, and hopeless, regardless of how bright a picture of it patriarchy tries to paint.

But finding the courage and strength to break out of patriarchal lifelessness is very difficult. Instead, patriarchal man works at changing facts to suit himself and fabricating symbols to represent his mind-sets. Man has made a male god to endorse male superiority. In the image of patriarchal man, he created an exclusively male god. This means that the sovereignty man exercises over women—and all "lesser" nations of men—is vested in him by a Supreme Being. Patriarchal man claims to be master by divine right! It is natural for a husband to be in charge of his wife.

So patriarchal man came. He came in disguise as Her lover and took the Goddess—the love and the goodness, the power and the glory, the technology and the wisdom of the Feminine—and yanked Her from Her throne. Throwing Her to the floor, with his boot upon Her belly, he leveled his sword at Her throat. To resolve the war between his desire for blood and his lust for Her, he decided to marry Her. What choice did She have? Obediently She now sat on a stool beside the throne from which *She* had reigned with compassion, wisdom, creativity, and competence, enlivened and stimulated by the Masculine. Man donned the robes of the Goddess, took Her wand as his scepter, and ruled with a cruel and ruthless hand. His reign was not enlivened and inspired by the Feminine. And this is the state of affairs today.

Patriarchal man changed the symbols that represent the creative life-force. He dethroned the ancient, all-powerful Creator/Mother Goddess who held the key to the mystery of life and death, and he replaced Her with his male gods. He excluded the Feminine, She who gives birth! from the symbols for creation. And he taught that "God," an almighty father alone in heaven, created.

And on earth, man the father created. By conceptualizing his semen as "seed," man made a major belief-changing symbol. By this symbol man isolated genetic power and attributed it to his "seed," making his contribution count for everything. The womb then counted for nothing. Just as his "seed" became the symbol for the reproductive life-force, so his male god became the symbol for the Creator of heaven and earth and all therein. "God" created from on high, as man created on earth. The creative power of the Feminine—symbolized by the power to conceive, to accept and assimilate a sperm, to develop a new and unique human being out of the substance of her own body, and to give birth to new life—is not mentioned in any patriarchal story of creation!

Man took over the feminine power of reproduction, an absolute biological absurdity. Patriarchal man then made a new symbol for woman: the earth in which man plants his seeds. Like the earth, woman is symbolized as being totally passive; she has no genetic power of her own. The power of passing on the genes belongs exclusively to the man.

She does not exist. Men may have daughters, but women do not have sons. They are the sons of men, man's "seed," and they inherit the wealth and power of the patriarchal family, the right to make money, the right to rule, and the right to belong to the "holy community," which alone hears and interprets the word of "God." Women have rights only as stand-ins for males; they inherit only according to male generosity, not by right. Man tells women (and all "lesser" peoples) what "God" has said and what it means. Man has assembled the world's bibles, just as he has written history and compiled dictionaries.

Thus man ousts women as possible representatives of the Supreme Being on earth, and he excludes the Feminine from having any divine power in heaven. Man, being the father, is therefore like "God": spiritual, high, pure, and full of light. Woman is earthy, low, materialistic, dark, and dank. By successfully excluding the Feminine from the godhead in heaven, man successfully casts women out of the "holy community" on earth. Women have no role in the symbol-shaping, money-making, history-writing community. Man has robbed woman of even a deity to whom she can pray. In a patriarchy woman is stripped of a divine power upon whom she can call. She must worship and obey a male god whose commandments demean her and whose laws condemn her.

Under the reign of the Great Goddess men and women saw the image of a splendid Goddess everywhere. There was a fearless and natural emphasis on the importance of one's sexual life. This emphasis ran through all religious expressions and even influenced the provocative dress of both men and women. There was an easy mingling of the sexes—the opposite of puritanical stiffness, segregation of the sexes even at parties, and the taboo against open sexual desire.

As long as the Great Goddess and her symbols lived in the active, idea-making faculty of men and women, an equality of human beings existed. A male divinity represented this equality in the heavens, in the shape of a young man who affirmed and stimulated the creative and active Feminine. Both the Great Goddess and her Adonis were worshiped as symbols for exuberant life. This exuberance of life and equality of people radiated into the daily affairs of men and women and affected the quality of family and community life.

Today we do not know what it is like to live in a society in which people normally consider each other equal. Not only did men and women think of each other as equals, they also considered neighboring cities and nations equal to their own. They all worshiped the Great Goddess, regardless of the many names they had for Her; they all were Her children, just as all were the children of their mothers. They all believed in the holiness of life, the value of each individual in a caring community, and the sacrament of erotic love. (A sacrament is the outward, visible sign of an invisible, inner grace.)

The concept of one people or nation or religion being superior to another did not enter "Western thought" until it was brought in (beginning around 2500 B.C.) by invading nomadic tribes from beyond the Black Sea in the north and from the Sinai Peninsula in the south. These tribes were by then accomplished warriors; warfare was inculcated into their way of life. They arrived with their patriarchal mind-sets, value systems, and ideas of god (or gods) very well developed. These tribes did not value civilization. They did not know the meaning of art or advanced agriculture, technology (road and bridge building), or architecture. They were content to live in their tents and care for their flocks, always fighting for the grassland of their neighbor. They did not know how to create wealth and preferred plundering as a way to gain wealth.

Under the Great Goddess, however, people created their own wealth and the wealth of their communities. And they were easily and unashamedly happy. Their material and spiritual needs, as well as their sexual and mental needs, were taken seriously. Their sexuality was considered good, and sexual desire was promoted and satisfied by the mores of their culture. From fully developed sexuality, men and women became joyfully spiritual.

Female sexuality was sacred to the Great Goddess. It was honored in Her rituals, which celebrated the pleasure-giving creativity of the Feminine. The women made cakes for Her with Her features on them. In Her worship, there was recognition of the necessary cooperation between the Masculine and Feminine Principles in the process of creation, in the enhancement of life, and in the regenerative enrichment of the individual. Her priestesses poured libations to Her with their husbands' knowledge and approval.

In spite of the increasing patriarchalization of the culture, as long as women's priestesses were as powerful as men's priests women had the right to mediate between humans and the Divine. They had the right to belong to the Supreme Being's holy community and interpret the divine word. And this power to address the Divine maintained women's essential equality as human beings.

No wonder patriarchy needed to extinguish the light of the Feminine. Her religion precluded any amassing of power and any mode of living that was based on domination and ranking. That is why patriarchy has systematically devalued anything feminine.

Patriarchy claims that female sexuality is evil. It says female spirituality is earthbound at best. Women are incoherent; they are incapable of real thought, decision making, or judgment. Their irrationality is absurd, bizarre, crazy, emotional, foolish, mad, muddled, nuts, rambling, babbling, preposterous, and ridiculous.

So much for the Feminine!

Even when man made that giant leap in abstract thought and could think of the Divine as Spirit, it was the spirit of a male god, born of a father and a son! He could not make the leap to Spirit/Love born of the erotic union of Man and Woman, because he had murdered the Feminine.

Having effectively disempowered Aphrodite, the symbol for the power of feminine sexual love and fertility, man debased sexual love: sex became a sin. Sexual desires, sexual intercourse, menstruation, and birth became dirty. After making Psyche into a goddess devoid of sexual power and "pure as the driven snow," man could then make woman-as-whore the symbol for the source of evil in the world. Thus he vindicated his moral and legal subjugation of woman's sexuality—the sexuality which had once been sacred to the Goddess.

With feminine sexuality out of the way and the Feminine cast out of heaven, man could then make the term "man" subsume woman. The word "man" became the symbol for all humanity. Thus man built into his system of thought a conceptual error of such vast proportions that it has nearly destroyed the entire human race and the planet upon which we live: man believes that he is superior and is divinely commanded to dominate others, amass power and armed might, and rule as he wishes.

How has man coerced woman into playing his patriarchal game, submitting to him, believing his counterfeits, worshiping his male God, and denying her own power and worth? He has used enough violence—slashing her lovely face, raping her, castrating her lovers, torturing her, and molesting and beating her children—to make the threat of violence real. Fear has allowed the dark, sinful concepts bred of male-oriented religions to enter into all aspects of life. Women, afraid, unconsciously internalized the myths and symbols of the patriarchy that enforced its rule and their subordination until at last being subordinate to the male seemed natural and normal.

How has patriarchy gotten men to play its foul game? Not just by giving them the right to rule, the right to subjugate women and enslave other men. Patriarchy has also used death and man's fear of death. The enticing reward that makes a man forsake his calling to be human is the patriarchal promise that if he obeys he will not have to die. Consciously, men believe the bestower of this false reward to be a father-god in heaven. But the one who imparts this belief to a man's unconscious is the patriarchal mother who envisions her son as god. That vision contains a lot of power, the more so because it is buried deep in the unconscious.

There are only a few phrases that clue us in to this unconscious vision. One is "No woman is good enough for my son." The implication is that he needs a goddess (in the image of his mother). Another phrase that gives us a clue is "the golden-haired boy," denoting the savior-god of redeeming light. With age the "golden-haired boy" becomes the "revered professor," denoting the father-god of almighty wisdom. And there are the jokes about the mother who thinks her son is god.

This vision leaves patriarchal man with two choices. He can be a god who won't die but who must live without a body (since gods don't have bodies); or he can claim his body and his masculine spirit—making him man enough to be able to love a woman—but then he would have to confront the fact that one day he is going to die, like everyone else. Thus, to ensure his immortality in patriarchy man has to deny his flesh, fight manfully against the devil (his own irrational masculine spirit that desires to live), and kill his humanity (so he can be a god). If a man forgets his mother (and loves a woman), he will die!

Though man calls his male gods almighty, they are powerless to help him. Man does not win the immortality he seeks by obeying them. Nor does he earn his happiness, his self-fulfillment. Man's marriages end in divorce or stagnate in dead-end roles; even his success is like dust on the tongue without the love he needs. His wars and disputes continue; his rapes and murders go unstopped by all the laws he has made and religions he has concocted. He shares the fate he has inflicted on Psyche: while he is alive he never really lives, so his death is final. His god cannot help him. He has condemned himself to live life as a truncated male!

In the darkness of patriarchy, Psyche has little chance of finding a real man to ravish her with his passionate, masculine love. She is cut off from her erotic love and so from any possibility of becoming a fully conscious human being. Psyche does not have a prayer in patriarchy. In an unconscious state, Psyche could not even claim the anger of Aphrodite, which would oppose masculine oppression. She is chained to the rock of obedience, sacrificed to an unquestioned masculine power system. In rampant, unrelieved patriarchy, with no Feminine Principle to make it more agreeable and compassionate, more loving and joyful, the torches of the light of the Feminine are indeed extinguished.

The terrible irony is that patriarchy has changed the Feminine into the symbol for darkness, rather than the symbol for the light that shines in the darkness. Without the light of the Feminine, both men and women perish, buried alive in a daily hell. But remember darkness cannot put out the light of the moon, nor can it stop the light of a burning candle from shining. We might have to live through the darkness of the moon, but rest assured it shall wax once again. The light of the Feminine is the light of light that darkness can never extinguish.

THE FIRST AWAKENING

Psyche's father had chained her to the rock. And he, his queen, and all of his court had left her for Thanatos, the monstrous Lord of Death, to claim. Not one of them cared enough or had courage enough to dare to defy the value system that denigrates, vilifies, and discounts the Feminine. But Aphrodite cared. The heart of the Goddess broke with an unbearable sorrow when She looked at this wonderful, beautiful, sensitive girl, full of grace and spirit, whom man had cast aside as expendable.

No longer could She tolerate such waste, ignorance, and blasphemy. The Goddess of the power of feminine love was not going to let Psyche be caught in the web of patriarchal subjugation. Patriarchy might try to disempower Her as a Goddess, making Her into some bitchy sex symbol or an aging beauty, but She was not powerless yet. And She was going to exert her power. Though She did not yet know the exact details of what She would do, She had the courage and the strength to dare to defy the system that turned reality inside out and called lies truth. The Goddess of Love was going to fight for love and for all mortal women who would also dare and defy.

It was critical that Aphrodite take this opportunity to restore the psychological and spiritual impact of erotic love. Patriarchy was taking over. Although She was Goddess, She did not know ahead of time what the outcome of Her actions would be. She had to take a risk. Aphrodite had to use totally irrational means: the full power of unconscious, chaotic, fervent, and uncontrolled femininity. She had to call on the power that patriarchy tried to say was limited to intuition.

Aphrodite called in Her son, Eros, the handsome god of love. She ordered him to go and shoot Psyche with one of his golden-pointed arrows to ensure her falling in love with Death. He was delighted to shoot anyone.

To save Psyche from the daily torture of commitment to an increasingly passionless marriage, and from the state of unconsciousness it exacts, Aphrodite sent in Her son, telling him to shoot Psyche with one of his arrows so she would fall in love with Thanatos, the monstrous god of death. This was total irrationality! However, this act would paradoxically free Psyche from her marriage to death (her subjugation by patriarchy); it would endow her with the life-giving properties of erotic love. It would restore passionate sex as the most meaningful of all ways to express personally the power of her spirit. And it would reestablish the truth that erotic love is holy.

But in order for Eros to rescue Psyche, Aphrodite Herself had to act irrationally. She had to renounce the only honor bestowed on women by patriarchal values, the very hallmark of feminine sexuality within a patriarchy: Her motherhood! She had to relinquish Her vision of Eros as Her perfect son, and release him from blind obedience to Her. By disavowing Her motherhood in order to set Her divine son free, Aphrodite exposed the lie in the patriarchal concept of motherhood as the crowning glory of womanhood.

The crowning glory of womanhood is woman's ability to act independently. It is her ability to express her love, her sexuality, her intelligence, and her spirituality in whatever ways are available. By renouncing patriarchy's "honor," She disdained masculine approval. She exploded the belief that woman is man's property, the incubator of a man's "seed," and the caretaker of man's progeny. Womanhood no longer depended on motherhood.

Aphrodite's example sets human mothers free from the false vision of their sons as gods (and their daughters as goddesses), and it sets the sons (and daughters) free from bondage to that vision. It frees both mothers and children from the awful burden of being perfect (perfect supermoms and perfect superchildren). And it frees women from the false notion that their own worth depends on the "divinity" of their husbands. (Only gods beget gods and goddesses.)

By sending in Eros, Aphrodite gave him the unconscious, irrational opportunity to break his bonds to patriarchal motherhood. What the Goddess did was throw Her son into a situation in which the patriarchal image of man as some sort of superior, godlike being would not work! Aphrodite had to count on Psyche's beauty and sexuality to arouse Eros's desire. If he wanted to experience the joy of his sexual desires, Eros had to become incarnated as a man. He would have to sacrifice his "godhood" in order to ravish the woman he loved erotically. He could not use his "divinity" as an excuse for his fear of being wholeheartedly man.

Eros went unknowingly into this situation as his Mother's "good boy," the obedient, unconscious executive of patriarchy. What he was about to face was the most terrifying creature a patriarchal man can ever face: a woman with whom he can fall passionately, irrationally in love. The power of the irrational, which he would encounter in falling in love, was the same illuminating power of the Feminine. They both have the power to destroy all of patriarchy—the patriarchal family, the patriarchal state, and the patriarchal religion. And, most terrifying of all, they have the power to slay a man's patriarchal self. But the only way for a man to gain the courage to grow outside of his own system of controls is by tasting and savoring the intense feelings generated by falling madly in love and wanting more. If he has the courage to seek more love and to let go of more control, then a man can develop his manhood and learn to love the abundance of his masculinity.

THE FIRST AWAKENING OF EROS

So Eros, borne upon his mighty wings and needing no instru-
ments of earth, soared by. But seeing the object of his aim, he was
smitten by Psyche's beauty. Flinging control aside, he abandoned
himself to the joy of his sexual desire. In his passion, Eros accidently
pricked himself on one of his own arrows, and looking at Psyche
again, fell madly in love with her. Without further thought or ado,
he decided to claim her for his own. He called his good friend,
Zephyrus, the god of the west wind, and asked him to lift Psyche
gently from the rock and blow her down into his valley of paradise.

Eros, borne upon his mighty wings, symbol for the
mighty power of the irrational spirit in the Masculine, was
really rolling on his own! He did not need any earthly
instruments (rationality, the laws of logic, or reasoning) to
soar into the heavens. Indeed, they would have only kept
him earthbound. A man's irrationality is what can light up
his way like lightning in the sky. Eros would have laughed
at any marriage readiness tests, any quizzes to see if he was
really in love. The idea that cultural standards or religious
ideals could guide him to the woman he would love was
ridiculous! And above all, when a man is borne upon his
mighty wings he does not need to capitulate to unconscious
femininity; he does not need to ask his "mother" to find out
what he wants.

Soaring through the light and the dark, the past and
the future, Eros was stopped short in the present: he *saw*
Psyche. He was smitten by her beauty. The *otherness* of her
femininity carried him away. It made him keenly aware that
she was the consummate opposite to his masculinity. He was
excited by the magnificence of her nature; her sexuality was
driving him mad! The "she" he had seen did to him what
he had intended to do to her: the full force of her female
sexuality pierced the god's heart, and he wanted her. In hot
desire, Eros flung control aside. The heat of his passion
dissolved his patriarchal image of the ideal man/god. In his
loss of control, Eros irrationally pricked himself on one of
his own arrows and, looking at Psyche, fell madly—irrationally—in love with her.

For the first time Eros wanted to be a man. The way a man first tastes the power of his manhood is through the irrationality of falling in love with a particular woman whom he ardently desires to love him erotically. That means he wants a specific woman to love him, not as some pure goddess or some naughty "lady of the night," but as a woman in charge of all her personal sexuality.

This kind of desire is very different from the "romantic" love of patriarchy, which sings of the glorious day when "all the things you are are mine." When a man wants the woman he loves to love him erotically, then he sings of the joy of beholding his beloved in the freedom of her selfhood. Patriarchal values that denigrate the *spiritual* power of sexual desire reduce it to the perverted desire to possess.

But sexual desire that is connected to the spirit seeks to relate to the *other*, not to control or dominate the *other* in any way. To relate to another is to encounter the *other* in a conscious and passionate intimacy that allows both man and woman to increase and intensify their self-identification and autonomy.

This kind of passionate desire frees a man to experience the glory of his masculinity within himself—not just in his genitals, but within his mind and feelings and all of his body. His sexual desire makes him conscious of being man, conscious of his personal self, his individuality, and conscious of the uniqueness of the woman he is beholding. When a man can assume this degree of consciousness, he has broken asunder the bonds of patriarchy and assumed his power to become a man.

Unlike the real power of the Masculine, the power patriarchy bestows on man actually robs him of the might of his personal masculinity. He can worship woman or fuck her, but he is forbidden to penetrate her with his wonderful masculine spirit. His power system forbids him to love her and want her erotic love in return. Though patriarchy may grant him the moral and legal right to subjugate women to his control, *he does not have the power to become exuberantly man.* The power patriarchy gives a man kills the Feminine he needs in order to become fully acquainted with his irrational, masculine spirit.

What every man fears in losing control is being controlled, losing his power over others, and losing power over himself. He fears being dominated by his almost uncontrollable sexual desires (which he should be able to express in a wholesome, sexual freedom), and he fears the control this might give to the woman he desires. But the truth is that upon falling in love a man has to face the fact that he has been controlled by his "mother" (and all her substitutes) all his life. "She" keeps his fears of the power of his sexual drive (or lack of it) at bay.

If a man can remain obedient to his "mother's" vision of him as a divine son, he does not have to face the hard task of becoming a man. His "mother's" vision of him provides his false sense of immortality and his false sense of security, which protect him from his powerful sexuality. Obedient, he does not have to face being alone or being afraid of his death—gods do not die. Obedient, he does not have to consciously respond to his sexual desires and his capacity for erotic love. Obedient, he does not have to worry about his lack of sexual prowess in his old age. He can think of himself as spiritual, noble, intellectual—anything but physical (and vulnerable).

No wonder rational man is so terrified of woman! She will "make" him lose control. She will "make" him vulnerable. She will "make" him disobedient, and the disobedient deserve to die. So patriarchal man "plays it safe" and denies himself his erotic nature rather than risk falling in love and being out of control. Better to marry a nice, compatible girl who, stuck in patriarchy, is dead to her sexuality. Then he can control his intense desires, be obedient, and forever avoid the fact that he does not love his own masculinity.

Obedience is the easy way out, and control is less arduous than conscious responsibility. However, such obedience robs a man of his body. A spiritual being does not have a body. If there is no body, a man has nothing to love with. But without erotic desires there is no awakening of true sexual identity, no sexual "I am," and no power to be a man. His obedience eliminates his chance of becoming a passionate man who is capable of ravishing a woman with his erotic love.

But the bodily desire Eros felt in his groin denied his bodiless godhood! He wanted Psyche. The force of his irrational love awoke Eros from the sleep of enforced control, rational thought, and logical behavior. Without further thought or ado, Eros decided to claim this woman for his own. He forgot to remember his mother's orders. He was no longer chained to blind obedience! In the grip of the irrational power of love, his need for his mother's patriarchal vision of him and his godhood had vanished.

Though Eros was not yet conscious that he had disobeyed his mother, his disobedience nevertheless freed him to taste his manhood. His masculine irrationality had been awakened from the sleep of his conscious, rational control. Though he was unconscious of what he was doing, HE WAS DOING IT! The significance of what Eros was doing was beyond his understanding. By becoming a man, the god of love had triumphed over Thanatos, the god of death! When he had flung his "godly" control aside and pierced himself on one of his own arrows, he fell erotically in love and his erotic love overcame the power of Death, Psyche's espoused husband. However, since it was the blasting power of the unconscious that caused his "awakening," Eros remained unconscious of it.

Without the arrows of Eros to penetrate us with irrational love, our spirits lie in limbo. There is no compassion, no caring, no sense of self, and no sense of *otherness.* It is erotic love flowing through people which makes them most human. Without erotic love we live death; joy, the pleasure in being human, and the meaning of life are all dulled to a grayness that hides the glorious colors of being alive. Being in love is being "touched" by the god of love, and it makes men and women feel alive. Erotic love is what makes us taste the goodness of our creation, our uniqueness, the unrepeatability of the beloved, and the sweetness of life. There is nothing more wonderful than being in love.

In love, Eros forgot his mother and his godhood. And in forgetting, he disobeyed the Goddess. Instead he called his friend, Zephyrus. He confided in him, asking the god of the west wind to lift Psyche gently off her rock of suffering and blow her down into his valley of paradise. (Erotic love requires a period of courtship.) If Eros had taken Psyche while she was still chained, he would have violated her innocent love. It would have made no difference that he, not Death, had taken her. So Eros called in his friend, Zephyrus, to be the go-between. That Zephyrus was glad to do his friend's bidding shows us the special quality of male friendship. Each friend was glad to do the other a favor. Patriarchal marriage effectively ends such friendships because men are supposed to own their wives' sexuality. They are supposed to be in control. When people are obsessed with possessing, they are unable to create relationships that they can share and enjoy.

THE FIRST AWAKENING OF PSYCHE

After the last sound of human footsteps had died away, the lovely bride sat weeping in fear and trembling. But instead of teeth and claws and rape, she felt the soft, cool breath and downy wings of Zephyrus, who did his friend's bidding. Puffing out his cheeks, he blew her down into a beautiful green valley and laid her softly on a bank of violets. The sweetness and peace of the moonlit valley eased Psyche's fears for the moment and she fell asleep.

Zephyrus, the god of the west wind, symbolizes the wind of the masculine spirit. His breath was soft and cool, and his wings were downy. The force of the masculine spirit when relating to the Feminine is soft and gentle, cool and light, and his might is downy, like those delicate feathers found on a bird's breast that protect its heart. Such is the true creative force of the Masculine.

So Zephyrus did the bidding of his friend, the god of love. The masculine spirit serves love. And just so could the spirit of man unchain woman from the rock of dying. If man chose to, he could have his spirit blow her down into the lovely valley where green things grow, where life is. (He could let go of control, unchain her from her living death, and let her be free.) Zephyrus laid Psyche on a bank of violets, symbol of the innate goodness in the Feminine Principle and the incorruptible innocence of woman's love.

Psyche went to sleep in the moonlight. She slept in the light of darkness that man cannot put out. For the moment her fears and trembling were gone. Her tears were dried and she smiled in her sleep.

Fears in the human heart, however, are hard to erase, and in the morning when she awakened, there they were. The sight of a beautiful grove of tall trees took her mind off of her troubles, though. In the midst of the trees she saw a most wonderful palace. The great arches of the roof were supported by golden columns, the walls were covered with silver carvings, and the floors were mosaics of precious stones.

Timidly Psyche entered. She could see no one, but she heard low voices as if fairies were talking.

This invisibility represents the truth about patriarchy. No one with a patriarchal mentality can see or be seen. Individuality is not allowed. And no one is supposed to see the real self of another. Such exposure is considered vulgar. Everyone must conform—from the highest ruler to the lowest slave. Psyche could see no one, because there was no one to see. In the realm of patriarchal, "rational" consciousness, people are so underdeveloped that they are invisible.

She came upon a room of unearthly beauty where a table was laid for a feast. Evidently only one person was expected, for she could see only one chair and one place setting. Psyche, half afraid, sat down, whereupon she was waited on by invisible nymphs. There was a chorus of singing, and then she heard a single voice singing to her, accompanied by the lyre.

Psyche was charmed by the beauty of the palace, the lovely food, the music, and the service. In her wonderment, she forgot her fears. The myth paints a beautiful picture of the difference between the way a man falls in love and the way a woman falls in love. The way a man's inhibitions are overcome (and his desires aroused) is different from the way a woman's fears and inhibitions are overcome (and her desires aroused).

We can see how Eros's desires were aroused by *seeing* Psyche. His inhibitions vanished. Hot desire, loss of control, pleasure, and the irrational act of wounding himself on his own arrow "made" him fall in love. For Psyche the route to erotic love was not so direct. It was not seeing Eros that aroused her. She did not see Eros for a long time, and when she did, it was an entirely different kind of seeing. Unlike men, women do not tend to get sexually aroused simply by looking at the opposite sex. In Psyche we see that a whole gamut of factors played a part in decreasing her fears and arousing her sexual desires.

The beauty of the place, the tall trees, the morning sunlight, the golden columns and arches, all created a special atmosphere for her. Playing with the thought that the man who dwelt here must be handsome and strong, rich and imaginative—like the palace he had created—generated warm feelings all through her body. But "handsome" did not apply only to looks; it also meant the sensitivity of a man who could envision such loveliness. And "rich" did not necessarily mean only material wealth; it also meant the power of intelligence and drive that make up an exciting man. The beautiful music filled her heart with tenderness. And the single voice singing reassured her, filling her with an un-named yearning. All these things opened Psyche's heart to being touched by the Masculine, because in all of these things Psyche experienced the power of Eros's maleness.

As darkness came to the waiting twilight Psyche began to tremble, for she feared that the owner of this place would prove to be the dreaded monster of the oracle. Then she heard footsteps coming lightly and quickly to where she was sitting. Her flesh froze in breathless fear. But the voice that spoke to her was softly musical and excitingly masculine. The touch she felt was gentle and enamoring.

How Psyche loved that zeroing-in power of Eros, the irrationality of a man in love! The beginnings of love stirred in her heart because Eros first loved her. Now Psyche was ready to hear. And Eros spoke.

"Beautiful Psyche, do not be afraid. This palace and all it holds are yours if you will consent to live here and be my bride. The voices you have heard are the voices of your handmaids, who will

obey your every command. Every night I will spend here with you,
but before dawn can light the sky I must fly away. Do not ask to
see my face or to know who I am. Only trust me; I ask nothing
more." So, though Psyche could not be sure that this was not the
voice of the monster, her fears were allayed enough and she consented.

Eros had successfully courted Psyche. To his great delight, he had aroused her full sexual desire. Psyche wanted
Eros. Their yearning for each other created the poetry of
their relationship.

But Eros had unwittingly presented her with the same
patriarchal marriage contract he had saved her from: "If you
obey me, I will love and support you." Psyche was ready to
consent to anything; she desired Eros in all the heat of the
sexual passion he had aroused. She heard only the promise
of love. Neither Psyche nor Eros was aware of the trap into
which they had fallen.

Then Eros made love to her. It was the most beautiful thing that
had ever happened to Psyche. With his arms around her, Eros told
Psyche how beautiful it was. So, although Psyche could not see Eros,
his loving her confirmed the magnificence of her sexuality and assured
her that masculine sexuality was good, not something to be feared.

Psyche's consent to her sexual desires and to Eros allowed
Eros to make love to her. This was powerful sex. It changed
both of them in a way that neither could ever completely
undo. Eros, as the god of love who had become a man in
order to love Psyche erotically, confirmed the goodness of
their sexuality and the beauty of their sexual intercourse.
Psyche, by accepting this confirmation and reassurance, re-
fashioned her views of sex. Instead of accepting patriarchy's
censure, she saw that sex was something with which to love,
something to make people feel good and happy.

Eros came to Psyche every night. He called her by her name,
and her heart pounded new life through every particle of her body.
He touched her, and she felt the earth quake. He made love to her,
and volcanoes erupted fire, pouring hot lava even into the soles of
her feet. Until this time Psyche had never known she had a body;

now she knew beyond rhyme and reason. "I don't know who
you are," she told him, "but I love you passionately, as I love
life." As their bodies vibrated pleasure, so their hearts were filled
with joy.

This first lovemaking between Psyche and Eros was "in
the dark"; it was unconscious. Their passion sprang from the
fountain of their human sexual instincts. It did not make
any difference that they were not yet fully conscious of each
other as individuals, that their lovemaking was not yet personal. *As their bodies vibrated pleasure, so their hearts were filled*
with joy. This first lovemaking was like play to have fun with;
like joy to laugh with; like delight to love with. (And no
matter how deep a relationship may grow, erotic love never
outgrows play to have fun with.)

Eros had taken the first step; he had ravished his bride
with his most passionate sexual love. But that was as far as
he could go at this time. He did not know there was anything
else. All he could be was the rescuing, ravishing hero. He
was in the dark about his function as a fully developed man.
He could only love Psyche between dusk and dawn.

For the time being Psyche was content to be in love
with Love. She did not yet know the difference between her
young love "in the dark" and the power of fully conscious,
erotic love. She said, *"I don't know who you are, but I love you*
passionately, as I love life." Although her feelings almost over-
joyed her, they were still outside of her self. She could not
yet connect them to the meaning of being who she was.

Nevertheless, this kind of lovemaking was the first
awakening of Psyche from the sleep of her girlhood. She had
said a passionate "yes" to her sexual desires and to Eros. And
she knew she had been ravished by her wonderful hero. She
had become consciously aware of her body as the vessel that
contained her love. In experiencing passionate masculine
love, Psyche felt the intense pleasure of being visible to the
other, naked in both body and spirit. And this feeling awareness of her body freed her passion from the prison into which
patriarchy had enclosed it: the prison of her mind. Freed to
be the sexual woman she was, she swung with the pleasure

of life, which her passion had given her. In her ardent, bodily connection with Eros, the fires of her spirit had been lit. And it would be her spirit which would transform her sexual experience into knowledge and into love of her self, her lover, and her Goddess.

Psyche could never return to her girlhood or to the ranks of unravished brides. For she now knew the difference between being an unravished girl and being a ravished bride. Psyche had felt the earth quake at Eros's touch; she had felt the heat that caused her blood to throb through her body. And she knew why.

(For an individual person the experience of hot, passionate love may or may not involve sexual intercourse or even physical touching. The touch demanded by impassioned love may be the barest whisper of fingers brushing; it may be encountering the eyes of the beloved; it may even be the transcendent touch of soul touching soul. But always it is the irrational communion between man and woman who have each been pierced by some Extraordinary Power which produces the intense emotion of being in love.)

In all the mastering might of passionate love, Psyche began her consciousness of self, a self in the flesh. The basis for self-identity is the sexual "I am," reflected in the face of the opposite sex. He, her human *other,* called her by her name. An individual's name is the greatest personal symbol of who a person is. How sweet is the sound of it upon the lips of the beloved. It opens the door to the love for self and calls a person into being. And how grim to hear one's name called in that demanding tone created by commitment and duty, by right and privilege. It slams the door shut on the self.

Through Eros's love for her Psyche had become a woman, the absolute *other* of a man. But until Psyche could see Eros as her definitive *other,* see him and love him as the unique man he was, she could not *see* her self; she could not know who she really was. For she could not give birth to consciousness of her inner masculine self, the *other* who lived within her, without knowledge of an earthly *other.*

Through erotic love Eros had been initiated into irrationality. Falling madly—irrationally—in love with Psyche had awakened him to the exhilarating vitality of the unconscious. He was now unconsciously awake to something beyond the rational. Somewhere in his depths he knew that there was more to being man than the earthbound, anesthetized, patriarchal consciousness allowed. But until wide-awake consciousness of Psyche's love could free him from his mother's house, from the patriarchal values that had put his masculinity to sleep, he could not develop his full, exuberant manhood.

Eros was himself humanly dependent on Psyche. He could not achieve his autonomy without her. He could not know who he really was until he could recognize and love Psyche as his human *other*. Half-awake, man cannot give birth to consciousness of his own inner woman, who would connect him to his soul, teaching him to love his masculinity and trust the authority of his inner voice. But the fact remains: Eros had claimed Psyche as his bride. He had ravished her with his passionate, masculine love that went way beyond the rational! He was at least unconsciously awake.

Psyche, on the other hand, had been fully awakened from the sleep of her girlhood. To be an adult, a woman must break free of her unconscious dependence on the archetypal mother. She must differentiate herself from the patriarchal ideals of the "Earth Mother" and the "Eternal Virgin" mother; she must reject the idea that they represent true femininity and pure sexuality. In the sleep of girlhood a woman is unseparated from the patriarchal mother's great bosom of undefined, oceanic femininity.

But Psyche had been awakened from this sleep. She had become acquainted with the passion of being a woman, a ravished bride. Psyche's experience of Eros's passionate penetration of her had awakened her to a new knowledge of herself: she knew her body as both the vessel and vehicle of her love. She now knew that the Holy Spirit of Love lived in her body.

Through the awakening that passionate love provoked, Psyche was now prepared to enter adult womanhood. Keats's "still unravished bride of quietness" had been ravished. Psyche could no longer be quiet. She had become alive, knowing and wanting to know. (And this was just what patriarchy did not want.) She was ready to face the shadows that the distorted light of patriarchy throws.

So far, so good. Aphrodite smiled.

THE INVASION
OF PARADISE

Most of the time Psyche looked forward to Eros's coming with delight, but there were times when the sound of his wings filled her with terror.

Psyche had delighted in being in love with Love. She had relished being ravished, and she knew it. But she was not telling anyone, not even herself. If she were to acknowledge her erotic nature, she would have to acknowledge the fact that she was unacceptable to patriarchal culture (and—worse—that it was unacceptable to her).

When Psyche yielded to Eros's passionate masculine love and fell in love with Love, she took on an entire culture, not just one man. All of the unravished, obedient, conforming women, as well as all of the "play-it-safe" men, were against her. In a patriarchy nobody wants a woman who is alive, sexual, and spirited; who accepts and delights in her own physical nature as well as in the differences between herself and men. No one wants a woman who sees, listens, and hears; who asserts the power of feminine consciousness—her intellect and her intuition.

When a woman discovers her self through sexual love, she comes face to face with an ugly reality: it is the nature of patriarchy to destroy a person's self. Patriarchal doctrine asserts that physical urges, especially sexual ones (which everyone has), are sinful, wrong, and dirty. Believing this destroys the fountainhead of a person's deepest feelings of self-worth. Desecrating human sexuality—calling any sexual expression not sanctioned by a patriarchal authority evil—contaminates the well-spring of an individual's original subjective self-identity and autonomy. The repression of sexual desire damages the basic physical center of self respect; it damages one's sense of the goodness of the body and makes people ashamed of their bodily feelings.

Patriarchy has taught women that to give way bodily to sexual desire for a man without some sort of prior magical fusion (such as marriage, or at least being in love) is promiscuous at best (and really a sin). Such behavior constitutes what respectable (patriarchal) society calls fornication or adultery. But the truth is that being unable to use one's sexual desires is a disability.

Psyche, like women today, was required to submit to a system that demanded that she silence her own adult passion. She must deny her immediate feelings and give up the right to use her sensuous, erotic capacities straightforwardly. She must stifle herself until she had no idea of who she was. At best she must postpone her desires until the "right" man and the "right" time came along and their union could in some fashion be legally and morally sanctioned. Women have become so accustomed to the dark of darkness that they do not know they are unconsciously controlled by a system that owns their sexuality and regulates its expression.

Everyone has a legitimate desire to be accepted. Therefore Psyche was tempted to regress. She thought about how to make herself acceptable (in patriarchal terms) by insisting that Eros was a monster or a bad boy and that he "made" her do it. It felt safer to Psyche to shun her erotic nature and just play like she did not have a pussy at all! Men might be erotic, but nice ladies never were. But Psyche had to assert her self and assume responsibility for her erotic love. If she denied her feelings and gave up her right to her sexuality, she would never grow up; she would just grow old.

But in a system that morally and legally subjugates women, Psyche felt overcome with a sense of helplessness, of having no honest authority as an adult, of having no right to assert herself, no right to become a fully conscious human being. Not only in relation to the culture as a whole or as she experienced it in daily living did Psyche feel this; she also felt helpless, with no authority as a person, no right to exert herself in her personal relationship with Eros, the man she loved! This made her feel as though she had an empty space inside her heart that she could never fill (except perhaps with fear or hopelessness).

Dealing with the weight of being squelched sapped the energy that Psyche needed in order to grow up. At the same time her empty hole of fear made her want to revert to the only ways she had ever known, submitting more than ever to patriarchal demands. It is much safer for a woman to believe the patriarchal lie that sexual desire needs some sort of validation than to admit her honest sexual feelings. What's she going to do with them? She tries instead to melt into a feeling of closeness no matter how contrived with the man who excites her sexually. Thus, she loses the ability to distinguish personal love from sexual desire (both of which are good and which can be combined). Sure it's wonderful to be in love and have sex as an expression of that love, but it is also great to have sex just for the fun of it. The important thing is to know the difference. If Psyche continued to try to make herself acceptable to patriarchal values she would lose access to her source of self-worth—the goodness of her sexuality.

Patriarchal authority, whether religious or secular, teaches that life lived in the spirit is higher, nobler, and more virtuous than life lived in the body. Celibacy is supposedly a higher estate than marriage (which allows people to have sex if they have to). Patriarchy praises a kind of "reasonable" love that buries a person's spontaneous affinity to life in the body. But repudiation of the body—a silencing of its urges and a denial of feelings—does not alter the fact that life in the body is all the life we have!

Until people acknowledge the irreplaceable joy of the body and delight in the most delicious of all pleasures, they cannot experience the fullness of Spirit. This burial of pleasurable feelings and bodily yearnings helps people to tone down any deepening sense of their individuality. By living life on the surface as good, conforming people, they avoid the deeper experience of self—consciousness of the incarnation of the Holy Spirit in their bodies, which produces profound physical joy! What they experience instead is a dis-ease of the body and an anxiety of the soul.

Psyche, in becoming more and more aware of her self, was left alone every day with her unknown fears. Unacknowledged, these fears had the power to undo her. They left her feeling bad about herself, uneasy and anxious, and thus susceptible to the seduction of patriarchy: if she were "good" and obeyed, if she were "good" and denied her sexuality, if she were "good" and buried her body, then she would feel good about herself again. But Psyche could not deny her encounter with passionate, sexual love. Nor could she deny the intensifying awareness of self and the feelings of self-worth that this encounter caused. However, "sometimes the sound of his wings filled her with terror."

Psyche was doubly afraid. She was afraid of the unseen power of the irrational masculine spirit; the "sound of his wings." In former times the power of the masculine spirit was seen. Like Zephyrus, men had used it openly. But patriarchy had suppressed it, and suppressing, distorted it so that now more often than not it was used negatively—to crush the Feminine and clobber other men. So Psyche was instinctively afraid of the irrational power of the masculine spirit that could charm or seduce her, protect her or possess her, help her or hurt her. And she was also afraid of being devoured by the invisible monster of the oracle. She was afraid of losing her identity in a marital union with Death. Psyche felt intuitively that her very selfhood was threatened. And it was.

When, out of fear, she passively accepted sensual self-denial or failed to exert her self on her own behalf, she felt oddly humiliated and horribly dependent. When she forced her bodily feelings into the unconscious, there was no way she could effectively assert her self. They were not there to guide, instruct, and support her. Psyche was doubly afraid, and in both cases, she was afraid of something she could not see. She could not identify what was wrong with her or what was wrong between her and Eros, because by patriarchal standards everything was O.K.

But Psyche knew that things were not O.K. Why must she stay at home? If the palace were indeed hers, why couldn't she leave it and return to it? Why was staying at home "proof" that she loved her husband? Eros came and went as he pleased (or so she thought). And if he had really given her all these things, why did she sometimes feel uneasy or hostile? And why did Eros seem more and more preoccupied or even bored when he was at home? Why did he lash out at her from time to time? Why did she sometimes feel the guilt of an unnamed anger?

The myth shows us the double-headed monster of what patriarchy calls holy wedlock, which had been in their "paradise" since their relationship began: Psyche's unfaced fears and unrecognized anger, and Eros's unconscious, patriarchal demand for her unconsciousness and obedience (which kept Psyche's fears boiling below the surface). Most of the time Psyche kept these fears at bay, but....

What was happening to their bliss? The myth points to the evil in the seemingly innocent estate of holy matrimony, but which, in reality, has within it undivulged crimes. The ethic of holy wedlock is obedience to a contract (called vows). The marriage vow "If you do this, I will do that till death us do part" enslaves woman and exterminates man. And the morality of the holy estate of matrimony is a meaningless "sexual fidelity" that cripples the spirit of both sexes, while it ignores an unholy infidelity to the sacredness of human individuality and freedom. Blind obedience is what kept Eros demanding and Psyche unconscious. And a gross infidelity is what eroded their love and sapped its vitality, robbing their relationship of energy. But neither Psyche nor Eros was conscious of what was going on.

The motive of holy wedlock (or any form of coupling in a patriarchy) is fourfold; it is to protect the supremacy of the male "seed" (meaning that women are considered nothing but incubators), to guarantee male privilege, and *to institutionalize the moral and legal subjugation of women*. At the same time, this holy estate (patriarchal marriage) imposes cultural shame about the human body. This shame weakens the inner core of a person's sense of self. Unconsciousness of the source of this shame keeps both men and women submissive to patriarchal power. Psyche had good reason to be afraid.

Contrary to patriarchal belief systems and local customs, the holy estate of matrimony is not divinely ordained; it is only socially sanctioned. Wedlock is the product of "reasonable," patriarchal love: love which is tamed, mild, modest, and barely passable as love; it is a love that is self-centered, controllable, shrewd, and sober. It is the antithesis of erotic love. Erotic love contains double passion—the passion of the Feminine and the passion of the Masculine. It is other-oriented, yet nourishes and gratifies the self. There is nothing "reasonable" about it; it is irrational, beyond law and logic, and it is sent by the god of love.

Erotic love wants the paradox that is inherent in the mystical union of flesh and spirit—the mystery of eternal love existing in a warm human body. Aphrodite wanted Psyche to be able to yield her self to a man who loved her passionately and who wanted her impassioned love in return. The Goddess wanted them to experience, in their own limited, particular relationship, the unlimited glory of the unconditional love of Divine Spirit. Passionate sexual love is the strongest, most enduring basis for a deep, personal relationship between man and woman. For from it flows the spirit; love is spirit. Such love comes in varying degrees of intensity and can be expressed in a thousand different ways; sex is only one of those ways.

In wedlock, holy or not, the best that men and women can do is share their external interests. Without impassioned love, they need things and activities in common. To generate energy in a "reasonable" relationship people have to rely on their concerns about their houses, their children, their careers, their churches, or their tennis games. When mutual interests are not enough, they have to create problems to distract themselves so they won't have to face their lack of erotic love. Problems give meaning to their lives. But in a patriarchy the favored way of avoiding the issue of erotic love is never to let it happen in the first place.

Aphrodite knew, as does the unconscious Feminine, that the nature of the Feminine is spirit/love living in woman's flesh. But in patriarchal belief systems, spirit/love is isolated from the flesh. They claim that a person cannot be sexual and spiritual, especially at the same time. Women are taught to lock their love feelings in their thoughts or their souls. They must ignore any feeling in their vaginas, any bodily yearnings to be held or to hold another body. Men have the choice of locking love feelings in their minds or in their genitals. They must ignore their desire for intimacy, their desire for deep feelings. But in reality the body is a sacred place, the tabernacle of the Divine Spirit and the proper container for feelings of love. Feelings in the body communicate to the brain, telling it of sexual desire, desire for closeness, and desire for joy. Erotic Love can grow from these desires, communicating to the human spirit the boundless love and joy of the Divine Spirit.

The bond of flesh and spirit is a powerful mystery. And in order for Psyche to grow she needed to find ways of expressing this mystery in concrete daily living. For this woman to become more and more aware of who she was and for Eros to become more and more aware of who he was, and for them both to become more and more aware of who they were together, they needed the freedom to express their sexuality consciously, passionately, and individually. Without sexual expression their spirits would burn out.

Erotic love cannot exist in a climate of control, and neither can the Spirit. Psyche and Eros loved each other because they had been touched by some Extraordinary Power, not because they had become husband and wife. This kind of loving—passionately, consciously, and individually—is diametrically opposed to the ideal of patriarchal union, which is a fusion of the sexes into a couple, a monolithic conglomerate, wherein the identity of each is lost in a spiritless, sexless, and passionless coexistence.

When the Feminine Principle inhabits the consciouses of both sexes, the royal authority is love. All else is subservient to it. Love is Spirit, and the climax of creation is the incarnation of Spirit in human beings. The essence of being human is the ability to manifest the mystery of the bond of flesh and spirit. The job of erotic love is to pull together its two forces: love as bodily and love as spiritual. Sexual feeling—and the emotions of happiness, gratifying work, and worship with which it resonates—is what provides the unique opportunity for the erotic connection of body, mind, and spirit. It is love between the mind and body and spirit that unites the three aspects of being human into a united whole, but without losing the identity of each part. *When this three-way connection occurs, it gives birth to adulthood.* Such conscious passion provides the best way to end the outgrown need for one's mother or father. At the same time, it provides the good feelings about the self that produce the courage to be.

Erotic love is the manifestation of the Spirit that fosters both human autonomy and personal intimacy. Erotic love sets us free and allows evolution to proceed. What Psyche needed to know and what every woman needs to know is that patriarchy is *not* a necessary step in our human development—as individuals or as a society. Patriarchy is at best a detour. To grow in an erotic reality demands activity according to the honesty of pleasure. This includes the pleasure of the reasoning, self-reflective, and inventive activity of the brain; the pleasure of planning, adventure, and imagination; and the pleasure of the physical poetry of our bodies. Pleasure is its own reward; people were created to experience pleasure. (That is what makes pain a miracle: pain tells the human organism something needs fixing! quick! so that pleasure, the natural state of being human, can be restored.)

Aphrodite would not accept, therefore, compulsory, gender-defined roles. The antagonistic behavior between the sexes provoked by patriarchy was abhorrent to her. Such attitudes and behavior destroy pleasure. They split the sexes into warring camps and result in a sick symbiosis between man and woman. The deep, inner Feminine Principle in Psyche, represented by Aphrodite, was going to upset her and cause her anxiety whenever she started to sell out and accept a patriarchal substitute for love. The Goddess scorned the requirements of contractual union: cooperation, respect, commitment, comradeship, compromise, and consideration. Even when added up these are anything but love.

In each of the requirements for patriarchal union of any kind, including the holy estate of matrimony, there is a hidden, self-centered catch that destroys erotic love and mutilates the identity of each partner. With cooperation the hidden catch is "I'm perfectly willing to cooperate so long as I have my own way." With comradeship it's "Let's do all the things I like to do; if you don't know how, I'll teach you; don't bore me with the things you like." With consideration the hidden catch is "You watch out for my feelings; you apologize to me for all the things you do and say that I don't like, and I'll forgive you—but I don't forget." With compromise it's "I'll compromise if I get the big end of the deal, and if I don't I'll make you miserable." With commitment the hidden catch is "You fulfill your obligations to me and then I'll fulfill mine to you, and we'll be in love forever; but if you default on yours then I have a right to default on mine; look at all I've done for you, you unappreciative bitch, you lousy bastard."

And the tragic catch in "reasonable" love is "Make me feel good and then I'll make you feel good." Gratifying a comrade is a sick substitute for impassioned love. It is nothing more than a dutiful performance, done in hopes of ensuring a meaningless fidelity or of proving a man's virility. Sex ceases to be an act of love. It becomes the tool with which to control women, and the only weapon women have with which to bargain. The notion of conjugal duty *profanes* the act of sex; the thought of "having" to do it is repugnant.

Eros and Psyche did not "have to do it." They were swept up in their love, and sex was the way they expressed it. In patriarchal marriage each is forced to love the other, the grimmest possible contradiction of love. Patriarchal marriage virtually robs sex of its spirit-fueling spontaneity. Thus it effectively excludes love from a woman's destiny, and the Feminine from a man's destiny.

With no flesh in the spirit and no spirit in the flesh, men and women are devoid of their sexuality and spirituality, unconscious in a hell which neither of them can avoid. Everyone's paradise is invaded—not accidentally, but by design. We live in a culture that must rule out erotic love, the value of the Feminine, and the personal power of the Masculine in order to survive.

But something of cosmic proportions had shaken the foundations of patriarchal repression and unleashed the healthy forces of evolution: in intense pleasure Eros had ravished Psyche, and Psyche had yielded to passionate sexual love. In sweet delight she had received the power of passionate, masculine love and rejoiced in her sexuality. She had been changed! And so had Eros.

The only way Psyche and Eros could deny what they had experienced was to die by refusing to grow. That option was always open to them. But if they did not deny their experience of erotic love and continued to expand their consciousnesses and increase their love, then the foundations of patriarchal repression were shaken indeed, and the evolution of man and woman could not be stopped.

The unwritten history of Western culture is the story of the Psyches and Eroses who refused to die.

THE SISTERS,
THE SHADOWS

Psyche had it all (inside of patriarchal values). Perfect daytime life: her beautiful palace, servants, and a lovely garden. Perfect nighttime life: a wonderful, sexy husband and abundant lovemaking. If she needed to exert her prestige, she had aristocratic breeding, social status, spiritual grace, and political clout (her father was king). And she was pregnant with Eros's divine child. The only thing that was missing was Psyche. Though she had been awakened, she had been awakened "in the dark." She still did not know who she really was because she did not know who Eros was. Nor did she know the identity of Love. *Outside* of patriarchal values, she had nothing.

So Psyche had to dream, for that is all one who is unconscious can do. Most women in patriarchy want to dream. Fantasy gives them an escape from the reality of having to live death. They do not want to know who they are. It is too painful. So they look for THE man, THE job, THE palace, or THE career that will make them happy. They want something or someone to take responsibility for restructuring the past, making their current lives perfect, and ensuring their futures.

Psyche had every woman's dream. But, dreaming, she had not changed her role from that of her girlhood: she was obedient, dutiful, and docile (or she was pouty, lazy, and bitchy). Just as she had not confronted her father, she had not confronted her husband. Nor would she be able to confront her mean, self-seeking sisters when they came looking for her.

Psyche faced a turning point. She could muster the courage necessary to realize the imperfections of life and take responsibility for who she was—a ravished bride, awakened from her girlhood, alive and assertive. Or she could refuse to change and join instead the ranks of the unravished brides, blaming others as she looked outside of herself for the perfection she thought would make her happy—the "right man," a fulfilling career, a beautiful house, and social position.

If Psyche wanted to experience the passion of being woman, she would have to wake up in the daylight and respond consciously to herself, to Eros, and to their marriage. That meant she would have to disobey her husband; she would have to break her marriage vows. (This is very different from rebelling.) Psyche was going to need great courage. For the fact remains that in a patriarchal society ravished brides are not acceptable; nor is it permissible to know and ravish one's husband. She would find no support, no instruction sheets, and no maps. Patriarchal cultures (including ours) offer no road upon which women can travel to self-hood—they never have, and they never will. Psyche was on her own.

One day, when she was gathering roses within sight of the rock to which she had been chained, she saw her two sisters weeping and crying out in mourning for their dear, dead sister. Psyche believed that in spite of their unkindness in the past they really loved her, and she was moved to pity. So that night, when Eros came to her, she asked him if she could see her sisters to let them know she was alive and happy. Reluctantly, Eros gave his consent.

Eros warned Psyche that she was in grave danger and reminded her of the consequence should she try to find out who he was. But the graver danger, which Eros was unaware of, was that Psyche's sisters, upon seeing who she had become, would do all they could to destroy her—and to hell with him. And the hell Eros would be consigned to is the hell of every patriarchal man. Without the worth of the Feminine and the authority of erotic love, man is reduced to living either in his head (which he mistakes for his spirit) or in his genitals (which he mistakes for his sexuality). Instead of developing his multifaceted being, patriarchy insists that he choose one or the other.

The next day Zephyrus blew the sisters down into Psyche's garden. They seemed more surprised to see her good fortune than glad to see her. But Psyche, in her joy, did not notice their jealousy. She did not know that each sister was miserable in her "good marriage." One sister was married to an older man who treated her with a condescending tolerance. The other was married to an invalid boy who made her responsible for his welfare. They asked her a good many questions, particularly about her husband. Psyche only told them he was away hunting.

Here came the sisters, marching into war! And tragically, this is the ugly truth of what patriarchal control does to the sisterhood of women: it makes women band together to keep other women—those who do not fit the picture—out! Their intent is not only to ostracize the ravished brides—the openly sexual women—but to destroy them.

Unravished brides can always spot a ravished one, and how they despise her! They will plot and connive and do everything in their patriarchal power to ridicule her erotic love and destroy any feelings of self-worth she has. They fabricate lies about the ravished bride, slandering and condemning her. And their patriarchal society listens with ugly relish, believing the absurdity of their rank rumors. They encourage the results of patriarchal subjugation of women—self-pity, suspicion of men, and feelings of helplessness. They will say and do anything to distract her from finding out who she is.

And they generally succeed because their prey is so unconscious of their evil motives that she believes their opinions are right and their behavior well motivated and she does not believe they are really slandering her. Psyche's sisters were not bewailing Psyche's death; they were bewailing her good fortune and their miserable marriages.

The oldest sister represents the Eternal Daughter of a Spiritual Father. She holds her husband responsible for all her good, for liberating her from all she had not liked in her father, or for acting like the father she adored. She also holds him responsible for all her miseries. Either way, she turns her husband into her father.

This way of relating locks the man into superior attitudes and condescending behavior towards his "little girl." She cannot allow her man to be human. He cannot have, much less share, any hopes or fears, any pain or weakness. The female, both inner and outer, has prejudged all of his feelings. His passion is locked in a prison of rights and wrongs, do's and don'ts. This kind of relationship also locks the woman into acting like she is eternally obedient, pious, unconscious, and asexual—but obviously "spiritual" (and feeling like a victim).

The other sister represents the Eternal Mother (Caretaker) to her Divine Son. This way of being and relating holds the woman responsible for the relationship. She allows her man to "be in school" forever. Coddling an eternal boy, she has substituted a son for her husband.

This locks the man into relating to the woman as a begging, whining son whose emotions are dependent on his mother's moods. If she is happy with him, he is happy. If she is disapproving, he feels like nothing. As a god/boy a man cannot know his masculine passion, because he remains unincarnated. As a god, his body is useless to his passion; as a boy, his mind is useless to his masculinity. He is an invalid, an invalid male, a worshiping wimp who holds himself responsible for all his mother's mood swings. By taking on that responsibility he is playing god—an act which helps him believe he will not have to die.

This arrested way of relating locks the woman into being the eternal know-it-all, the love-it-to-death mother to everyone and ravished bride of none. She remains unconscious and asexual (and feeling resentful), no matter how many orgasms she might have.

Consumed with jealousy, hate, and fear of any woman who had found a man who could ravish her with his passionate masculine love, the sisters could barely hide their malice. But Psyche, in her joy at seeing them, did not see their viciousness. She happily showed them all the wonders of her palace and gardens, her clothes and jewels. She refused to see that her sisters, along with all the other unravished, conforming women in a patriarchy, were not her friends. Psyche should not have trusted them. Blind and deaf to her sisters' jealousy and malice, she left herself wide open to being kicked from behind.

What Psyche did not know, and her sisters did, was that she was different; she had been changed. Their worst fears had been confirmed: Psyche had found a man who knew how to ravish her with his virile love. But Psyche chose to be oblivious to the fact that her sisters had not been ravished (regardless of how much sex they had had). She refused to see that her sisters had never had what she had, and that if they could not have it they did not want her to have it either. Psyche could not acknowledge the difference between her sisters and herself, because then she would have to acknowledge her sexuality and awakened sexual appetite. Only sluts, whores, and brazen hussies have a sexual appetite.

Obviously Psyche was going to have to disentangle herself from all the patriarchal images of womanhood and the arrested ways of relating to men and to women. She needed to become aware that all her images of the perfect patriarchal female were going to stop her from becoming conscious, from becoming more and more erotic, from becoming more and more powerful. Psyche needed to see that if she chose to remain blind to their real intent, these patriarchal images of "the good woman" were going to kill her. And the collective values of patriarchy which deny women their sexuality, their spirituality, their intuition, and their bodies are still pervasive in our culture—in movies, in books and magazines, on TV, at the Post Office, and in the schools. There is no area of life in our patriarchal culture that does not make women feel somehow diminished and incompetent (whether consciously or unconsciously).

It is abhorrent that in patriarchal societies women have to renounce the values of the primary mode of their beings! It is repugnant that they must instead embrace a system that denigrates the worth of the Feminine Principle and project onto themselves images of a "good" that are false and malignant. In such a society Psyche could not possibly have found out who she was. Nor can women today. Psyche was special (as is every woman who has been loved): she had delighted in being ravished, she wanted to ravish her man, she wanted more and more erotic love, she liked this new consciousness of her self, and she was even capable of thinking! But to admit all this in a patriarchy was to set herself up to be destroyed.

During tea the sisters probed and poked. They questioned and insinuated. And they got Psyche generally agitated—especially with their questions about her husband's identity and whereabouts. Psyche fudged and told them he was out hunting. But Psyche did not know who he was or where he was, and at the time she did not want to know. Knowing who he was would have meant addressing the growing imbalance and disharmony between them.

What Psyche's sisters were doing by asking her about her husband was going after a woman's most vulnerable spot: her sexuality. Human sexuality is the wellspring of a person's self-identity. ("I am a girl" and "I am a boy" are among the first self-identifying sentences in the human language.) Our sexuality is our primary source of innate self-respect. Making a woman feel that her sexuality is tainted, ugly, or bad is the way to break her down.

Patriarchy teaches woman to fear her sexual desires: they are something shameful and any expression of them outside of the marriage bed is called fornication or adultery, sins worse than murder! So women try to hide their erotic longings and repress their sexual feelings. What women want naturally—to be ravished—is what they fear most and try to hide. But if something is hidden long enough, the owner will forget where it is hidden and the object will be lost forever. And if feelings are repressed long enough, they will atrophy.

But without good sexual feelings women have no way to reach a consciousness of the goodness of their sexuality, which is the basis of their power to *be*. If her sisters could have gotten Psyche to deny her sexuality and conform to the patriarchal picture of womanhood, they could have robbed her of her power. And patriarchal society would have been "safe" once again. For if Psyche had found out who she was and discovered the value of her sexuality, she also would have found her power. And that is the most unacceptable thing of all to the patriarchal mentality—a sexually powerful woman.

If Psyche had not been afraid of the power of her sexuality, she would not have had to use unconscious manipulation to deal with her sisters' questions. She would have been able to ask Eros outright: "Who are you? My keeper and my judge? What do you do all day? What's this 'doing it' only at night business? Fuck me in the morning." But Psyche was stuck in the patriarchal picture that told her to pose as spiritual daughter or eternal mother. For modern-day Psyches, patriarchy offers another role that also denies women's sexuality, thus keeping them powerless: "imitation men," women who take on the masculine values of patriarchy and who devalue and despise the Feminine.

The sisters also represented the mean, ugly side of being female—the side which is provoked by the patriarchal necessity of relating to one's husband as if he were a god (most women are unaware of the unconscious motivation for this). It takes a man, patriarchy tells us, to redeem a woman from the sin of being born woman. The inferior status she is born with is like a hereditary disease. Only a man can cure her; *only a man can make her legitimate as an adult*; and only a man can alleviate the pain caused by the empty hole in her heart. As a godlike being, he is the one who confers goddesshood, her ultimate security. If a woman is a goddess, then she has some control over her male-dominated life, some control over her fate. She is in charge here. This sense of power, false though it is, feels like the ultimate security for which all humans yearn: the assurance that they will not have to die at all, much less alone. Each unravished sister had to pretend to herself (as well as to everyone else) that her husband was perfect. Only then could he remain a god who would bestow immortality upon her.

Women are afraid not only of violence but also of the elusive fate of *not-being*, of not being effective, of not counting for anything, of not being allowed to live. So they convince themselves to believe the patriarchal lie that men can save them from this fate, and they obey the masculine demand. Each type of patriarchal woman keeps herself as unconscious as possible (intelligent and well-read but unaware of her self) and as asexual as possible (whether sexy in appearance or prim and proper in appearance). Fear of being degoddessed breeds envy, hatred, and jealousy. And tragically, it cuts women off from the healing love that comes from the feminine caring of other women, the passionate goodness of woman.

Psyche needed to be aware of both dangers: the danger she faced by not recognizing patriarchal women, and the danger of patriarchal men who relate to women as spiritual fathers or divine sons. Such men do not know how to trust, support, or respect the Feminine. And they certainly do not know how to be embraced by the feminine goodness—a goodness patriarchy calls evil. They are the worshiping wimps and the ridiculing jocks. A "spiritual father," when confronted with an erotic woman, becomes a judging, blaming, criticizing domestic tyrant. And a "divine son," when confronted with an erotic woman, becomes an adoring, possessive, moody mama's boy. These men are the willing father/son substitutes who abdicate their roles as lovers and husbands. They leave the women in their lives and the woman-self within unravished and malnourished.

What women do not know is that men do not have that feminine feeling. Men do not know what it feels like to be passionately, lovingly penetrated. Unravished men and their masculine authorities tell women there is no such feeling. And patriarchal women, being obedient creatures, believe what is not true about them. No wonder they are scared of their sexual feelings: they feel something that they have been taught does not exist! Psyche desperately needed to become aware that these distorted pictures of perverted, disfigured men and women arrest the development of a woman's sexuality and obscure her consciousness of feminine power.

The sisters' first visit was innocent enough on the surface. But the fact was that Psyche chose to remain blind to their real motives because otherwise she would have had to confront not only them but also Eros. Instead of challenging Eros's control, Psyche reported everything to her husband. Again he warned her. He told her that if she continued to see her sisters there would be a disaster. If she tried to find out his identity, he would take her out of paradise, fly away, and leave her all alone. And their child, who was now on the way, would be born mortal instead of divine.

Though her sisters' questions agitated Psyche about who her husband really was, she decided she wanted to see them again. She had grown tired of being alone, waiting for Eros to come home. She was bored with picking roses. After again warning Psyche, Eros gave his consent.

Once more Zephyrus blew Psyche's sisters into her paradise. This time they were ready for her. They zeroed in on her unfaced fears. Who was her husband? They told her he was the monster of the oracle. (*Oh god,* thought Psyche. *You mean I've had sex with a monster? And enjoyed it?!*) She kept her face blank. She told her sisters how kind her husband had been to her. But they were insistent. "Do not be fooled by his kindness, Psyche. The people of the valley have seen him coming every evening at dusk."

Rank rumors are the toys of malice—no matter how sweetly, how lovingly, how earnestly they are told. They betray a heart overburdened with hate, envy, and jealousy; they reveal a self that is unloved and underdeveloped. Psyche, like the rest of patriarchal society, believed the rumor. The sisters had her where they wanted her. They told Psyche that the horrible monster/husband she was married to was going to devour both her and her baby. (*Oh god!* Her worst fears—fears of being devoured by man—were being confirmed.)

Their description of coming events made their advice sound so reasonable: whet a knife to fine sharpness and ready a lamp with oil. If they proved wrong, all Psyche had to do was put down the knife and extinguish the lamp. But if they proved right, she would be able to behead the monster and save herself and her child. How logical! The way to save herself and her baby (her new life) was to emasculate her man: cut his head off from his body.

Psyche was now much more than agitated; she was terrified. Poor Psyche could not rid her mind of the fears that she had kept at bay. She could no longer ignore the question of who her lover was. Who had so sexually excited her? To whom was she giving her love? Who was the father of her child? If all were well, why was her lover so anxious to keep her hidden? Why did he come to her only at night? Why didn't he want her to see him? Why was he either mad at her or bored with her? And, with panic rising in her throat, why did he have wings?

Of course, Psyche had no way of knowing that Eros had to keep both of them hidden for fear of his mother's wrath. He was afraid Aphrodite would find out he had disobeyed Her orders. He had not shot Psyche with one of his arrows but had fallen in love with her instead! She would kill him if She knew! (Or so he thought.)

And that is the reality of patriarchal society: man is afraid of his mother. A man cannot allow his mother to see his passionate, sexual desires. He is afraid she would "kill" him if she knew. And unconscious, like Psyche, women do not know that. Unconscious of her self, Psyche had no way of becoming conscious of Eros and his fears. From infancy every man is afraid of his mother's rejection. He thinks that without his mother he will die. And when he is a child, this is true. She is the goddess who not only bestows his very life but also protects it with her own.

So insistent is this fear of death that boy children will even put up with the threat of the "sewing scissors": if the little boy displeases mother too much she will cut "it" off. In a patriarchal society, the mother can effectually emasculate the male who needs her promise that she will not let him die. How tragic is this hideous perversion of maternal love. And how tragic is Psyche's ignorance of it.

Like every man in a patriarchy, Eros had no way to escape his mother/goddess's vision of him. His fear of death kept him tied to his mother as a bodiless god and an immature boy. Patriarchy allows no power strong enough to encourage man to face his mortality; he remains dependent upon his mother for his ultimate security. Obedience or rebellion are his only options.

However, when a man becomes conscious of the value of the Feminine, he becomes conscious of the goodness of his sexuality; when he becomes conscious of his love for a woman, he becomes conscious that he wants her to want him erotically. When a woman loves a man in all the fullness of her passion of being woman, it can free him from the prison of his "godhood," and from his ungodly dependence upon his mother's vision of him. And when man accepts woman's erotic love, he can then love his own masculinity.

But since patriarchy destroys any consciousness of the value of the Feminine or the holiness of erotic Love, man must pretend that he is not erotic. He can be spiritual, or he can be some superstud. But in either case he must fight manfully against the "devil" (his irrational masculine spirit), the flesh (his own body), and the world (the goodness of life on earth) in order to obtain his immortality. A god does not have a mortal's body, nor does he have a man's masculine spirit. In the light of day, patriarchal man must deny the fact that he longs for a woman's erotic response to him. So Eros only came to Psyche in the dark.

Repudiating the passion of the human body as well as the passion of the spirit, patriarchal marriage encourages unconsciousness. On the one hand, a husband does not have to think about his sexual choice. He has a "right" to her, just as she has a "duty" to him. And on the other hand, patriarchal authority has invented the idea of sexual sin and coined words like lust, fornication, and adultery to scare people into living a passionless life. That way man can remain unconsciously but self-righteously obedient to patriarchal authority—more or less oblivious to the fact that it devalues the Feminine and outlaws erotic love but rewards him with his mother's vision of him as a god who cannot die.

In choosing to endure unconsciousness of the value of the Feminine, of his sexuality, and of his erotic love, Eros regained some of the control he lost when he fell in love. He returned to his "rational" state by denying his most prized irrational experience! And so does modern man. He goes back to the realm of unconscious femininity (his mother), where he thinks the promise of his immortality dwells. He goes back to the false images of the "good" Feminine that patriarchy projects onto the women in his life. Thus he thinks he controls death. But actually patriarchy controls him.

Until Psyche could see Eros in all the glory of his manhood—not as a god or as a monster, but as a man—she, too, had to remain "in the dark." Psyche could not liberate her self or her man from the prison of patriarchy until she became conscious. Psyche's real threat was not her sisters. It was the possibility that she might give in to the temptation *not* to question, to just let things stay as they were by remaining as unconscious as possible.

Psyche's sisters came to shake her foundation, and they did. Psyche had never felt a "duty" to Eros, but now she was beginning to feel a duty to obey him. Thus she was beginning to feel a desire to avoid him. She felt sick. Psyche could choose whether or not to discover the answers, but the questions were now in the open. Who was her lover? Why did he have wings? Why did he come to her only in the dark? And WHO WAS SHE?

DISOBEDIENCE: LIFE

Finally Psyche decided she must find out who he was, and an energy called courage began to rise in her heart. She would disobey her husband. She had chosen to see him.

Psyche's mean, ugly, unravished sisters had exposed her to the dead end of patriarchal marriage. She did not want to be an eternal daughter; she didn't want a spiritual father. Nor did she want to be an earth mother with a divine son for a husband. Psyche wanted Eros! But Eros was disappearing. Their relationship had gone as far as it could go in a patriarchal marriage.

It was no longer enough that Psyche knew what impassioned sexual love was. If she wanted to become more and more erotic and alive, she had to fight for it. At this point in his development Eros was powerless to save himself from losing his erotic love. And he certainly could not save Psyche from losing hers. Without erotic love there is no fuel for the spirit, and without the spirit a relationship shrivels and dies—as does consciousness of self. Psyche sensed the grave danger they were in, and she was scared.

Besides, some nameless, unrelenting power was pushing her, not letting her rest, asking leading questions, and daring her to find out the answers. This urge to know the truth was so strong, so demanding, so insistent that trying to ignore it was making Psyche feel sick, sicker even than the pressure to obey her love.

The fires of her spirit had been lit by Eros's impassioned sexual love. And her spirit burned with the desire to own her own body, explore her mind, and experience her soul. Psyche had to disobey. There was nothing else in the patriarchal system she could do. She could not be a "better" wife—more obedient, sexy, and efficient. Psyche felt like a caged lioness raging to be free. She had to disobey if she wanted to save her chance to be "touched" by the Divine, if she wanted to save her self, and if she wanted to give Eros a chance to save himself and his erotic love.

Psyche was finding that her obedience and her respectable behavior were destroying the passionate love she shared with Eros. She was bored and boring and becoming frantic. Eros was bored and boring and becoming punishing. Having experienced the pleasure of passionate, sexual love, Psyche wanted more. To hell with respectability.

For the first time, Psyche was ready to fight. And so conscious anger became her ready ally. Psyche stopped feeling sick. She stopped turning her unconscious rage against herself. She no longer had to express it unconsciously by withdrawing in silence or by lashing back. She knew that what she was feeling was wrath. And she knew the evil at which she was angry: a system that denied her her womanhood, that forbade erotic love, and that kept her man forever tied to obedience and fear in the dark of his patriarchal system.

Psyche's anger encouraged her to stand up for her right to know the truth, and it gave her the energy to fight for her self and her love. Psyche decided she was going to light her lamp and look at the man with whom she had been sleeping. Knowing that she could be caught, Psyche decided to disobey! What courage it took for this young woman to fight for her birthrights: the dignity of free will (the same kind of free will that the uncreated Deity has); her right to know, to search for knowledge about her self and her love; and the freedom to expand her consciousness.

With her knife whetted, Psyche was prepared to face the "monster" and kill him if necessary. And the first "monster" she encountered was the terror of her own sexuality. Like most women in a patriarchy, Psyche was terrified of her passionate, sexual love for a man—for his body and hair, his muscles and strength, his fatigue and weakness, his penis and balls. The fear hiding inside all "good girls," "sophisticated ladies," and "older women" is the fear of admitting to their capacity for full sexual love—a capacity patriarchy condemns.

And the terror lurking inside man is that he can be loved sexually by woman. He knows that if that happens, all hell will break loose. He will lose his control in the heat of her passion. He will become subject to the high power of irrationality. This power is the doorway to his true power and freedom, but before it he feels helpless. He feels that he must prevent himself from being loved at all costs. He will talk on the telephone for hours on end, work at anything that will consume his attention, become obsessed with tennis, golf tournaments, and workouts at the gym—anything to prevent himself from *seeing* woman and being loved by her.

Woman is terrified to stand naked in front of her man and say "I want." Man is terrified of a woman who stands naked and says it—because his mother, whom he passionately loved, could not say it. Who is this woman who wants? Psyche was asking Eros to do what his mother could not ask him to do. She was asking him to be something he had never been. So the "dark-robed monster" of patriarchy uses their own fear of sexual desire and erotic love to kill the passion between men and women.

As an obedient daughter in her father's household Psyche had not had to face the monster patriarchy makes of sexual desire; he was denied entrance. Nor did she have to face him when she was an obedient wife in her husband's palace; the monster was kept in "the dark." But as a woman who knew she had been ravished—penetrated by ardent, masculine, sexual passion—and who had delighted in being ravished, Psyche was prepared to face the "monster" of her own sexual desire.

Fully conscious of what she was doing, Psyche made preparations to disobey. She replenished her lamp with oil, and she whetted a knife to fine sharpness. A lamp lights the darkness, just as moonlight does. Both are symbols of the light of the Feminine, which alone can shine in the dark. Psyche could use only the light of her feminine self to see who Eros was. Only the "light of darkness" contained in the Feminine Principle can reveal the identity of love. The light of day, which excludes darkness, cannot reveal the identity of love. And oil, the fuel of the lamp, is the symbol for the spirit of the Feminine, which has to burn so that it can shine and heat and transform. The cutting edge of the knife is the symbol of the ruthlessness of feminine love. It is feminine ruthlessness that zeroes in on the reality of what is, disdaining rules and regulations about what should be, and slices through any falsehood to get to the truth of the matter. And feminine ruthlessness will fight against all odds to protect what it loves. Psyche would even fight her man to save their love.

This fighting spirit bolstered Psyche's courage to hold high her lamp and see who this "monster" was. Instead of letting her disobedience make her feel guilty, Psyche used the light it shed to expose the lie in the patriarchal illusions of being a "good woman." The light of her disobedience unmasked a long string of patriarchal deceptions: that to be "good" she could not be a passionate, red-blooded woman; that her body was "dirty" and needed cleansing; that sex was sinful and needed some outside authority to make it all right; that women do not like sex; that she was an asexual being whom man calls immoral or "mother"; that motherhood was the end-all and be-all of being woman and being married to a good man was the source of all her happiness; that woman was to blame for all the vicissitudes of life so she had better try harder and keep her mouth shut; that she could not think; that she was too beautiful, kind, and true to have a brain; that she was too sweet and noble to get angry; that she was helpless because there was no power in the Feminine; and, finally, that she was passive, dependent, and masochistic (the patriarchal ideal woman).

But it was not enough to expose the illusions of patriarchy: Psyche had to free herself from them. She had to "kill" them. By consciously changing her attitude from one of passive obedience to one of active desire, Psyche took the first step towards exterminating the patriarchal lies about women.

Now she was ready to kill the patriarchal "lord of death." And who was this patriarchal "lord of death"? Any man who would devalue the Feminine and outlaw erotic love; who would deny her her passionate sexual nature and purity of spirit; who would try to keep woman hidden in his palace as an adoring servant to his masculine ego; who would try to control her, telling her what to think, feel, and believe; any man who would withhold his irrational masculine spirit because he would not face and accomplish the tasks that would make him a man; who would worship her as a goddess and debase her as a whore; who was such a coward he did not have the courage to love himself as a man and her as a woman; or who "honored" her as "mother" but blamed her for all his ills, all the ills of his son, and all the ills of his society. Psyche was ready to kill any man who would keep her unconscious in his power system—the system which destroys woman and protects him—the patriarchal male who never became a man. That Psyche was ready to kill if necessary shows us the power of her passion to be, the strength of her determination to know Eros, and the urgency of her demand that she no longer be man's passive servant.

Eros came as usual after dark and fell asleep beside Psyche. Quietly she got up and, trembling with fear, lit her lamp. Taking the knife in one hand and the lamp in the other, she went to the couch where Eros lay. The light of the lamp fell full on his face—and in stunned amazement, Psyche saw no horrible monster or dark-hooded lord of death. She saw Eros, Love himself, the most beautiful of all the gods. Thick curls fell back from his wonderful face; his red lips were slightly parted in the sweet smile of sleep; his snow-white wings were folded, the down on them as delicate as the wings of a butterfly. His strong male body lay stretched out in relaxed trust. At his feet lay his bow and arrows. In her bewilderment and consternation Psyche dropped the knife and, trying to pick it up, accidentally pricked herself on the golden point of one of his arrows. Holding high her lamp, she turned to look at Eros again. Then, beholding him in all the glory of his manhood, she fell overwhelmingly in love with him.

Holding high her lamp, Psyche turned to look at Eros again. Wounded now by the arrow of the god of love, Psyche beheld Eros with a heart opened to conscious love. In the clear light of conscious disobedience, Psyche saw no devouring monster and no all-powerful, godlike husband. She saw a man in all the glory of his humanity; the Divine in man and man in the Divine. It took her breath away. Because of her courage to disobey, Psyche saw the reality of eternal love in a man's mortal body. And in that seeing, in that comprehending, Psyche fell overwhelmingly in love with him.

Being "touched by the power of the Divine," Psyche now encountered the full force of erotic love: she loved an individual man consciously and passionately. She loved a real, live man—not some romanticized picture of him, not some spiritual father or magic prince. And she recognized this man as one who had borne to her the image of Divine Love. This aspect of her love in no way negated the fact that Eros was her earthly lover.

In recognizing Eros's identity as man, Psyche recognized her own as woman. Her very flesh, alive with the Divine Spirit/Love, had recognized the incarnation of that same Spirit/Love in Eros's flesh. She felt the flow of Spirit in Eros's body resonating with the flow of Spirit in hers. And she desired him with a force of sexual love she had never known before. There was scarcely a drop of her blood that did not hammer and throb within her. The tremendous assertion of the Spirit in her own flesh and the intimate realization of the holiness of human love sobbed through her chest and out through her throat.

Psyche's comprehension of Eros, illuminated by her erotic love, was a clear declaration of the human identity of the god of love. It was also a declaration of the divine identity of this mortal maid, Psyche. The Divine Being lives in humans, and humans live in the Divine Being. This love story could hardly be a more emphatic affirmation of the mystery of the incarnation of the Holy Spirit.

Falling in love with a human male opened Psyche's eyes to his irreversible, essential, and equal *otherness*. And in looking at that human *otherness* through the eyes of erotic love, Psyche caught a glimpse of the total *Otherness* of Divine Love. In her knowledge of their sexual difference and *otherness*, Psyche uncovered the secret of Divine Love. Divine Love is the total *other* of human love. It is manifested for no reason except that human beings could taste its sweetness in the erotic love between man and woman, the earthly opposites of each other. Psyche saw that the symbol for the mystery of the Divine Spirit/Love could not be a lone "godhead"; it had to be a "God/Goddesshead." The passionate, sexual love between man and woman reflects the mystery of the Divine Spirit/Love. And so Psyche witnessed in her heart the great irrationality: that the Divine Love of the Supreme Deity is made visible and accessible to human beings through the erotic love between man and woman!

Psyche's deliberate act of disobedience was an act of love; therefore the Divine Love/Spirit revealed to her its mystery. And by knowing that mystery, Psyche now knew herself in a new way. She had lit her lamp and she had seen. Psyche had become consciously passionate and passionately conscious. She recognized her self—not just as a wife loving her husband, or even as a woman loving a man, but as a unique, unrepeatable woman loving a unique, unrepeatable man.

In beholding the maleness of Eros, Psyche felt the might of her femininity as a consciously directed force. In the heat of a woman's conscious erotic love, the male, the beast, and the god irrationally become one. She had lit her lamp with complete awareness of what she was doing. And ironically this conscious act led to her irrationally pricking herself on one of Eros's arrows. Her newfound erotic love initiated her into a consciousness of the power in the passion of being woman, which she could have known before. This is transforming knowledge, and it is irresistible—even if it is not constant or consistent. Psyche felt drunk with the holy, with the light and darkness of love, with the dancing joy of sunlight sparkling on the sea, with the sound of velvet-black night—with that something which is beyond anything a human can imagine.

Gazing at him in ecstasy, she bent down to kiss him. But her hand trembled and a drop of hot oil from the lamp fell on the god's shoulder. Burned, he awakened in pain and saw what had happened. With a reproachful look, he flew away to the house of his mother, Aphrodite, where he sulked, tending his minor burn.

Eros saw what had happened. He had always known who Psyche was, but now, by *seeing* him, Psyche knew who he was. Psyche, too, had become a "knower." Eros, unknowable as a god, had become known as a man by a woman! And he could not bear the intensity of her erotic love. It meant he would have to become conscious also of the meaning of being a man. So he flew home to Mama. Patriarchal man needs to have a mother who needs him in order to complete her patriarchal picture of being a woman. Then he can remain a "god" who is in control.

Psyche's knowledge of Eros as a man was a direct contradiction to the patriarchal mother/goddess's "knowledge" of her son as a god. Psyche knew Eros through his body; indeed, it was his body that revealed to Psyche who he was. A patriarchal mother/goddess knows her son only as "spirit." And as such he is not incarnated. He does not have a body. Psyche, knowing Eros as a man, was now conscious of the painful irony that man, as Divine Spirit incarnated in mortal flesh, must one day die. Psyche's new knowledge, the fruit of disobedience, was also in direct opposition to all of patriarchy, which promises some form of life everlasting in return for obedience to its demands. Instead of celebrating the body as the temple of the Divine Spirit/Love, patriarchy celebrates mortification of the flesh (a bodiless spirit and a spiritless body).

Burned by the hot oil, Eros felt his mortality. He was terrified of being known by Psyche when he did not even want to know himself. Knowing himself would mean struggling through the difficult tasks of differentiating and reconciling his inner oppositions: god and mortal, boy and adult, beast and spirit, man and woman. To complete these tasks he would have to face his own mortality and fallibility. He would have to admit that he was not superior, that like the rest of nature he was going to die one day. And—greater terror still—so was his love.

In revolt against Psyche's disobedience, he lashed out at her: he cast her out of his paradise and left her alone. He took away her palace and all her worldly goods. Worse, he took away his masculine confirmation of the magnificence of her sexuality and the purity of her spirit. According to his hate and fear, she was the source of evil in his world. She was guilty according to his laws and his god's commandments. She was dirty, awful, an unfaithful wife and a betrayer—but still an insignificant nothing. Then he flew home to his mother, Aphrodite, and there he sulked under the protection of patriarchy.

A woman who sees her man as more than just a partner in sex, more than just a bearer of the Divine image, more than just some romanticized version of a man—a woman who sees him as a male human being whom she loves—often initiates her partner into the pains involved in becoming a man. When faced with such pain, a man runs home to Mama (or some younger substitute). The fury, the resentment, the hurt, and the self-loathing that a patriarchal man feels when his woman becomes conscious is indeed an almost insurmountable mountain of pain. In a patriarchy it seems that the sexes cannot bring each other pleasure; they can only terribly hurt each other.

Eros was scared to death of Psyche, who had yielded her self to his penetration rather than surrendering to him. To yield was to give right of way by her own design. It was a conscious act, a conscious choice. When a woman yields her self, it is blatant disobedience against the patriarchal edict that woman belongs to man. Yielding is a direct confrontation: a woman's femininity confronts the masculinity of a man. In her disobedience Psyche was free to act; Eros, tied to his mother, was not.

By her action Psyche was insisting that Eros become conscious of himself as a man—not as some superior source of knowledge and goodness. Only as a man could he become conscious of her as a self, and only when he was increasingly conscious of her could he sustain his erotic love for her. What Psyche wanted was for Eros to relate to her as an individual, responding spontaneously to her unique expression of the passion of being woman with his own unique sexual response to her. She did not want him to react to her sexually as he would to any other woman. She wanted Eros to be conscious!

To define her thoughts and look at her emotions, Psyche spoke. And this is the voice of everyman's Psyche. If he wants life and power, he had better damn well listen. "Come on, Eros, grow up. I can't believe you are this threatened by my becoming conscious and knowing you. I love you. I don't love some immortal god, some infallible male. Relax. Be the mortal man a woman can love and care about, not a god she has to care for.

"You say you don't understand me, and you don't. You don't take the time or the energy or the thought. I'm telling you, Eros, no amount of worship, money, security, or understanding would be enough to keep me in this relationship. I stay in it because I want to. And that scares the purple shit out of you because you can't fathom such irrationality. So you have cast me out. And I have felt the full force of your anger and hate like a blast from hell trying to blow me off the face of this earth for becoming a conscious person. But the truth is that I have cast out your demand for my unconsciousness and my servitude; I have left you free! And you are running scared, back home to Mama and her promised immortality in the land of patriarchy.

"You act as if you could come back any time and resume living and loving me after you've rejected it all. Well, buddy, you can't. The meter has started; your time is running out. And when the crunch comes, you have to recognize the truth: you weren't there, Eros. In trying to live out your precious male principles and unreal ideals, in trying to keep your 'godly' image unblemished by the real world, you sacrificed yourself to the wrong god. And you blame me.

"Listen, Eros. I want to live. That is why I, your wife, have disobeyed your command to stay unconscious and be your adoring servant. I want reality: deep, profound reality. I want the reality of you, all the most personal parts of you, all the things that make you you. And I want the reality of me, in all the passion of my womanhood, to be loved by you.

"Oh, Eros, fill me with the power of your irrational love. Comfort me in the shadow of your wings. Play with me, Eros; play with our love. Life is too serious to take seriously. Let's dance in the moonlight and ravish each other in the light of morning. Look at me, Eros. I, Psyche, am your way out of the prison of patriarchy. Stop denying yourself; grow up and live!"

Psyche stands for all time in full opposition to the man who remains an underdeveloped male, a mother's son or a "spiritual father." She demanded that Eros risk taking the same heroic courage that she had taken, that he disobey so that he could know her as an individual by knowing himself as a man.

Eros, however, was determined to remain a god—denying his body, sacrificing his flesh, and remaining unconscious in order to keep his false sense of immortality. So Eros's last word to Psyche as he flew away to the fake immortality in his mother's house was that their child should be born mortal. The child would be born to die. Thus Eros took away Psyche's goddesshood.

Psyche stood naked in her mortality and prayed for strength. But she was now free from bondage to the male and to the patriarchal picture, in which motherhood is painted as the ultimate expression of her sexuality and goddesshood as the only expression of her spirit. If only she could believe her freedom!

In the knowledge of herself as man's equal *other* and the Divine's unequal but parallel *other*, Psyche encountered her self on a deeper level of understanding. She encountered her self as a separate self, separate from her role as Eros's wife and separate from collective womanhood. In this taste of selfhood, Psyche experienced the aloneness that portends death. She knew that she must die and die alone, and that one day her love would die. And she knew she was powerless to help. Death is inexorable and irrevocable. There is no automatic immortality—not even through one's children and one's children's children. Nor can a person's children keep that person's erotic love alive. If she wanted to live her life, Psyche would have to face the fact that she had to die. But in facing the fact of death, Psyche also found the freedom to follow her inner voice more and more.

Psyche's refusal to be the passive servant of the masculine ego and her demand for a full, passionate relationship cost Psyche her security. It cost her her palace and position, her handmaids and her husband—and it cost her her fake immortality. But Psyche had won a triple reward: she knew Eros as a man, she discovered the identity of Love, and she became conscious of herself as a separate self, an adult woman.

In the light shed by her disobedience, Psyche had really seen Eros. She had seen the Divine Being in man and man in the Divine Being. Psyche had beheld the humanity of the god of love! Then, in her amazement at what she saw, she had pricked herself on one of the arrows of the god of love and been opened to erotic love. When Psyche had turned to look at Eros again—in full awareness of what she was doing— she had fallen madly, irrationally in love with him. Alive to her erotic love, Psyche had experienced the full force of the Holy Spirit of Divine Love moving through her mortal body. And in that experience she comprehended the paradox that eternal love dwelt in human flesh, in a man's imperfect body that one day must die.

Consciousness of the incarnation of Divine Spirit comes only through feminine perception that has been awakened by the power of erotic love. Wherever the knowledge of this incarnation exists, you may be sure it was feminine consciousness (which can exist in men as well as women) that brought it to light.

Beholding their shared humanity, Psyche saw in Eros not a monster but the "beast," the loving animal in man longing to be free. In her erotic love, Psyche recognized the three components of man: male, beast, and divine. If only Eros could recognize and accept Psyche as his equal *other*, the fire of her love could transform his sexualness, animalness, and divinity into the glory of being man. And so it is today.

Only in the heat of woman's erotic love can the boy become a man, can the beast become a man, can the god become a man.

In encountering Eros as a man, Psyche experienced the mystery of human *otherness*. Seeing him naked, she had recognized him as her human opposite, her desired *other* in the woman-and-man pair. A pair constitutes a unit that can function only if both halves are present. Think of a pair of shoes, you need a right and left one for either to function, only as a pair do shoes work. So it is with man and woman; they need to be a united pair. But each half is still separated from the other half by unalterable sexual differences. The mystery of *otherness* is the mystery of erotic love, which unifies two equal but different *others* in a union that leaves each whole.

In the mystery of human *otherness* (revealed to her in her consciousness of her passionate, sexual love for a man), Psyche encountered the mystery of *Divine Otherness*. She could experience the love of *Divine Otherness* because she had first experienced love in human sexual *otherness*. And in her experience Psyche discovered the identity of love. The identity of love is the identity of the Supreme Being! The love of the Deity for the whole world makes itself most powerfully known through the erotic love between men and women. All expressions of erotic love—from the "lowest" movings of instinct to the "highest" communion of spirit with Spirit—are the tangible signs of the Supreme Being's love. Psyche's revelation of the identity of Divine Love changed the symbol for the Supreme Being from that of a masculinized "godhead" into that of a "God/Goddesshead." The erotic love between man and woman on earth mirrors the reality of the love in heaven.

The Supreme Being is infinitely more than any earthly image, but at the least It must contain the Feminine Principle as well as the Masculine Principle. Otherwise love and creativity could not exist in the Deity. That love which irrationally unites the opposites is what produces new life in heaven and on earth!

Through the mystery of *otherness* Psyche became conscious of herself as a separate self, an adult woman. In love with Love she had first discovered her body and its power.

This knowledge was the basis for her self-identity. Now in conscious, erotic love Psyche discovered her self and the power of her passion to be. She became alive to her self, which introduced her to that inner divine prompting which urged her to know, to risk and dare, and to change and grow.

Still today the "godlike" patriarchal male and the "goddesslike" unconscious female have blindly accepted patriarchal definitions of their sexuality. They have no awareness of their bodies, their spirits, or their emotions. Unravished and unconscious, woman locks her feelings, which alone can reveal her spirit/love to her, in her head. She has no more idea than Psyche's sisters had that her spirit/love lives in her body and that it is wonderful to be a sexual woman with brains and a passionate spirit.

Unconscious, man locks his feelings in his genitalia or shoves them into his unconscious and has no idea about his body, his moods, or his spirit/love. Without the love of his inner woman-self functioning consciously, he is powerless to connect his unconscious to his conscious or his body to his spirit. Therefore, unconscious, both man and woman remain unaware of the communion of body and soul, sexuality and spirituality. This unconsciousness prevents them from developing their selves. They have no awareness of the divine urge within themselves to know, to grow, and to be. So they don't.

By responding to the mystery of *otherness*, Psyche found that it lived within her. She became conscious of her man-self. Psyche, like every human being, needed to be awake to the differences between the sexes so that she could build a personality that was based on her sex but into which she could integrate the strengths and virtues of the opposite sex.

The first time Eros disobeyed he did so unconsciously; he forgot his mother's orders. The first time Psyche disobeyed she did so deliberately, consciously. What Psyche then needed to do was become aware that she had also disobeyed unconsciously—the masculine way—when she had delighted in being ravished and when she had invited her sisters to visit her. Psyche's task was to consciously integrate this masculine way, unconscious disobedience, into her personality so she could use it whenever she needed to. This would mean that she could allow her inner man to forget her orders and act spontaneously for her, just as Aphrodite had allowed Eros to forget Her orders and unconsciously act on Her behalf.

Likewise a man must so value the Feminine that he can integrate into his masculine personality the feminine ability to consciously disobey. He must allow his inner woman to disobey his commands for her unconscious fidelity; he must grant her uncriticized freedom, and he must see himself as woman does!

Alive to her erotic love, Psyche had discovered that the force of love in her body for her sexual *other* was a force of the spirit. Thus she comprehended the three components of the feminine self: her sexuality, her spirituality, and her body. The three are inextricably mixed, irrationally combining to make one whole. Take away one and the whole dies. Psyche now knew her self—her femaleness, her love/spirit, and her body—*as one indivisible person beholden to no man.*

The paradox was that Psyche only knew her separateness, her *otherness*, in relation to Eros, her *other*. She could become conscious of her own unique being and her feminine power only as she became conscious of the individuality and masculine power of the man she loved. However, she could only fulfill the relationship by disobeying the masculine demand for unconscious servitude.

In her expanding consciousness of self, Psyche had found the silver key: disobedience. It alone opens the door that patriarchy has locked. Psyche had turned the silver key, the door had opened, and she entered a new house, a new mentality. Her triple reward—intimate knowledge of her self, of man, and of Divine Love—became her new reality. Upon this sure foundation she could build a new house, create a new mentality, one that would be large enough to include all. By disobeying, she had left behind the old mentality, the ethic of obedience, whose morals are based on commitment and control, obligation and duty. She entered a new mentality: the ethic of creativity, whose morals are based on love, individuation of self, the reality of being human, and the unique value of each person.

There was no way Psyche could go back. Conscious identification with patriarchal values and unconscious fusion with a man were no longer options. Eros, for the time being at least, was left way behind, stuck in his mother's house and of no help to Psyche. She looked around but could see no path in the trackless plain.

But she was *alive,* intact; moreover, she had won a triple reward no man could take away. The only way she could lose her transforming knowledge was if she repented of her disobedience, repented of her hot passionate sexual desires, repented of her erotic love. Psyche could blaze her own trail!

ALONE

The beautiful palace disappeared, and Psyche found herself all alone on a deserted plain. Eros had taken away everything. What was she to do? She did not want to go back to her parents' house. She had known love, and she was no longer daughter but wife.

So we find our friend Psyche cast out of paradise, all alone on a deserted plain. Psyche had lost everything: her friends, her social status, her economic security, and—oh god, her love. The only thing left was the baby, now moving in her belly, and Eros had rejected their child. She was painfully aware that she was alone.

This scenario is no joke. It is the patriarchal reality of every woman who declares her right to be, her right to the dignity of free will, and her right to expand her consciousness and creativity.

Eros could divorce Psyche or choose to "keep" her, but either way he would cast her out. Regardless of whether a man leaves a woman or she has to flee the relationship, it is man's patriarchal attitudes that encourage and endorse his feelings of dislike, disrespect, and disregard for the Feminine; it is man's behavior that forces her out. Even if he "keeps" her, he keeps her out with his anger and hate. He will alternate between control and possessiveness on the one hand

and withdrawing and withholding on the other. He will become depressed, resentful, noncommunicative, and reproachful. And always woman is the object of his rational, "constructive" criticism. That is what women experience in a patriarchal culture even if they do not experience it at home—condemnation and punishment in some form or another just for being women.

There is no way to get around the patriarchal fact that woman's "original sin" is being born female. There is no way to get around the fact that in the world in which we live, women are the second-class citizens. To be born female in a patriarchal culture—in Psyche's time or today—means being born a "wrong." Man's birthright is inherent superiority. Men have the power and authority of being born male. Woman's birthright is inherent inferiority. Women are not born with the power and authority of the patriarchal male. According to the theological and philosophical precepts of patriarchy there is something intrinsically wrong with woman. (See the book of Genesis and the writings of Aristotle for starters.) No matter how good, how obedient, how loving, kind, and true they are, women cannot absolve themselves from the original sin of being born woman. No matter how smart and well educated they are, they cannot attain the level of respect that, as men, males automatically receive.

In a patriarchy the only sanctioned redeemer of those born female is man. Unfortunately, most women believe that lie. They think that if only they attach themselves to a superior being (a man) they will be absolved of being female and feel all right. However, the only real way to overcome the "sin" of being born female is to disobey the system that created the lie in the first place.

In choosing to see Eros, in choosing to become conscious of her self as woman, Psyche had to disobey. No woman who wants her destiny to include both her self and love can remain obedient to patriarchy. Like Psyche, she has to disobey. Therefore she, like Psyche, will be cast out of society. A lone woman does not have the same rights, respect, and welcome that a woman who is on a man's arm has. The fact that she is alone means she has been cast out, and if she has been cast out, then obviously she has done something wrong. She is hated and despised, rejected and denounced. She is ridiculed and scorned for being a woman alone. But Psyche remembered that she had also been ignored and disdained when she was attached to a man. Being rejected in one way or another is the price a woman in a patriarchy pays for her self.

Psyche had not expected to find herself cast out onto the street, friendless and penniless and homeless. She had not expected to find herself pregnant without a husband. And above all she had not expected to find herself loveless. She had been taught that married love, like parental love, was permanent and dependable.

Psyche was in no way prepared for the pain she felt when Eros blamed her for crimes she never committed and rejected her out of hand. To feel a deliberate hate coming from the most beloved person in one's life is the most self-reducing, self-annihilating feeling there is. The pain of being cast out, condemned, and reviled by the one she loved was so unrelenting that the grave would have been a welcome relief.

Blame was right there on the tip of her tongue, just as revenge was trying to get a foothold in her heart. Blame is seductive because it allows a person a sense of power. Blame that bastard Eros. Blame her jealous sisters. Blame her ineffectual mother; her cruelly impotent father; the blasted culture. Psyche was tempted to forsake her consciousness by abdicating responsibility and blaming anyone, even herself. But blaming someone would only have rendered her powerless; it would have led her straight to a bitterness that poisons the whole person. And revenge would only have gutted her love and left her sexless.

Psyche had been warned what would happen if she tried to see, if she tried to become more and more conscious. Disobedience had been her own choice. And there was no way of avoiding the consequence of disobedience in a patriarchy. She was cast out in the open on a deserted plain, face to face with her self, without even a rock to hide behind.

Psyche knew she could not escape her aloneness and pain. She could not return to Eros, making love in the dark, any more than she could run home to her parents. Nor did she want to return to her parents. Their house was no longer her home. She had been ravished by her man; she had disobeyed and seen the "unseeable." She could not return to being an obedient daughter any more than she could return to being a dutiful wife. And she would not run after the husband who ran home to his mother. His mother's house certainly was not her home! Nor was the house her patriarchal husband had once provided. All alone, Psyche had to face the fact that she did not have a home. She had no place to go to. The fact is that patriarchy has cheated woman out of a home that once was hers.

From time immemorial the woman had been the maker of the home. She had been the keeper of the hearth, the tender of the fire—the light and warmth of feminine consciousness that turned a cave into a home. The heat of the Feminine is like the fire woman used to change grain and water into bread, clay into stone, and raw meat into food. And the heat of her sexual fire turned a cold bed into a place of comfort, just as the heat of her erotic love turned a male/ beast/god into a man. While man was out hunting, woman became the image maker, drawing pictures on those ancient walls so that man could see what he had done and become conscious of it. She was the meaning giver. Woman was the gatherer and the sorter of the seeds that she would plant in the earth man tilled. She was the mediatrix, the go-between between humans and the Divine.

Man's job was to love woman and uphold the Feminine, to follow where she led and execute her policy, to comfort her when the vicissitudes of life seemed overwhelming, and to protect her with his love and guard her from anything that threatened her well-being. Her job was to guide man by her vision, to lead him by her courage and inventiveness, to protect him with her love and guard him from his aloneness and despair, to comfort him and encourage him to find meaning in the acts of daily living, and to leave him free to pursue his daily bread.

It took thousands of years, but the patriarchal mentality deliberately drove the Feminine out of the house—out of human consciousness, out of the culture, and out of individual lives. At the same time, man turned his protection into possession, he turned his guarding into controlling, and he usurped the life-giving force of the Feminine and appropriated it for himself. And woman, robbed of an identity, shackled man to her neurotic needs. "Take me where you go," she said. "Stay here and take care of me. Tell me what I should do." In a patriarchy, both man and woman are without a woman of the house and a queen of their dominion. They have no Feminine Principle operating in their mentality—in their house—and no feminine spirit, no queen, to transform their daily routine into happiness. And neither do they have the Masculine necessary to make woman fully Feminine.

Psyche began to realize what it meant to not have a "home." She had no consciousness of a feminine mentality over which to preside that was free of patriarchal counterfacts. Nor did she have a man to guard her "house," or an inner man to guard her consciousness from values that would corrupt it; she was bereft of the masculine spirit she needed to protect the treasure of her feminine way and to stimulate her creativity with his potency. Psyche did not have a queen, a director, to reign over her own consciousness, transforming the bits and pieces of life into a magnificent whole. She did not have one, because she was forbidden consciousness of what a real queen is and does.

In a patriarchy a queen is merely a stand-in, a deputy, for a king. And a woman's unconscious man-self is a stand-in for the collective patriarchal value system. Until a woman can become conscious of her inner man-self, he will merely parrot all the destructive values of a male-dominated society. In order to be a real queen a woman must know within her self the power of the Feminine to transform, to illumine, and to regenerate. A queen needs consciousness that these powers are hers in order to reign.

And a king without a queen is no king at all. Without the Feminine Principle (wherein his irrational wisdom dwells) he cannot go beyond the rational. His solutions to the problems of life are therefore limited to his linear, logically directed thinking. He is trapped in the ethic of obedience. He must punish all who disobey as well as criminals; and he must reward the obedient even if they are criminal. Every king needs a queen to give him vision before he can rule from the ethic of creativity. Without the feminine approach of a queen, a man rules as an executive, administering the laws man has made, rather than as a king, stimulating creativity and providing for the enrichment of life.

Homeless, Psyche began to struggle with the fact that she had nowhere to go, except inward, to build her house. But to make it a home she needed to find a man and a woman to put in her house. She needed to find an inner-man who would encourage the growth and flowering of her inner-woman. And she needed a new model of male-female relationships for her new mentality.

A man-woman relationship based on need was no longer very meaningful. Psyche may have wanted Eros, she may have yearned for him with every beat of her heart, but she did not need him. The charming, rescuing, ravishing prince had already charmed, rescued, and ravished her. She was conscious now of her womanly passion, and she was conscious of her man as a man.

A need is different in kind from a want. If a need is not met, we die. If we do not get what we want we may feel like dying, but we don't. Needs are what a person is dependent on; wants and desires are what a person is responsive to and responsible for. A real need is a life-ensuring urge that is built-in, like the need for food, water, and air. Psyche, chained to the rock, had needed Eros, just as every woman needs masculine passionate love to ravish her and awaken her to the life of her adulthood. But if Eros did not love Psyche now, she was not going to die.

However, it is hard to give up needs. To acknowledge the passing of a need, like a woman's need to be awakened from the sleep of her girlhood by a rescuing, ravishing hero, is difficult. The idea that what was once needed is no longer truly needed is terrifying; it means a person is left alone with her wants and desires, which change and for which she has to take responsibility.

"Oh, Eros, let me say I need you forever," yearned Psyche. "It is so much easier and safer to say 'I need you' than it is to say 'I want you.' When I say 'I need you' I belong to you and I do not have to face being really alone. Please don't make me say I want you, and for god's sake don't make me say I desire you. Because I don't desire you when you condemn me without even staying one minute to hear me."

Psyche was terrified by her feelings. Unlike real needs, her desire for Eros was not constant. Wanting him—wanting no one else in the world but him—*simply dissolved in his reproach.* Criticism and desire do not go together! Wants and desires are vessels for love, but they are not love itself. In her agony, Psyche discovered that these vessels for her love were not made out of stone—how quickly, without thinking, her lover could crush her heart, and how easily his angry criticisms could spill the precious wine of her desire.

Psyche was tempted not to feel her want, to deny her desire for love. If she did not want, then she could not lose what she wanted. If she could not lose what she desired, then she would not be really alone. But turning her back on her wants and desires would be tampering with a basic part of her self-identification process. Consciousness of our wants and desires not only makes us human but also makes us *think.* Ancient woman's desire to provide well for her children made her think of ways to make better tools and ways to sort out the best seeds to plant to end her endless gathering. If Psyche did not respond consciously to her wants and desires, then she would be abdicating her right to be a vitally alive person. She would forfeit the human capacity to move from differentiation to inventiveness, and on to creative thought. (And she would remain stuck in the culture that destroys the value of the Feminine and reduces the lives of women to the lowest levels of poverty.)

But if Psyche felt nauseated by her pain and did not desire Eros, then why did she feel such longing? Why couldn't she blame him? Psyche's heart plummeted to her feet and shot up through her head. She loved! Yet she could not obey his demands or tolerate his behavior.

Thus Psyche became conscious of the difference between her desires and her love. This left Psyche vulnerable: she was no longer dependent on the adolescent need to be awakened by love in order to create desire. She had to learn that the more she wanted and desired, the more human she became. At the same time, Psyche had to consciously accept the fact that fulfilling her needs and her wants and her desires was her own responsibility. She could no longer ask someone else to do for her what she could do for herself. However, in a patriarchy there is very little room for a woman to satisfy her sexual needs and her erotic desires, and there is even less room to satisfy her spiritual aspirations. And the room given her to earn a living is so marginal it leaves her squeezed out of the money-making arena.

Following the patriarchal picture of togetherness, both Psyche and Eros had desired to be taken care of. Each had felt a "need" to be held, to be nurtured, to be loved and petted and made to feel the excitement of the other. Psyche had wanted Eros to feel her pains and joys as his own, and Eros had wanted the same from Psyche. Each had expected to be fulfilled by the other. But no matter what they did to please each other, it was never enough. When people expect someone else to take responsibility for their basic needs and desires, the inevitable consequence is that they begin to experience pain in their relationships. And Psyche and Eros were not exceptions. So each had believed that their mutual lack of satisfaction was the other person's fault.

In deciding to see Eros, Psyche had pierced the veil of this false togetherness, this patriarchal idea that merely being together a lot creates the basis for desire. Of course it does not work that way. Psyche had to admit that erotic desire for one particular person was not permanent, and that it was not all-fulfilling. She had become bored in Eros's valley of paradise. And now she realized that there was no moral or legal code that could change this; no marriage vow could make the relationship meaningful or make desire stay.

Having become conscious of her erotic love, as differentiated from her desires, Psyche no longer loved Eros because he was her husband and he had made her his wife, thus redeeming her from the sin of being born woman. She loved him because, having seen him, she desired to love him. Psyche was now free to desire the man who was desirable to her. Passionately loving Eros as the individual person he was had become Psyche's choice.

This terrified Eros. If Psyche, whom he desired, chose to love him because of the individual he was, then at any time she could choose to love another—or even just desire another. Eros had no idea that love was not taken from one person in order to give it to another. He was ignorant of the fact that love begets love. (The more Psyche and Eros loved others, the more love they would have to give to each other. But that is a concept so foreign to patriarchal values as to be incomprehensible.)

Rather than face the vulnerability in being chosen by his love, Eros opted for control over her. He could see no power in vulnerability, only weakness and helplessness. He would tighten his control. But Psyche, in choosing to disobey, no longer fit within his patriarchal picture: he could not control her anymore. So out of fear and anger he cast Psyche out and ran home to Mama; he would not change and go forward.

Instead of running after Eros out of some patriarchal hope that he would magically change, Psyche stuck with herself and her aloneness and her pain. She had to learn that she must yield to her aloneness and her pain as to her lover. Otherwise she would have been right back in the patriarchal game, because she would have sought patriarchal means to relieve her aloneness and pain. By yielding to them, Psyche knew how to embrace them. And embracing them transformed them. It transformed aloneness from desperation into self-identifying knowledge, and it transformed her pain from self-destroying agony into the will to live.

Psyche was becoming a lady with some balls. She discovered that she could penetrate the reality of what was because she could contrast the falsehood of patriarchal mindsets with the reality of the erotic love she had experienced. She could begin to see the difference between the values patriarchy preached and the reality of what she was living. This was not exactly her former picture of herself—a well–cared for, docile princess—but she had to admit that she liked the feeling of power she got from taking responsibility for herself.

This attitude scares men to death, as it did Eros. First Psyche disobeyed him, and then she did not run after him, begging his forgiveness. How was he going to "keep" her (cast her out) if she would not be guilty? If she were not needy and dependent, what would happen to him? He could not be dependent on her either. If his little girl/powerful mother disappeared, so would his superiority and his security.

Suddenly Psyche was no longer Eros's idealized, all-good, all-accepting, all-perfect goddess, made in the image of his adoring mother. She was bad, rejecting, hateful—an immoral woman. When Psyche changed from a passive, obedient caretaker into an active, disobedient lover, she was asserting her essential and unqualified difference from the female vision in Eros's head.

Sure, Eros wanted Psyche back. But only as his cheerleader. He only wanted a woman who adored and admired his wondrous superiority and who needed him to take care of her (translation: take care of him). Most men, like Eros, feel justified in their wrath and in their punishment of a woman who refuses to fit into their picture of a perfect (patriarchal) woman. They really feel that she is an unfaithful wife (a slut) and that she does not love them. And unconsciously most women feel they really are victimized by their husbands.

In one fell swoop Psyche's courage to disobey had destroyed the patriarchal picture of husband and wife. No wonder Eros felt betrayed. Psyche forced the issue. She insisted that man is not betrayed by woman and woman is not victimized by man. Psyche would no longer tolerate artificial, unrealistic images of women and men. She demanded a conscious response from Eros. She wanted the real thing—a grown-up man. But Eros would not respond to her that way.

Instead he used all the weapons of patriarchy—other women (including the mistress of his own ambition), resentment, rage, jealousy, abuse, and guilt—to try to force her back into his harmful images of patriarchal togetherness. Whenever a person focuses on the "need" to be loved by someone else, he or she feels unloved very soon because the picture of how it is supposed to feel and look is somehow always crooked. And when a person feels unloved, he or she begins to act unloving.

What Psyche had to learn was that underdeveloped man felt unloved. Therefore he was going to act unloving. He desperately needed to maintain his imagined superiority. Whether consciously or unconsciously, he had to do all he could to sabotage her efforts; he had to keep his woman in her place. Psyche *needed* to become conscious of this. Otherwise she would feel that something was wrong with her. She would think his efforts to sabotage her were legitimate and sooner or later they would destroy her. Psyche had to avoid the seductive idea that Eros's hate and anger were personal, that she had done something evil. Eros's hate and anger hurt Psyche, but it was up to her to protect herself (and her love for him) with the knowledge that his emotions were not her responsibility. Her responsibility was to concentrate on her self-growth. Psyche's continuing development of her self was the only force that would get Eros to wake up.

If Eros wanted Psyche, then he too would have to face his aloneness and choose to develop himself. As she removed herself from his patriarchal picture, hopefully (but not necessarily), he would be urged inward where his woman-self dwelt. There he would have the opportunity to face his inner poverty—his infantile need to be needed, to feel important, superior, and in control. Only when Eros recognized Psyche, as she had *seen* him, would he be able to grow up.

Out there on that deserted plain Psyche had learned that she no longer needed to search for a mother or a father or a husband. She had lost her need to be parented by anyone. She had lost her need for a man. Alone, Psyche now encountered the legitimate needs of adulthood: the need to be a separate, self-identified person, and the need to connect passionately and consciously with other human beings. But no patriarchal man knows how to develop a relationship with an adult, sexual woman, because he is limited to a "need" mentality: his need to be a rescuing hero, and woman's need to be rescued and redeemed. Loving Eros, and having seen him for herself, Psyche now wanted Eros to see her. But that meant he would see her inability to obey him. He would see that she no longer needed him. He would see her autonomy. Thus, Psyche came upon the problem presented by her dual need to be both autonomous and intimate with the ones she desired.

In the patriarchal scheme of things, these needs are polarized; one cannot "rationally" attain both. "Rationally," these are mutually exclusive needs; one cannot be intimate and autonomous at the same time. Some autonomy must be sacrificed for the sake of intimacy, and some intimacy must be unattained for the sake of autonomy. Patriarchal societies claim that you do have to give up parts of yourself to be loved. In a patriarchy it is a game of either-or with compromise as the umpire.

But needs create the desire for what is needed. Psyche's adult need to be intimate created the mature desire for someone with whom to be intimate. Her adult need to be autonomous created the desire to be a self-identified, self-governing person.

These needs are real needs. If they were not met, Psyche would die. If she could not exercise her autonomy as a self-identified person, separate from all others, she would die. If she surrendered the authority of her self to the authority of others, even the authority of the man she loved, her personhood would wither and die. However, if she could not experience intimacy, then knowledge of her self as a self would die. Psyche, like every human being, had to find a way to fulfill these two adult needs.

But she was up against it. In her first conscious awareness of these two opposing needs, all Psyche could do was be aware of them. In her state of underdeveloped consciousness, there was no way yet for Psyche to find an answer to the dilemma these needs posed. What she had to do was concentrate on her self and resist the temptation to despair.

The only arena that afforded this opportunity was Psyche's aloneness. It allowed her to deepen and expand her consciousness of her self as a female human being. It forced her to become mindful of her independent, self-governing power. But she also needed others to mirror her face so that she could see her self. To accurately reflect her feminine self, Psyche needed a clear picture of what it means to be a man. Thus she had to find a way to keep the patriarchal meaning of man from distorting her image of masculinity. She had to learn to differentiate her inner man from all the men in her life, including Eros, and from the Masculine in the culture.

Fortunately, aloneness offered Psyche the opportunity she needed in order to deepen her contact with her inner man, increasing her ability to establish a passionate and conscious connection with masculine love. And in developing that connection, she would discover her self in relation to that love.

It was there, in her inner man-self, that Psyche would find the power to bring to life and to empower her femininity. In her aloneness Psyche experienced a deepening consciousness of the strong, passionate, masculine love for her self that lived inside her. And this consciousness would become increasingly the enhancer of both her autonomy and her ability to be intimate.

By accepting her aloneness, Psyche experienced an important truth: to be loving, autonomous, and intimate precluded her from assuming any part of her lover's inner pain. One of the simplest and most sanctioned ways to avoid aloneness and responsibility for self-growth is to try to solve someone else's troubles. But Psyche refused this role. Nor did she try to make anyone else responsible for her feelings and thoughts. Aloneness forced her to accept responsibility for her self, knowing she stood free of the childhood need to be taken care of.

By becoming conscious, Psyche had unmasked the patriarchal illusion that she and Eros could relate only as two unconscious, unequal, polarized sexes. Alone, Psyche knew different. Alone, she knew that she and Eros were two separate individuals who were equally free to be penetrated by erotic love, to be touched by the power of Divine Love.

Alone, Psyche was free to make her inner home the place where her inner Masculine would marry her beautiful inner Feminine in a love that was beyond law and logic, beyond myth and magic. Alone, she was free to find the real queen who would reign over her life, the queen who would connect her conscious and unconscious realities to form the meaning of who she was.

PANIC

P*anic exploded in her mind. Since she was now her own person Psyche decided she would go to the river and throw herself in. But at the riverside she met the cloven-footed god, Pan, sitting by the river playing his magical flute. He saw that Psyche was about to drown herself, and he came and played for her. His music dissuaded her. He told her she must pray.*

So, praying, Psyche went from one deity to another, but no one would help her because they all feared Aphrodite's wrath.

Changed forever by the knowledge that her erotic love had brought her, Psyche was alone. By her conscious disobedience Psyche had discovered that the Divine Love of the Deity is made visible and accessible to human beings through the erotic love between man and woman. She had seen—and by seeing, known—the "unknowable": the Spirit of the Most High is made flesh in a man's body; God/Goddesshead is incarnated in man as well as in woman.

Therefore, Psyche could no longer find meaning through a patriarchal value system: attached to reason, it sees meaning only in the external data of life. She could no longer experience life merely on a material and biological level. Psyche had liked her palace, her beautiful clothes and jewels, and all the security she had had. She had liked being a respectable and respected wife; but she now knew that these things were not the ultimate meaning of her life. And she also knew that even her approaching motherhood, which was exciting, could not define her existence.

The rational approach to life limits people to viewing reality according to no more than what can be seen with the eye, heard with the ear, touched with the hands, tasted in the mouth, or smelled with the nose. From the rational window it had looked illogical for Psyche to be unhappy. She had had all life could offer. It was logical for her to say she was sorry and return to her husband's house.

But Psyche's new knowledge had changed her view of reality. She saw that life included all the external data patriarchy acknowledged but that it also included a great deal more. Now she saw with her inner eye as well as her outer eyes; she saw life from the window of irrationality as well as from the rational window. It was her irrational, impassioned love that transformed the externals of daily living into an inner reality, the meaning of which was beyond law and logic.

Psyche could not change her new knowledge; nor could she stop its transforming effects. She passionately willed to know. Her passion for knowing was like her erotic love; it exceeded all rationality. It aroused an intense devotion to the quest for knowledge and a loyalty to the truth as she experienced it. By deliberate thought and design, by intuition, reflection, and perception, Psyche sought to know the unknown. Mindful that her knowledge would transform her values, her goals, her sense of morality, and her love itself, Psyche still had to respond!

Her response to Eros, as well as to her self, was to learn to value the Feminine Principle with all her heart and mind and strength. But first she had to find out what it was. Her patriarchal mentality had devalued the Feminine Principle until it existed only as negatives. Once she uncovered the great wealth of feminine values she could develop the self she had found. Only then could she sustain her side of the erotic connection. What Eros did or did not do now had no effect on her erotic love and the individuation of her unrepeatable, unique self. Waiting for Eros to change would not save her from patriarchal death.

What Psyche had to struggle with in the heat of the day and face alone in the cold of the night was that the Feminine she sought—the magnificence of her sexuality and the purity of her spirit—would never be acceptable in the culture in which she lived. She could either murder her self or live out her allotted years knowing she was unacceptable! She could be obedient to a system that does not allow woman to become a fully sexual, conscious female human being; or she could be an outcast. To have to capitulate to the patriarchal value system that violated her only verified her oppression.

Just like Psyche, a woman of today has little choice in a patriarchy. She has no way out of being born female. The laws of patriarchy debase her. There are few laws that really protect her, though some have been written lately to try. There are laws that will protect a man's wife, his mother, his daughter, his sister.... but there are few laws to protect a conscious, sexual woman alone. Credit card companies take away a widow's or divorcée's credit cards when they are in her husband's name—even if it is her money that is the credit behind them. And since their wealth, managed by her husband, gave him the power of their money, she has no way of reestablishing credit for herself.

That she has no credit of her own accurately reflects woman's lack of credibility in a patriarchal society. It does not give her even the right to her own body. Though rape is considered a crime and is supposedly punishable by law, few women win a trial. And the torture they are put through by the patriarchal system of justice is often worse than the crime.

The issue of who is "right" or "wrong" merely camouflages the graver issue: that women are born "wrong" and men are born "right." Women can never be "right." As long as they are female they are always disabled. Professional women must always work much harder than men. They must dot every *i* and cross every *t* because all their colleagues, even other women, expect them to be wrong. Everyone is waiting to catch them in a mistake. And there is no religion to comfort them. There is no religion which honors women as much as men. She has no God to turn to in which the Feminine is included. In a patriarchy the "She" does not exist, either in heaven above or on earth below. *Woman* is the alien of aliens. In Western patriarchalized culture, she is the unwelcome intruder in a male-dominated world.

Can a man ever understand the tremendous physical exertion of courage it takes for a woman to face the reality of her existence in Western culture? The pain a woman experiences as she discovers her patriarchal fate is almost overwhelming. She has no acceptable avenue for expressing the passion of being woman outside of motherhood and wifehood. She may have a brilliant career, but neither she nor society can accept it as an expression of her femininity. Nor can she or society accept any expression of her sexuality or spirit outside of the patriarchal picture. The energy generated by a woman's intense feminine sexuality—the fire of her spirit and the creativity of her mind—has no legitimate outlet in patriarchy. There is no word for the feminine equivalent of a "stud," which denotes masculine, exuberant sexuality. All of her energy is blocked—cut off at the source—to fit into a patriarchal mold. And then it is repressed to fit into a patriarchal damnation—the damnation of being woman.

Like a sock in the belly, the magnitude of her plight hit Psyche full force. Panic exploded in her mind. Her first brave faith gave way, and sobbing in despair she saw that she could not obey, she could not limit her self to a patriarchal definition of femininity. She could not care for man, nurture his projects as she nurtured his children, while denying her self and obeying his almighty godhood. She could not accept the supposed righteousness of exclusive love. It sucked. The act of denying her passionate love, which reached out to all who were dear to her, all who inhabited her earth, crushed her heart until her blood ran dry.

Panic exploded again as Psyche saw herself turned into a robot that played back the patriarchal video. No! She could not go back. She had to keep growing. The only way she could have stopped the process of her transformation was by dying. Psyche just wanted to close her eyes and think of something else—just work herself into exhaustion; diet, eat, or drink herself into oblivion—anything to drown herself in the waters of unconsciousness. So Psyche made for the river to throw herself in.

At the riverside Psyche stopped short. What was this music that resonated deep in her heart? Then she saw Pan, looking half man and half goat, sitting on the riverbank playing his flute. Strange that his cloven feet did not alarm her. Instead, the sight of them filled her with the same kind of love she had felt when she had first seen the beast in the man she loved. And her heart opened again to the almost inescapable joy of life itself. The power of Pan had reached out and touched Psyche, revitalizing her life-force through the intensity of his own. She was on the other side of panic.

What was this power that so swiftly affected her? How could it change her overwhelming despair into a new joy for life? The power of Pan represents the power of positive male sexuality, to which the power of feminine sexuality naturally responds. The life-force of Pan resonated with the life-force in Psyche.

Positive male sexuality is expressed in men who are earthy and sensual, who know about their bodies and like to be in them. Pan represented the life-force as it is expressed through the body and the senses. The ancients in their wisdom invoked him as the symbol for the forces of nature, and as the male principle that is needed to bring fertility and abundance to earth. A man who could receive the power of Pan recognized that his purpose as a male was to bring about abundance in himself, in his women, and in the earth.

But Pan was much more than a fertility god. He was the archetype for the hunter—the symbol not of killing but of seeking and pursuing his prey with single-minded purpose, just as a person who hungers after knowledge must pursue it. Pan is the god of all quests for truth—whether physical, spiritual, artistic, scientific, or social. He is the inspiration that motivates the pursuit of knowledge of the unknown.

Pan symbolizes the untamed male presence that refuses to be domesticated, compromised, diluted, made safe, molded, or tampered with in any way. It is this invisible and untamable spirit that arouses the passion for knowledge, that insists on finding out, that goads one into pursuing the unknown. The untamed male presence in each of us generates the longing for freedom and the yearning for its expression. It takes great effort to ignore and suppress this longing. This spirit lives in every human being—whether they know it or not, whether they can relate to it or not.

The acknowledgment and release of this spirit brings about a buoyant, energetic attitude in people. Such people know they are supposed to be happy here on earth. They know that if they do not enjoy their sensuality—even the struggle for growth, knowledge, and freedom itself—they will not find a home in the joy of heaven.

Obviously the kind of power we see in the god Pan poses a direct threat to the authority of a patriarchal society. According to the values of a male-dominated culture, release of this spirit is considered evil. And whoever commits this "sin" deserves to be punished by "God," the "Almighty Father"—or by any of his secular substitutes.

But the repression of humans' untamable spirit and the suppression of humans' wild extravagance (*not* mechanized industrialization) cause robotism—that dull, mechanized, monotonous way of living with other people who have also been made into robots. It was the spirit of Pan moving in Psyche that made her revolt against turning herself into a patriarchal android.

By removing human sexuality from the worship of the Divine, patriarchy disconnected sexual expression from the untamable Holy Spirit of Divine Love. It domesticated what was made to be an expression of Divine Love and glory. It tamed what was made to be an expression of the wild extravagance and the holy waste of heaven. With human sexuality disconnected from its Divine source, patriarchal values removed its meaning. It profaned what should be sanctified, seen as glorious and mysterious. No longer did the expression of human sexuality reflect respect for life and personhood or love of the universal Feminine. Disconnected from the value of the Feminine Principle, sexuality takes on the negativity and power struggles inherent in a male-dominated culture. What might have been the most satisfying, the most heavenly and healing experience of human life—lovemaking—became instead a harmless, mundane activity (at best!).

Violence and armed aggression, the very things patriarchy says it fears from Pan-like wildness—unshackled sexuality and an untamable spirit—are, rather, extreme reactions to the suppression of the human spirit and the repression of human sexuality. But the untamable spirit in the male sexual presence is not violent; it is aggressively caring and tender. Nor is his wildness mere annihilatory aggression; it is the kind of "foolishness" and play from which creativity is born. The music of Pan's flute is irresistible; it makes people laugh and sing, dance and celebrate the joyful holiness of life. (And patriarchal religions do not celebrate life, they seek to control it.)

The myth is pointing out, in vivid images, the fact that panic is a reality—and one that Psyche had best not avoid. We view panic with such distaste and alarm because it is not rational, and we have been taught that we should trust only what is reasonable and logically thought out. Trust a weirdo like Pan? A person's got to be crazy! A "sane" person takes out a piece of paper and lists all the pros and cons in order to know what to do. Well, that just doesn't work very well for a woman, because it gets in the way of her intuition. It blinds her to Pan. She cannot even hear his music.

The feminine need to go through panic has no parallel in the masculine way of being, and most males simply do not understand this feminine need. Nor do they understand the need for panic that their inner woman has. And so they just squelch it and get heartburn (or worse) instead of the answers they seek. They try to dissuade woman or teach her another way or ridicule her. Little vertical lines on a woman's upper lip are often a sad, telltale sign that the use of the masculine way of a "stiff upper lip" is not appropriate for a woman.

Psyche's situation was desperate. There was no logical, rational way out of her plight. There was no "road less traveled" for her to tread. She had no rights: no right to consciousness, no right to exist as a free woman, no right to protection, no right to food or shelter, no right to life or love. All her "rights" were contingent upon the male in her life and the men in power. Even anger at her plight, at this time, was futile.

Only the raging, shivering shock of instinctive panic can break a woman out of the deadlock caused by trying to use masculine logic in an illogical, cruel situation. Only panic can break her out of the prison of despair that such rationality produces. Like a bombshell, panic ruptures all rational thought.

If Psyche had tried to avoid panic, she would have remained powerless, stymied, emptied of all creative thought, forever caught in the patriarchal web. But when she accepted her fears and tears, not dodging her feelings but going through the panic, she got back in touch with her feminine power and wound up more than victor—for no one was defeated by her gain. There are no losers in feminine power, only winners!

Thus Pan initiated Psyche into "panic"—the irrational way of finding an opening in a blank wall. Panic opens the door to self-growth, joy in living, and pleasure in being human.

He told her she must pray. Pan taught Psyche to transform her panic into prayer, to bring a light touch to her work and sexuality. Pan told Psyche to pray, which is a way of dealing with a hopeless situation that is very different from keeping a "stiff upper lip." But praying is more: it is the way to tune in to the irrational power of self.

So, praying, Psyche went from one deity to another—but all refused to help her. They all feared Aphrodite's wrath. And rightfully so, because each of them would have given Psyche the wrong advice. Though Psyche was ignorant of the fact at the time, one day she would learn that thanks should be given to Aphrodite, who protected her from the wrong powers with the intensity of Her anger.

What Psyche had to learn now was which "god" to pray to. Which power one chooses to tune in to is critical. But more critical is the praying itself. *In the midst of praying, Psyche ceased to be a victim!* She refused to react to her situation according to patriarchal mind-sets or the prescribed behavior patterns of a victim. She repudiated blame and recrimination, vengeance and spite. She repudiated repentance and patriarchal forgiveness. By teaching Psyche to go through panic, the irrational Pan introduced her to the power of prayer. Prayer is the activity of the transforming power of irrational knowledge (knowledge not attainable through rationality). It is also the first movement of autonomy.

Psyche was moving!

THE OTHER SIDE
OF PANIC

Finally Psyche decided to go to Aphrodite Herself, thinking that the mother of Love might be kind to her for Love's sake. But Aphrodite was very angry. She had learned all that had happened. A sea gull, Her own bird of the ocean, had flown to Her and told Her everything. Aphrodite blamed Psyche for all that had passed.

Aphrodite gave a bitter, tyrannical speech. Psyche was reduced to nothing. She was told that she was a good-for-nothing slut, that even the job of a scullery maid was too good for her. But Psyche bore the Goddess's wrath. She stood there and took it.

Finally Psyche realized she must go to Aphrodite Herself. Only the Goddess of unformed, chaotic, feminine love and beauty can teach a woman how to develop her feminine self. A woman's deep, inner femininity, which contains her unique capacity to love, is the only force that can teach her how to become conscious of the love and support of her own inner man, her inner Masculine Principle. It is he who will then cultivate her femininity, infusing her personality with his masculine strength and spirit, coaching her and encouraging the individuation of her self. This development of her self is the only way out of the web of patriarchy.

So our friend gathered up her courage and went to Aphrodite's house hoping that Eros's mother might be kind to her for Love's sake. But the powers of the deep are not kind; they are ruthlessly effective. Though Aphrodite was going to make Psyche go through hell, She was also going to cause her to grow into a mature, beautiful woman who stood free from any system whatsoever.

A sea gull had told Aphrodite all that had happened in Eros's valley of paradise, and once again the Goddess blamed Psyche for everything. A woman's unconscious feminine being is somehow informed of the goings-on in the conscious mind. The part of Psyche that she had not differentiated from all other people, the part that was still part of the general herd, would dislike her difference from everybody else. It would unconsciously (and accurately) blame the difference on the part of her that was in the process of becoming conscious. The part of her that was unconscious of her subservient attachment to patriarchal values made her feel anxious about her struggle to be who she was.

If Psyche had chosen to remain unconscious of the difference between reality and the patriarchal picture, she would have blamed herself. The patriarchal picture held her responsible not only for herself but for Eros and most everybody else as well. But her needless guilt would only have complicated matters. She was really responsible only for herself, though she could choose to be *responsive* to Eros and others.

Patriarchy wants "responsible" citizens who will feel guilty if they do not willingly obey whatever the system commands: get married; don't get married; have babies; don't have abortions; don't have babies; do have abortions; go to war; hate enemies; obey your father; honor your husband's superiority; work hard and pay taxes. It makes no difference whether the patriarchy is democratic socialism, democratic capitalism, or Russian or Chinese communism (or uncommunism). All systems want citizens who are educated to feel responsible. What no patriarchy wants is *responsive* citizens who are autonomous, who think for themselves and ask questions, and who relate to others.

Psyche was well on her way to becoming autonomous and responsive to the people around her as well as to her environment. So Psyche got what every woman gets who dares to disobey: the fury of the unconscious, collective, undifferentiated female who has allowed patriarchy to subjugate her. The malice of an unfulfilled, sexually unconscious woman is without equal. In a tyrannical speech, Aphrodite lit into Psyche. In victorious self-righteousness, She called Psyche all the ugly names She could think of.

Aphrodite's blame echoed the blame of all the unravished brides who hated Psyche and of all the conforming, play-it-safe, patriarchal men who bitterly resented her. Both blamed her for man's inner poverty. She had failed to fulfill man's patriarchal expectations; she had not met his needs, satisfied his wants, or gratified his desires.

It was extremely difficult for Psyche to hold her own and not give in to the blame dumped on her. Everything in a patriarchal society tells woman she is RESPONSIBLE. She is responsible for her husband's well-being, her father's well-being, and the well-being of her boss, brothers, and sons. If one of them is grumpy, overweight, underweight, depressed, or not doing well, then it must be her fault. She is a slut; a good-for-nothing, godforsaken whore.

But Psyche bore the Goddess's wrath! Pregnant and out of shape, disheveled and poorly dressed, Psyche stood before the Goddess and endured Her rage. She withstood the irrational fury the unconscious can generate. In the majesty of her humanness, Psyche did not apologize, explain, or justify. No matter what Aphrodite called her, Psyche would not repent of her erotic love and the knowledge it brought her. She would not say no to her self for the sake of safety. Psyche's standing there and taking it was an act of great courage and irrational hope.

By bearing the Goddess's wrath, Psyche offered to all women unlimited hope. In spite of the authority of the gods to punish and condemn her, in spite of the power of men to rape and ravage, disown and junk her, the *feminine self irrationally prevailed*! And so it does today.

By her courage, Psyche stopped the chain reaction with which unaware women automatically respond to the pressure that the feminine unconscious exerts. She demonstrated that by having the courage to be who she was, she could withstand the demand that she repent and conform to patriarchal values. What Psyche did was remove herself from patriarchy's judgment scene; she refused to categorize herself or let herself be categorized.

Most women do not crumble under the bombardment from the men in their lives or from the Feminine-destroying Masculine in the culture; they crumble under the barrage of garbage that their unconscious collects from the cultural value system and spews back at them. Look at all the battered wives who can "take it." What a woman finds harder to take is criticism from other women (the fear of being ostracized by her own sex) or the criticism of the Goddess (who is the final authority of the Feminine in the culture).

But most destroying of all is her own feminine criticism of herself, the patriarchal Goddess within. Paradoxically, it is the voice of her inner man-self that condemns her. Being unintegrated into her critical awareness, it is his voice that echoes the voice of patriarchal femininity and tells her she is a failure as a wife, as a mother, as a woman. It is his voice that tells her she is unfaithful, disloyal, a slut, and a whore. By becoming mindful of her inner man, Psyche changed the tune her inner man sang to her.

On the other side of panic, Psyche found herself in a new, conscious relationship to her self. For the first time Psyche experienced herself as a human being who could be self-determined! She was beginning to feel the force of what it means to be a self-governing person. She had not given way before the fury of the Goddess; she had held her own. Psyche realized that she had a self who could stand up to irrational power and bring it into her consciousness without letting it destroy her. And she could stand up to patriarchal man.

The other major change in her relationship to her self was this: she knew that by her bravery she had commanded the respect of her inner man and that he had stood by her when Aphrodite had condemned her. Psyche was catching on to the fact that she could have an inner masculine presence whose voice no longer put her down.

In a new relationship with her self, Psyche was now able to begin to formulate new mind-sets and new patterns of behavior based on her experience and the new values evolving in her. No, she would not carry Eros's inner pain as her own; she would not let him sap her strength or use her energy; she would not take the blame for his problems or for the problems of society. She would not kowtow any longer to the obedient, submissive, patriarchal women who condemned her or to her militant acquaintances who also condemned her. Nor would she relinquish to the Goddess the first fruits of her disobedience: her erotic love and her transforming knowledge.

Panic ushered in her autonomy, because it forced Psyche to let go of rationality. On the other side of panic she found her self, intact. But she also found that she could rely on the irrational (panic) as a way to find an opening in a blank wall. Following rational control, rules, and regulations does not reveal the self or the path that an individual should take. Ironically, going through irrational panic left Psyche free to use rationality as well as irrationality to cut her own path.

On the other side of panic Psyche also found the key to her autonomy and to intimacy with the opposite sex: a deepened awareness of her inner masculine presence. It was not through self-discipline that she became conscious of her animating function, for that would have led to despair or self-righteousness. It was not by directed, rational consciousness, for that would have led to self-limited and self-limiting knowledge. Nor was it by a "reasonable," holy, and living sacrifice, for that would have led to unreality and non-being. The only way Psyche could become critically aware of her inner man was by yielding her feminine self to the process of becoming conscious of her unconscious (much as she had yielded her self to Eros in conscious, passionate, sexual love). And that is just what Psyche did. It was not a preplanned strategy, however; it was simply what her emotions led her to do.

Allowing herself to be penetrated by the unknown, by the unconscious, as she had yielded her body to be penetrated by Eros in passionate love, is the feminine way of learning truth. This does not preclude the conscious use of both rational and irrational means; rather the yielding is the framework for the conscious use of any means. This was what happened to Psyche as the result of going through panic: she gained an expanded awareness of her man-self and the deep, masculine, erotic love that lived within her.

Psyche found that becoming conscious was as passionate a process as her love affair with Eros had been. She passionately willed to know the part of herself that does not ordinarily enter critical awareness—the part that remains unidentified, unnamed, and unmentioned. Only by using the two halves of being human—the yielding feminine and the penetrating masculine—could she know the unknowable. So Psyche needed to expand her vital awareness of the presence of her inner man by yielding to his presence. Then she could consciously use rational means—deliberate thought, critical analysis, and design—as part of her personality to penetrate the unknown. And she needed to acknowledge and treasure the value of her feminine self so that she could consciously use irrational means—perception, reflection, and intuition, which are inherent in a woman's primary mode of being.

Psyche had yielded and in that yielding stood: she had not repented. For the first time Psyche's inner man-self served her. And it felt great!

DO-OR-DIE TASKS

But Psyche bore the Goddess's wrath. She stood there and took it.

At last Aphrodite relented, but only so far as to prescribe several nearly impossible tasks for Psyche to do in order to earn her deliverance from death and the return of Eros. These were do-or-die tasks; either Psyche would succeed or she would die. And Aphrodite planned for her to die.

Psyche stood there. She did not give way before the Goddess's wrath. She did not repent of her disobedience, nor relinquish her erotic love, nor renege on the transforming knowledge it revealed. Psyche was not being defiant. She was being faithful to her vision of love and to the dignity of being human. She did not surrender to the almighty majesty of the unconscious, because she had gained enough of a sense of herself. She withstood the pressure of the patriarchal values that dictate (and judge) feminine behavior. She refused to accept the guilt caused by disobeying those collective values. Instead she bore the conflict between the intrinsic truth of her self and the internalized judgment scene of patriarchy.

Therefore Aphrodite relented. But She relented only so far as to assign Psyche four impossible, do-or-die tasks. Aphrodite could not have relented at all, however, if Psyche had not first achieved a strong enough sense of who she was. And no woman should dare to attempt Aphrodite's tasks until, like Psyche, her individuality has been sufficiently developed. It must be nurtured by her responsiveness to the high calling of erotic love: by her courage to disobey, to suffer her aloneness with dignity, to accept panic, and to learn to pray.

Psyche had not given in to the temptation to blame someone or run home (either to Eros or to her parents). Not wanting to spend the rest of her life in pain, she found out that she could remember the happy times and cherish the love she had had. She did not have to let Eros's rejection negate all the good she and Eros had experienced. Psyche had indeed left behind the mentality of obedience, which dictated that one act of disobedience condemns all of a person's motives and that one wrong step (i.e., a display of sexuality) contaminates the whole—whether that whole is a person, an experience, a relationship, or a mind-set. She had entered the mentality of creativity, which does not contend with evil but seeks instead to see the good in all the bits and pieces. She had thus become a candidate for attempting the four tasks of becoming woman.

Aphrodite, Queen of Heaven and Queen of Earth, Sovereign of the Sea, represented the highest level of feminine love—the highest level of sexual, spiritual, and mental love. She represented the very love in heaven to earth come down as well as the love brought up to earth from the depths of the sea. It was Her love alone that, receiving the Masculine, could create new life out of the substance of Her Being, just as new life is created out of the substance of a woman's body.

Thus the Great Goddess was known as the Creator of heaven and earth and all therein. It was She who filled the lives of Her people with joyous pleasure and graceful beauty, with the sound of music and singing and dancing. She protected Her people with the strength of Her rage, roaring like a lioness who is relentless in the hunt. And best of all, She gave them the gift of sexual desire and erotic love so that they would never have to be afraid of dying: they had already experienced a taste of heaven in their human love. They knew where they were going!

She was the Eternal Lady who burned all evil: Lady of Fire and Rebirth! She was the guardian of the truth and justice of the universe. She tied a cloth about Her eyes so that She could not be prejudiced. Her word reflected Her pure Spirit. She was the composer of the inaudible music of the stars, and the conductor of the cosmos. She was the giver of the unalterable Laws of Life and Death. As long ago as 2580 years before Christ there is written evidence of Her insistence upon kindness: Happy is the heart that has given bread to the hungry, that has given water to the thirsty, that has given clothing to the naked, that has given a boat to the shipwrecked. A happy heart is light because it has done good deeds, after the love that lives therein.

The heart of the Goddess was the place where moral judgments were made. It was She who weighed the heart of each who had died to test its lightness. It was She who judged. It was She who waited upon the holy mountain to welcome those whose hearts were light enough to allow their souls an everlasting peace. And the Almighty Goddess reached out Her arms to those whose hearts were heavy, holding them close to Her love and consoling them until they could rid themselves of the heaviness of their lack of love or of the weight of man-made judgments. Then, light of heart—liberated by the Almighty Compassion that lives in the Feminine—they could let go of guilt, in the forgiveness of the Goddess, and live in everlasting peace.

But a barbaric patriarchal mentality began to invade this civilized world. From beyond the Black Sea in the north and from the Arabian Desert and the Sinai Peninsula in the south, these barbarians invaded Old Europe and Anatolia and all of the civilized world. They imposed their mind-sets and value systems by brute force. They devalued and vilified the power of Her love. This patriarchal mentality replaced the Goddess's love with the cruel judgments of their god—a god of war, plunder, and rape; a god of judgment and punishment. These savage, uncouth warriors scorned the magnificence of feminine sexuality and defiled the purity of spirit in the Feminine Principle. They drove the value of the Feminine underground into the unconscious, making it a commodity that man owned.

Now, thanks to the selfless gift of Aphrodite and the courageous spirit of Psyche, consciousness of erotic love had broken the hold that the patriarchal mentality had had on Psyche. But Aphrodite knew that in order for Psyche to sustain the break and go on to the individuation of her self, she would have to learn how to develop her consciousness forever. She would have to grow out of the mind-sets and belief systems of the patriarchal culture, which debased the feminine half of being human, desecrated human sexual desire, and defiled the holiness of erotic love. Only then could Psyche become an unimpaired and comprehensive woman.

Aphrodite's task was to set the stage for the rebirth of feminine consciousness in the world and also to force the growth of a different kind of woman, different from the kind that patriarchy allowed. This new woman would be one who had reconnected with the love and power of the Goddess by consciously integrating her Masculine Principle into her feminine personality. Such a woman's consciousness of her inner man-self would enable her to form her own inner love relationship; she would not have to depend on a man even for erotic love. This woman, unlimited by patriarchal morality, would then be able to love a man erotically (and freely). She would be able to build relationships based on wants and desires instead of need, and based on the individuality of each person instead of some projected image.

So Aphrodite relented. She gave Psyche four impossible, do-or-die tasks to perform as the condition for her deliverance (the individuation of her self) and the return of Eros (the return of the Masculine to the Feminine).

The first task was the sorting of the seeds. Psyche had to differentiate herself from all other women as well as from the Feminine in the culture. And she had to differentiate her inner man from all other men as well as from the Masculine in the culture. She had to discriminate her own needs, wants, and desires from patriarchal values and belief systems.

However, it is impossible for a woman to sort the seeds in a patriarchal society. Patriarchy claims that this is a man's job! Man, in his omniscience, will sort the seeds. He will logically process all the relevant information and tell woman what is in her unconscious, what is from her past, and what is from her future. Using his rationality, he will tell her what her value is, to whom she belongs, and what she should be thinking, feeling, and believing. He claims that he is able to speak for her, that he knows what is in her mind, her heart, and her spirit.

But the truth is that patriarchal man is incapable of sorting the seeds for a woman. Limited by patriarchal lies, he cannot even sort his own. What the patriarchal mentality does not grasp is that information that is available emotionally is not also available intellectually. Irrational knowledge is not attainable by rational means. Consciousness is the product of the activity of the human soul as well as the human mind. The soul is the aggregate of all the irrational components of a human being; it functions independently of the intentions of the conscious, rational mind.

In order to accomplish her first task, therefore, Psyche could not rely on rationality. The rational, scientific method of man is simply inadequate to sort the seeds. And being inadequate, it is also inaccurate. Psyche had to rediscover the feminine way, the way of irrationality. The irrational way takes over where rational means end. It arrives at solutions to problems and explanations of reality that supersede those of logic or reason. And it can meticulously sort the seeds of a woman's soul for her.

Learning to sort the seeds led Psyche to her second task: facing masculine power. Psyche had to gather the golden fleece from the sun rams. Among the illusions patriarchy fosters is the lie that women can obtain power (the golden fleece) only by using masculine means. Women are taught that they are powerless to do anything, to get anything, or to be anything without masculine power. And the horror is that women believe this lie. By panicking, Psyche found the feminine way, the indirect way, of obtaining power. She collected the golden fleece without confrontation or struggle with the sun rams.

And this led Psyche to her third task: filling the crystal vessel with the water from the Fountain of Forgetfulness, which was at the top of a mountain that was higher than any man could climb. No man can accomplish this task; there is no masculine way. Nor could Psyche do it by masculine means. As she climbed the mountain, she began to shed all the patriarchal laws and commandments that held her captive. Psyche came face to face with the true nature of patriarchy: the polarization of the sexes and the deadweight of historical inertia. The polarization of the sexes destroys impassioned love and the personal knowledge of the Deity it brings. And the dead weight of historical inertia destroys self-growth and the further evolution of humankind.

At the top of the mountain Psyche faced three sets of monsters. If she could face the monsters without hating and blaming the Masculine or despising and rejecting the Feminine, then she would irrationally gain access to the power of the masculine spirit and so be able to fill the crystal vessel.

In a patriarchy it is easy to see the Masculine, because it is explicit. It is not easy to see the Feminine though, because it is devalued. Psyche could not use her feminine spirit until she was able to forget all the lies that patriarchy had used to deprecate the Feminine.

If Psyche could succeed in obtaining the waters of forgetfulness, then she would be able to reclaim her feminine spirit and free it from patriarchy's contaminating lies. She would be able to use for her own creativity the tools of her spirit—intuition, all-inclusive love, the ability to sacrifice, and the ability to feel. Furthermore, the masculine attributes that lived in her inner masculine—perspective, rationality, and success—would be able to penetrate and animate the tools of her spirit.

This then led Psyche to her fourth task: the descent into hell to obtain Persephone's immortal beauty ointment, and return it to Aphrodite unopened. If she succeeded, she would win her deliverance from death and Aphrodite would have to return Eros to her. But since Psyche followed her erotic love instead, there was a different ending.

The tasks that Psyche had to complete are symbolic of the work a woman must do in order to become a fully developed woman, one who is conscious of her passion for being human. Accomplishing the four tasks teaches a woman how to identify and develop a consciousness of her inner Masculine. The return of Eros symbolizes the return of the Masculine to the Feminine so that masculine love and strengths and virtues, incorporated into a woman's personality, can serve her. Psyche's consciousness of her inner man was the means through which she could get in touch more and more deeply with her life-renewing femininity.

The life-renewing power of a woman's deep, inner femininity is the same power that the Great Goddess has! And that power includes the invincible strength of Her creativity; the lustiness of Her love; the allure of emotional honesty and the trustworthiness of Her feminine judgment; the might of Her spirit, which burns all evil; the sparkle of Her joy; the ferocity of Her protectiveness; the energy of Her ruthless truth; and the intensity of Her irrational mind.

That is the kind of power that belongs to every woman (and to every man, through his inner woman-self)! And that is the glory that has taken the whole force of patriarchy thousands of years to quell. What a waste of talent and creativity, love and human compassion! But energy cannot be destroyed. And the power of the Feminine Principle, represented by the Creator/Goddess of Love, remains unconquered. It is intact and available for any of Her daughters or sons to use according to Her laws of the holiness of life, the goodness of human sexuality, the gift of sexual desire, and the sanctity of erotic love.

A woman's inner man-self is not like a sidecar, an addition to her being that she pulls alongside her. It is not merely something she fills with masculine traits, taking them out as needed as if they did not belong to her. These masculine attributes already belong to every woman. And the same is true for every man: his inner woman, and all of the feminine values, are already part of him. The properties of the Masculine Principle function in a woman as part of her being female, just as the properties of the Feminine Principle function in a man as part of his being male.

But if a woman remains unconscious of this masculine function, she will be subject to masculine rule and inexplicable animosity. She will feel bitchy and touchy; she will snap at people or withdraw from them. She will feel an undiagnosable fatigue and malaise, causing her to whine and complain. But a woman *can* become conscious of her inner man, in which case "he" will function on her behalf. Then she will feel animated, full of energy, and enthusiastic.

If a man remains unconscious of the value of the female-self living in him, he will remain under the rule of the unconscious Feminine. The more "macho" he becomes, the stronger will be her rule. He will become moody. He will find life devoid of meaning, and he will experience his love as futile. He will feel inexplicably rejected and abandoned, belligerent and ugly. He will feel overly aggressive, or gloomy and depressed. He will act controlling and possessive, jealous and rejecting. He will demand and condemn. And he will hate himself with a self-loathing he cannot cure.

But a man *can* become conscious of his inner woman, in which case "she" will function on his behalf. Then he will feel loved and accepted. He will be in charge of himself, liberated from the compulsion to control others. No longer will he be subject to irrational moods; instead he will be in conscious contact with the irrational. His life will be full of meaning, and he will delight in his love.

A woman's consciousness of her inner man is what connects her to her animal life so that she can feel at home in her body. When a woman is at home in her body she feels playful, vivacious, intense, and joyful. The other side of being vivacious is her animal ability to be as ruthless as a mother tiger protecting her young. A woman needs to be conscious of her ruthlessness, her authoritative hardheartedness. That is how she can protect those she loves and urge them to grow up. And that is how she can cut through the lies patriarchy has taught her. Then she can spot the attitudes that separate the mind and the spirit from the body, debasing the body and relegating it to dirty jokes and shabby novels. Feminine ruthlessness reestablishes loving conditions by restoring the worth of the body as well as the feminine spirit.

Many modern Psyches live outside their bodies. They have no idea of what it feels like to live in a body. They starve or stuff their bodies, they work them out to the point of exhaustion or mush about moving as little as possible. They even have trouble sleeping in their bodies. And their poor bodies, so hated and despised, just keep on breathing in and breathing out, dumbly hoping for their persons to start living in them, loving them, and caring for them. Bodies don't know whether they are ugly or beautiful; they just want to be loved.

In addition, a woman needs to become acquainted with her man-self. It is through her inner man that her feminine instincts are confirmed and brought to life so that they can serve her. If she has no consciousness of her inner man, then her instincts remain useless to her. No amount of mothering or fathering, religious faith and discipline, or philosophical education can get her in touch with the wisdom of instinctive femininity. Instinctive femininity is not the same as acting instinctively with no consciousness of one's instincts and no understanding of the consequences of one's emotions, thoughts, or behavior. But when consciousness of erotic love opens the door to a woman's awareness of her inner Masculine Principle, the erotic love between her and her inner man can get her in touch with her life-saving, seed-sorting, instinctive feminine wisdom!

These are crucial tasks. They are do-or-die tasks for women today, just as they were for Psyche. Either Psyche would succeed or she would die. If Psyche had not accepted the work she had to do in order to achieve a new, expanded level of consciousness, then her previous level of awareness would have shrunk and her level of aliveness would have died. If a woman fails to complete a certain stage of consciousness growth, not only is her growth arrested but all her preceding stages of development sour and turn against her.

It would have been lovely if Psyche—having so courageously disobeyed and then faced her aloneness, having lived through panic and confronted the Goddess's wrath—could have taken her trophies and gone home in victory. But if Psyche had tried to do this, all her work would have been for naught. Her courageous confrontation with Aphrodite would have degenerated into a pathetic scene, with Psyche despising and rejecting her own unconscious femininity and vainly attempting to justify her actions. Her panic would have deteriorated into unconscious hysteria. Her aloneness would have become unbearable loneliness, while her blaming would have expanded into bitterness. Her disobedience would have degenerated into mere rebellion and fruitless struggles to defeat men.

If Psyche had refused a task, or had failed at one, she would have ceased to expand her consciousness of her inner Masculine Principle. Her feminine strengths and virtues would have remained unimpregnated, therefore, by her inner man's respect, encouragement, and love. And her masculine strengths and virtues would have turned against her. The power of her primary Feminine Principle and her secondary Masculine Principle would have weakened and died. Her femininity would thus have been desexed even as her masculinity was emasculated.

But worst of all, Psyche would have been forced to give up her erotic love. That is the inescapable consequence of not growing. She would have had no expanded consciousness in which to hold the increase of her erotic love, so it would have burst its container. And if Psyche had lost her erotic love, she would have lost the fuel of her spirit. Without fuel her spirit would have slowed to a stop, and Psyche would have had to live death.

Therefore, Aphrodite could not tolerate failure. These *had* to be do-or-die tasks. But why would Aphrodite plot Psyche's death? What was the matter with Her?

Aphrodite remembered a better time, a time of free erotic love, a time which had produced compassionate sharing, joy, a richness of life, and great artistic and technological outpouring. But She now saw only a world of incomplete, unhappy men and women who were incapable of sustaining erotic love.

The tasks She imposed on Psyche, though deadly, offered Psyche a chance to attain an abundant life as a fully passionate woman. The deadly tasks also offered the return of Eros—an evolved man who could love her and be loved by her. This part of the myth signifies a woman's potential deliverance from a ghostly lover who seeks to keep her an unravished bride, an incestuous father who seeks to keep her an eternal daughter, a eunuch son who would keep her an eternal mother, or a play-it-safe husband who would keep her a neutered wife. As an undeveloped self, Psyche would have been condemned to live life as an impaired, limited woman who was married to death.

The Goddess *had* to plot Psyche's death, because without the cruel urgency of Aphrodite's do-or-die tasks Psyche would have been hard-pressed to make herself take the risks and do the work necessary to develop her self. Aphrodite had to think up each task as if She intended it to kill her. Only the prospect of dying could compel Psyche (or any other person) to go against patriarchy, to go through panic and find a solution to each task, and then to submit to the arduous work of completing it. And, paradoxically, a part of Psyche did die in the completion of each task. But it died so that something new could be born in her. Psyche's self-renewal was dependent on the death of the old.

Aphrodite, representing a woman's deep, unconscious self, was the only power strong enough and insistent enough to force Psyche to expand her self-awareness until she stood free from bondage to an unconscious and asexual life. A woman's urge to become whole comes from her unconscious feminine instincts and her dynamic femininity. It does *not* come from her inner man, or from the urging of any actual man, or from any masculine thought or religion in the culture. If Aphrodite could not get Psyche to change, no one could!

Tackling Aphrodite's tasks was the only approach that could shake Psyche up enough to get her to change. It would force her to transcend her enslaving patriarchal mentality until she could establish a new mentality in a new and unfamiliar land. Most women, still in bondage to their own patriarchal mind-sets, desire to be free but are unwilling to tackle the tasks. They do not want to accept the risks and do the strenuous work it takes to become free. And they are as scared of a new and unfamiliar land as their patriarchal men are.

What Psyche had to face at the beginning of each task is what each woman must ultimately face: the fact that she must either risk her life or accept a living death. And she must either risk losing her love or accept passionless commitment and powerless sex. She must risk her life as she knows it in patriarchy, but she must also take the risk that she might get caught in her own psychological depths and die. She could get ensnared while sorting the seeds, trapped by some aspect of herself that takes over all other aspects with a demonic force; she could get killed by the sun rams, whose golden fleece she must get; she could run from the terror caused by the monsters who guarded the fountain and never reach the waters of forgetfulness; or she could keep on trying to pull the dying man out of the river and never get Persephone's immortal beauty ointment.

Psyche had to accept the paradox that in order to live she had to risk her life over and over again. If she did not risk her life, she would die. And, even more frightening, she also had to risk her love. For although a woman's growth is the only thing in the current system that can persuade a man to change and grow, he is always free to dump her, to take away her "palace," and to cast her out and remove her from the ranks of respectable women.

That is one of the realities of patriarchy: man has the power to make a woman become something she does not want to be—subjugated, dependent, alone. (No woman wants to be a divorcée, even if it is the only way she can save her self.) Man has the power to declass woman. Though woman has the power to hurt or even kill man, she does not have the power to declass him. Though she may be able to divorce a man, she cannot make him a second-class citizen. She cannot cast him out or subjugate him or make him become something he does not want to be. Woman cannot make a man a whore.

In the process of accomplishing these tasks, Psyche had to become a hero! But she had to violate the picture she had of herself as a good, god-fearing, obedient woman. In her own mind she was not some warrior maiden, disobedient and willful. She was not some political activist, militant and determined.

But through the completion of each task Psyche learned more and more about how to become a responsible "I," a person who has courage enough to be responsive to her own needs, wants, and desires. In that increasingly honest response to her self, Psyche learned two things: to stand up for her self, responsive to her own reality, and to be more responsive to Eros as he was. And bit by bit she also learned to be responsive to the Divine within herself as well as the Divine within others. Psyche was daring enough to refuse to conform and courageous enough to assert her divinely given sexuality, intelligence, and spirit. And it was by accepting the consequences of her daring and her courage that Psyche became a hero.

With the completion of each task Psyche exposed in more than one way that the laws of men and the commandments of their gods were nothing more than a convenient escape, a subconscious alibi. Laws and commandments provide excuses for violent behavior and play-it-safe existence: for not living life, for not taking risks, for not becoming human. They are man-made answers to quell the anxiety of living and the fear of dying. They are designed to depower erotic love, and to empower patriarchy so that it can perpetuate itself.

Psyche had to become a hero in order to free Eros (and her own inner man-self). Only the erotic love of a full-blown woman, who sees no limits to her love, has a chance to penetrate a dominant male like Eros. Without such penetration a male can never become a fully conscious, pleasable man. Only a man who has been penetrated by a woman's erotic love can bring to birth his consciousness of his inner woman. A male who needs to be needed, who is afraid of being desired as an adult male, is not a man. Such a male is incapable of an adult relationship built on desiring and delighting in a conscious *other* who also desires him. It takes a real woman to make a real man—a man who is courageous enough to dare to not conform, courageous enough to love and embrace femininity, and evolved enough to be loved and embraced by the Feminine. But even a real woman cannot make a real man out of a worshiping wimp or a cop-out bully. A male must have the courage to change and grow in order to be a man. (And only the power of her erotic love can free a woman's inner man-self from the patriarchal value system. Her erotic love is what causes her inner man to defend her, support her, and love her, guarding her from the ugly labels of patriarchy.)

Any woman in Western culture who wants the right to her own sexuality and her own spirit has to become a hero. Like Psyche, she has to dare to not conform, because there is no royal road to consciousness. Each woman must find her own way, panicking and yielding to gain masculine strength for feminine love. A woman's bondage, as well as her man's, is not due to patriarchy alone. It is also due to her own unwillingness to be a hero.

However, Psyche's heroism went beyond the patriarchal heroism of self-discipline, willpower, reward, and glory. It went beyond masculine brute force, which must slay the dragon, and beyond the patriarchal concept of the triumphant victor and the subjugated loser. Psyche slew no one. Psyche's heroism evolved out of her developing consciousness of her inner Masculine. It evolved out of her courage to accept emotional and psychological conflict. And it evolved because she learned to live without answers, rejoicing instead in the continual search for knowledge. Hers was true masculine heroism; it dared to go on even in the face of death.

By accomplishing each task, Psyche became able to incorporate within her self irrationality and rationality, consciousness and unconsciousness. She learned to bear the tension arising from the dialogue between these "opposites." Aphrodite's tasks would teach Psyche how to let her conscious be intimate with her unconscious while she maintained the autonomy of her expanded awareness.

By loving Eros, Psyche maintained her femininity while developing her masculine mode of being. The ability to love erotically while developing masculine strengths and virtues is the only way a woman can become more and more woman.

In the patriarchal system both men and women are taught to develop the Masculine without loving the *other*, without respecting and valuing the Feminine.

But in bed with Eros, Psyche had discovered herself becoming conscious of her self—a woman self! By yielding her body to be passionately penetrated by Eros, Psyche could consciously receive (and incorporate into her self) masculine passion, encouragement, and respect for her femininity. (And so can any woman, whether or not she has a man. It does not depend upon the man to whom she may or may not be attached. It depends upon her love for the Masculine and her reception of the goodness of masculine sexuality as well as her own sexuality.) By yielding, Psyche could assimilate the masculine strengths and virtues she needed in order to express the power of being a passionate, creative woman. If Psyche were to let go of this knowledge of passionate masculine love for her, she would lose her foothold on the path that led to her freedom. She would return to the patriarchal way: developing the Masculine while rejecting and despising the Feminine!

Aphrodite's ulterior motives now become clear. Laying out Psyche's do-or-die tasks was not only to force woman into expanded consciousness. It was also to free man from the shackles of the patriarchal system he had created and from the power of the unconscious Feminine (which looks like his mother). What Aphrodite desired was women who were women—those who had successfully incorporated their Masculine Principle into their being woman—and men who were men—those who had successfully incorporated their Feminine Principle into their being man. Only such men and women are able to sustain erotic love so that a new reality can be born.

SORTING THE SEEDS
I

On *the morning of the first task the Goddess pointed to a great heap of seeds: the food of the doves that drew Her chariot and of the little blue birds that accompanied Her on Her journeys. The heap was composed of wheat, barley, millet, and other kinds of seeds all mixed together carelessly. "Take these," said Aphrodite, "and separate them grain by grain. Place each kind by itself, and finish the task by nightfall." And off She went in grandeur, Her sapphire chariot pulled by Her white doves.*

Psyche was face to face with a giant heap of seeds, and she had to sort them out by nightfall or she was going to die! The poor dear looked around for some help. Maybe Aphrodite would change Her mind or Eros would see the error of his ways and come to help her. But Eros had not erred by patriarchal values. And Aphrodite certainly was not going to change Her mind. What Psyche and every woman has to face is that she alone must successfully complete each task.

The seeds symbolize the contents of a woman's heart, all those non-physical things, both conscious and unconscious, that make up a person. They also represent a woman's talents and potential, her feelings and thoughts, her instincts and desires, her intellect and her independent spirit. Sorting the seeds represents Psyche's becoming conscious of who she was as a separate individual, apart from anyone else. The purpose of such sorting and separating is paradoxical: it is to differentiate the self from all others and increase autonomy so that the self-determined person may connect more intimately, more consciously, and more passionately with others.

Psyche had to learn how to stay attached to her feelings of love and affection while detaching from relationships, from the values and mid-sets of others, and from the expectations and demands placed on her by her family, her friends, her lovers, and even herself. She also had to unmask her needs and wants and desires. She had to recognize them as private and distinct from cultural injunctions, realizing that her desires arose from her feelings, her needs from what was necessary to sustain her life, and her wants from what she thought about her feelings and needs. (It is very important for a woman to keep quiet about what she wants, because the easiest way for patriarchal man to control her is by depriving her or granting her her desires.)

Patriarchal man tells woman that she is incapable of sorting the seeds and that he alone can do the job. But if Psyche continued to believe that or that the only way to sort the seeds was according to patriarchal masculine values, she would be giving man the power to continue his domination of her. Without knowledge of her self, she would just be imitating someone else's ideas and reenacting prescribed patterns of thinking, feeling, and behaving. Without the inspiration of her intuition, the logical process would sap her energy. It would focus on controlling all the people in her daily life and examining the content of all her problems. She needed to rediscover the feminine way of sorting the seeds. She had to learn to trust the mystery of her inner voice and to depend on her intuitive instincts, because they alone released the energy she needed for self-growth.

By accomplishing each task in the feminine way, Psyche would find the tools she needed to expose all the patriarchal values that she had absorbed and which had cheated her out of being herself. By learning who she was, what she wanted, and what she desired, she would gain confidence in her self.

And then she would be able to develop a different way of communicating with her self. Successfully completing each task would increase and support Psyche's new awareness of the value of her womanhood, her right to exist, and the power in her unconscious reality.

Until Psyche could sort the seeds they remained all mixed up and she remained ignorant of who she was and what she needed, wanted, and desired. But in a patriarchy the seeds are worse than mixed up; they are mislabeled, miscolored, disguised, and denied. Without her knowing it, these deceptions affect a woman's feelings and her sense of self-esteem. They affect her behavior and her personal relationships, her sense of humor and her level of stress. They further confuse an unconscious woman's identity, and this misguides her faith and actions.

These mislabeled seeds represent all the "shoulds," all the "do's and don'ts" that woman has been taught. They also represent all the false images of the good, images which depict the model patriarchal woman. (A "good" wife should have dinner ready for her husband whenever he wants to eat. A "good" mother has perfect children. A "good" female employee makes work her life and is never absent.) These miscolored seeds deceive people into feeling they might be doing something wrong at any minute. In a patriarchy the level of anxiety is very high.

Enforced by fear, anxiety, guilt, and shame, the ethic of obedience (to patriarchal values) forces men and women to adopt false fronts and disguise their true feelings. *Man is afraid of losing control, and woman is afraid of losing man's approval.* So woman denies her personal reality; she twists her self into different shapes and forms, like a pretzel, always trying to please. And man vetoes his personal reality and clones the patriarchal image.

The great delusion patriarchy perpetrates is that by obeying, people can avoid sorting the contents of the unconscious. But we are more answerable to the unconscious than we are to any moral or legal code. The unconscious is our source of inspiration, truth, and creativity. It is the wellspring of the urge towards wholeness and individuation. If a person refuses to answer to the unconscious, its power will turn negative. When a person denies the unconscious it simply hides its content, but it nevertheless relentlessly dominates the person's thoughts, emotions, and behavior. Psyche was not only blind to everything in her self of which she was not aware; she was also ruled by it. The self-discipline that obeying exacts lets a person feel in control, but in fact it is the unfaced unconscious that does the controlling.

Most women take their cues not from inside themselves but from role models. Because they have deserted their inner selves, many of today's Psyches are living the roles they play and cannot nurture the selves they have hidden. They are starved in terms of intimate relationships with themselves. And they are starved in terms of the relationships they have with the whole culture—a culture which does not nourish the Feminine. Women are starved for a sense of their value, for concrete help, and for recognition of their competence.

Patriarchy deprives women of the nurture that every human needs. Women have neither the benefit of the Masculine nor the benefit of the Feminine. Though men may from time to time nurture other men, it is rare indeed to find a man nurturing a woman in a patriarchy. (Men view female will as something to be curbed, not supported.) Besides, women do not seem entitled to male nurturing. Feminine will and energy are expected to go to the Masculine and not be squandered on women. Any endeavor of a woman's that might make her come home tired, absorbed in her thoughts about her work, self-reflective, or hungry, is considered bad. A woman is expected to be there, rested and energetic, ready to serve her man when he comes home tired and self-absorbed. A woman is expected to nurture masculine endeavors because a man's work is more important, more vital, and more meaningful, and he *deserves* the ministrations of his wife. Women are expected to nurture masculine talents—the talents of the men in their lives as well as the masculine in themselves.

Women cannot even find nourishment from the Feminine Principle, their primary mode of being. The Feminine has been so devalued that women cannot find the love and support or the power and glory that should be theirs. They, too, fear female will and leave their own female endeavors undernourished. Female talents seem lusterless and narrow even to women, next to the well-fed, well-exercised talents of men. But malnourishment is not recognized as a limiting factor; it is assumed that a woman's creativity is inherently deficient. But when a woman is hungry and thirsty her creativity is severely limited, just as a man's would be.

In a patriarchy there is no love that accepts a woman for the self she is. There is only approval (a poor substitute for love) for the roles she plays. Therefore she, like Psyche, does not have a true mirror in which to see her reflection. She believes the distorted image she sees, and she trusts the negative judgments given by others. Patriarchal woman knows only one way to stop the judgmental voices from yelling at her, and that is to do what they tell her. And what patriarchal culture tells her in every ad, video, magazine, and movie is that the way to find approval is to try harder, be stronger, be more loving, be adaptable and flexible, and do better. But the double bind is that the more she tries (in the masculine way, of course) the more she is cut off from her feelings and her life-renewing femininity.

Psyche must not hide her true feelings from her self, for it was from her heart that her actions came. She had to find a way to allow her feelings to come alive so that they could nourish her inner self with the enthusiasm and spunk she needed. Only then would she be able to create a lifestyle that would materialize from consciousness of her self. How tragic to find out later that the lifestyle she had lived had evolved out of her own blindness to who she was and her own fidelity to a false value system.

Before she could free herself to love her body, respect her mind, and honor her spirit as holy, Psyche had to critically question the religion, history, and symbols of patriarchal culture. She had to question a church she had loved, an education she had respected, a flag she had saluted. Patriarchal belief systems maintain that patriarchy is a necessary stage, for the development of individuals as well as the evolution of culture. They contend that without patriarchy humans would not have learned logic or reason or consciously directed thinking but would have remained in some ill-defined, pre-conscious state—a state in which recognition of personal individuality, the "I am" consciousness, was impossible. But couldn't men (and women) have learned these processes and concepts of self without devaluation of the Feminine, dese-cration of erotic love, and war? Perhaps people already knew these things before patriarchy arrived.

Could a god who ordered the rape, murder, and subju-gation of women, who allowed no mention of the Feminine in his godhead, be a loving god? Could one half of being human be destroyed without the other half being mutilated and invalidated? Could man, by driving the value of the Feminine from the memory of every man, woman, and child, get rid of his longing for what he was created for—to be the lover of woman, the protector and cherisher of the Feminine?

How do we measure the devastation patriarchy has wrought? In dollars? Or in the lives that have been sacrificed in man's wars, rebellions, and acts of terrorism? Or is the loss of human talent, human generosity, human creativity, and human love so immense that only the Deity can withstand such tragedy?

Psyche wanted to crawl into bed and pull the covers over her head. But she had to become acutely aware of all the insidious ways that her patriarchal culture had seduced her into believing its lies—believing that war was necessary and that adultery was worse than murder. She had to allow herself to feel the way patriarchal values sucked her into the bottomless pit of nonbeing and inferiority, depression and anxiety, denying her self and her right to exist, and abdicating the full use of all her talents.

She had to become consciously angry at what was going on, because she needed the energy of positive anger in order to combat the sweetly reasonable rationality that masked the harshness of patriarchal judgments. She needed to clarify the reality of her love so that it could encourage her to stop identifying with the roles she was supposed to play. Otherwise the feelings of inferiority and guilt, anxiety and despair, would destroy the fabric of her personality. And that would leave Eros without a real woman who had a face he could see and a personality with which he could connect.

To counteract the denial of the unconscious that patriarchy encouraged, Psyche had to become critically aware of how it made her feel to avoid confronting her own unknown. And it felt as though someone were holding her down, as though she needed to run from some terror but her feet were stuck, as though she were carrying an unbearable burden that she did not know how to get rid of.

Our friend, like every woman, needed some tools to remove all the mistaken labels. They hampered, limited, and retarded her; they judged her negatively and burdened her with anxious concerns. She needed a method for circumventing all the rigid requirements with which she had shackled her self, and she needed a way to shut up the inner voice that recited all the terrible things that might happen if she should try to please herself. Psyche needed a voice that would give her permission to be and do and feel all the wonderful, restful, reassuring, and challenging things available to her.

She had to learn how to exercise her "O.K." function in the face of the hate and prejudice of patriarchy. It is O.K. to relax. It is O.K. to take your time. It is O.K. to be imperfect. It is O.K. to cry. It is O.K. to be loved. It is O.K. to be human. It is O.K. to be God's crowning glory. It is O.K. to be woman!

A woman's disassociation from the patriarchal picture begins with falling in love and being surrounded by passionate masculine love for the Feminine. Psyche did not begin to separate her self from the roles that patriarchal values directed her to adopt until she had tasted her passionate love—drinking in masculine *otherness* and allowing her self to be ardently and intensely penetrated by the single-mindedness of masculine erotic love. Without carnal knowledge of her love for man and his love for her, Psyche could not have found the courage to disobey. And without disobedience Psyche could not have begun her exit from patriarchy. It was by disobeying that Psyche gave herself the gift of differentiation.

Without differentiation she could not have identified the voice of distorted authority issuing negative injunctions: "Don't! Don't do that! Don't be! Don't change! Don't be different! Don't be sexual! Don't be joyful! Just go back to your house and be good." Without differentiation she would have internalized this voice. She would not have recognized the fact that it was just the voice of the patriarchal value system.

Because of the negativity of patriarchy, negative voices have more impact than positive ones. Without differentiation the loud noise of false superiority hammering out criticisms and barking out domination drowns out the sound of goodness and kindness. Without differentiation Psyche could not have heard, identified, or encouraged her "angel" voice, the voice of her inner man: "I am really sorry, darling, that you get put down so much. You don't deserve it. You are really a good person, and I see how much you love the Holy Spirit. I know how much you want to please those you love and do everything right so your dear ones will be happy. I want you to know that I know how smart you are, how sweet and how charming. I want you to see how talented and lovable, how good-natured and full of energy you are. I want you to know what a hard worker you are and what a joy you are to be around."

Thus, in a patriarchy a woman must not only sort the seeds of her self (which is hard enough), but she must also sort out all the mislabeled, miscolored seeds that patriarchy has disguised in order to deceive her. She must separate the reality of her self from all the false identities and false blame she had bought as true. If Psyche could identify the roles she had been unconsciously playing, then she would be able to discard those she did not want and consciously adopt the ones she chose from her heart. The ability to repudiate patriarchal roles would enhance her autonomy. If Psyche could find a way to detach her self from the seductive illusions of patriarchal roles while still remaining attached to the people she loved, she would be able to redefine herself in her own terms.

But in order to do this she would have to relinquish all the criteria she had formerly used for judging her thoughts, emotions, and behavior. This required a radical severing of her self from all the guidelines that had tied her safely to the shore. Until she could establish within her self the values that were meaningful to her, based on her increasing ability to distinguish reality from patriarchal lies, she would feel frightfully adrift. Learning to listen to her self, however, would give Psyche a different perspective. Then she would be able to develop new guidelines and create different standards by which to measure her self.

And she had to rehearse her new values daily, because the insidious temptation a woman faces hourly is to judge herself by patriarchal standards—what her husband expects her to be and wants her to do, what her children are supposed to need, what the current vogue is among liberated women... The price of nonconformity is guilt. Psyche had to find a way to become so alert to the feeling of guilt that she could abolish it the minute it struck.

She also had to understand the fact that although it is logical to solve problems by discussion, it is impossible to communicate with a man (or a woman) who is stuck in a patriarchal mentality. She had to know on a gut level that it is impossible to change anyone else's mind-sets, emotions, or behavior. She had to give up the reasonable idea that if Eros could just see things from her point of view then he would change. He would not be so cruel, because he would see how much he was hurting her. She had to forget the rational notion that if women and men were equal in the workplace then men would change their minds about the superiority of the male and his right to subjugate women. Patriarchal man will not change because of any attempts to get him to see the consequences of his behavior. His rape of the environment, his defilement of the only planet known to bear life, and the bloody consequences of his devaluation of the Feminine all continue.

Psyche had to learn that she was the only person she could change. She had to learn to depend on irrationality and creativity, instead of logic and predetermined conclusions, in order to promote and accomplish change. Then her irrational femininity could administer her intellectual processes, which were meant to support, articulate, and interpret her intuition. This is hard to do in a patriarchal culture because people are taught to scorn irrational ways. Intuition is hard to trust, and a weirdo like the god Pan is definitely out of vogue. But the minute Psyche tried to lead with her head, using reason, logic, and control to sort the seeds, she was doomed to fail. The contents of a person's heart are beyond logic and defy rational definition.

To affirm her personality in all its completeness, Psyche had to learn to differentiate her needs and wants and desires from the patriarchal values embedded in the collective unconscious. These values are all day long broadcast in all the media. And she had to differentiate her self from her family, her friends, and her lover. Then she would be able to identify her innermost self. Sorting the seeds would force her onto a passionate path: the way of an open heart, a way that would necessitate difficult choices and demand devotion to her vision of erotic love, devotion to Eros, and above all devotion to herself. However, the accomplishment of this task would allow Psyche to so separate her self from any exterior source of identification, that *she* would become the conscious source of the ever-changing identity of her changeless self.

Psyche would find that differentiating her self from her family was often a painful and disorienting process. Regardless of their imperfections, Psyche really loved her mother and her father; she even loved her mean, self-righteous sisters. These family loyalties are among the strongest earthly ties a person has. This new awareness of the separateness of her self shook up Psyche's earliest memories of being loved, and it opened her up to an almost unbearable sense of her own death. To shake up the source of a person's identity feels like nonbeing itself. And realizing that there is some perverse force operating on an unconscious level that pushes people to be like their parents is disorienting to a person's self-image.

The only way Psyche could overcome this unconscious programming was to sort out the differences as well as the similarities between herself and the members of her family, and to use her sense of humor whenever she could. Laughter is a wonderful remedy for pain, and it also puts things in a different perspective. But she had to realize that her individuality was more than the sum of these differences and likenesses.

She also had to differentiate the thinking patterns and emotions that were caused by events that had taken place in her childhood from the thoughts and emotions that were caused by current events alone. Otherwise she would be forever recreating her childhood and deserting her adulthood.

Of course, events of the past always color current emotions. Psyche's job was to distinguish what was from her past from what was appropriate to the present (according to her evolving new values). Then she would not have to afflict herself (or others) with inappropriate emotions, with the demand to be taken care of, or with the futile search for someone to give her what her mother and father had not. And she would be free to use the energy of her appropriate feelings: free to be angry at patriarchy in any form; free to love as many people as possible but still be mindful of who she was, who they were, and what her priorities were; free to enjoy her sexual desires and appreciate her spiritual insights. By paying attention to her emotions she would learn that she had the authority to choose what she would feel.

At her stage of development it was no longer appropriate to blame her inadequacies on the deficiencies of her parents. Nevertheless, she had to look at the hurts she had experienced in her childhood. No matter how loving a parent is, there are always gaps between what a child wants and what that child gets. Psyche needed to get in touch with the little girl she had been so that she could see that it was this little girl, still living inside her, who got so frightened when men became dominating or abusive.

As children, all of us believe our parents' opinions of us. And as adult children, people project the authority of parents onto those who are close to them (such as husbands and wives). And then they believe in their surrogate parents' opinions as if they were truth. What affected Psyche was not so much what others said or did but the way she took it. Psyche needed some tools that would allow her to sort through the negative messages she had unconsciously internalized. She had to sort out and discard these hurtful messages so that she could hear and accept the positive ones. Only then could she become a competent judge of herself.

At the same time, she had to recognize that one of her jobs as an adult was to become a separate, autonomous person who could lovingly reconnect with her parents (if they wanted to reconnect). Reconnecting was not her parents' job. A lot of inappropriate anger is unleashed against parents and their surrogates (such as husbands and wives) because adult children unconsciously want their parents to do the job of reconnecting for them. It was appropriate for Psyche to separate this kind of anger from the positive anger whose energy is usable.

Psyche could no longer define herself in terms of her group of friends, her social class, or her religious or psychological support systems. Support groups of any kind are worthwhile for a limited time, but beyond a certain point they begin to limit the individual. Submerging one's self in a group is an enticing prospect. Being identified as part of a congregation of like-minded people is much easier than standing alone. The thoughts and emotions of the group replace the arduous task of sorting the seeds (thinking for oneself and feeling out the emotions that are truly personal). How safe it feels to be a member of a proven tradition, an exclusive religion, or a powerful nation!

However, it does not matter how high-minded the purpose of a group is or how dedicated the members are; it is still a group, and in a group everyone plays a role. The support of friends who are also learning to stand alone and sort their seeds is different; such friends maintain their own identities. And evolved, non-patriarchal professional help is also different.

But modern-day Psyches often get trapped in feminine support groups—both the traditionalist type and the militant, feminist type. Traditionalist groups encourage a woman to be a man's woman—content as his adoring helpmate and the mother of his children, submitting willingly to patriarchal laws of state and commandments of religion. These women are told by the authority of their groups that fulfilling these womanly roles is the consummate gratification for women.

Militant feminists, on the other hand, only reinforce how oppressed woman is and how cruel and abusive the patriarchal system is. They offer women no way out. Instead, they encourage women to hate men—the very people women must love in order to grow in consciousness of self. As long as a woman's energies are marching into war (or beating a quick retreat), she has no energy to find out who she is and what she wants.

If Psyche had fallen into the trap of hating all men just because *male dominance* is hateful, if she had stopped loving Eros, then she would have lost access to her consciousness of her inner man. Likewise, if she had fallen into the trap of waiting for men to become good guys, she would have been simply giving in to one of the distractions patriarchy used to keep her unconscious and unchanged (a "rational" hope that Eros would automatically change). In either case Psyche would have stopped changing; thus, she would have forfeited all the masculine strengths and virtues she needed to integrate into her personality in order to express her femininity.

Psyche could not be defined in terms of her husband's family. Nor could she let herself be defined in the most seductive way of all—in terms of the family she and her mate formed. One of the most fraudulent of all patriarchal delusions is this: not only is a woman's ultimate self-identity limited to "wife" and "mother," but worse, her identity to her husband is limited to "wife" and to her children it is limited to "mother." Psyche was not allowed to exist as an individual. But if she could not *be*, then neither could her husband or children. Limiting her womanhood to the roles of mother and wife limits the selfhood of her husband and children as well; it limits them to their roles as "husband" and "children."

In the last quarter of the twentieth century it is still easy to see a wife living in her husband's shadow. Indeed, it is expected. But it is not easy to see the process whereby a once rather self-sufficient woman comes to depend on what her husband has to say about who she is. Nor is it easy to understand why she lets him tell her how to act, what to believe, even what she wants. Psyche knew she was not afraid to live alone. Why did she give Eros the power to make her unhappy, when she would have been quite happy if she were not attached? This question made her see also how much of her energy was consumed trying to make an unpleasant person happy.

In sorting the seeds difficult questions come up. Why does it seem impossible for a woman to be happy with a man unless she knows that he is, at that very minute, happy with her? For a woman the male-female relationship seems to revolve around how the man feels about her. Is it that a woman is happy with a man—and with herself—as long as he is happy with her? A man can know he has made his wife unhappy without being upset in his inner being as a man (although he may be somewhat distressed). Psyche could be very happy with Eros, doing whatever he was doing, as long as he made her feel good about herself. Everything was O.K. as long as there were no criticisms, no put-downs, no ignoring—as long as they were laughing and talking or snuggling and sleeping. But when he was unhappy with her it felt as though she were being destroyed, as though her world were coming to an end—as though she were going to be chained to the rock again. But this did not make sense to her, since what terrified her was the thought of living with a man who accepted his "responsibility" for her but who no longer loved her! Could it be that her acute anxiety was aroused because she accepted his patriarchal labels and believed she was what he called her? Did his criticisms echo those of her father, whose rejection could have cost her her life?

And the questions do not stop with wifely dilemmas. Why, for instance, doesn't a woman feel that she has accomplished anything at the end of a day, even when she knows she has done even more than required? Why doesn't she feel fulfilled when she has a brilliant, productive, meaningful career? Why does she feel incomplete as a person when caring for her children? What is the matter with her? She loves her children dearly, even passionately. And she loves her husband. Why is it that a career of listening to complaints about school and work, trying to make everyone around her happy, settling differences, and negotiating compromises doesn't feel as though anything is taking shape?

What every woman is faced with is the fact that no one—no mother or father, no husband or child, no group of friends—can help her sort the seeds of her unconscious. No one can give her permission to be happy. No other person can discover what is in her heart. No other person can define for her which values are meaningful to her or what it is that she wants to take shape. Psyche would have to see that she could live quite happily without man's permission. She could not, however, live without her self.

Pursuing her urge to achieve wholeness demanded that Psyche no longer define her self in terms of a man. Not even a man she loved. In order to continue the expansion of her consciousness, she had to free her self-growth from the limits of her husband's values. His needs, wants, and desires were not her own, nor was she responsible for fulfilling them. She had to open herself to her own personal potential. In order to claim her self, Psyche had to begin the differentiation of her self from her lover (husband). Lovers stop growing—and they stop loving—if they do not differentiate themselves from each other. Psyche had to learn how to be faithful to her self so that she could love Eros more erotically.

This kind of sorting did not necessarily mean she had to become unattached to her loved one. Rather it meant focusing on what her own values were. She had to pay attention to what she wanted to do, what the connection was between her feelings and her thoughts, and what her behavior said about her self—about her faith, her hopes, her loyalties, and her loves. So often when people feel the urge to achieve wholeness, which requires painful differentiation, they misinterpret their feelings and think that they must live apart from the *other*. They erroneously believe that divorce is the only option open to them that offers the chance for freedom and autonomy. But if they would just hold fast to their course of self-growth, sorting their own seeds, they would come out on the other side with their relationships intact (and in all probability improved). If the relationship has *not* improved though, then divorce is a viable option because the seeds have been sorted. Freedom and autonomy are first and foremost internal states; they must operate in the heart or they do not operate at all.

When a lover seeks fulfillment only through the other lover, one becomes the first-class partner while the other drops to second place. The first-class partner feels put-upon and the second-class partner feels victimized. Whether the second-class partner is ambitious or is copping out makes no difference; most first-class partners feel that the whole burden of responsibility for the happiness and welfare in their relationships rests upon them. And most second-class partners feel they are never appreciated for all they give.

To sort the seeds Psyche was going to have to recognize that if she settled for second best (for any reason whatsoever), then she was going to be treated like second best. She could not depend on Eros's success to make her a first-class citizen. And anything that is not best for an individual is second best, even when it is a loved one's best. A woman's heart may sing for joy for her husband's newest success. But if her smiling plea is "All I ask for myself is that he include me in his life," then she is unconscious of the contents of her heart and unconscious of what she is doing to her self, to her man, and to their relationship. She is putting herself in second place. She is making her man resent and fear her. He has to work too hard to bear the burden of success, and it is her second-class position that keeps him in a first-class position. What she is doing to their relationship is aiding and abetting the destruction of their erotic love.

Unlike patriarchal married love, which is a contractual agreement, erotic love between two autonomous people generates ever-unfolding possibilities and ever-increasing energy. Thus, each person in love needs to have an ever-expanding consciousness of self in order to contain the increased energy of erotic love and to process the unfolding possibilities of intimacy. This means each must be doing something that is personally fulfilling.

When a man and a woman in love are expanding their consciousnesses, when each is doing what is personally fulfilling, values and mind-sets drop to a secondary position in their relationship. Though living in a patriarchal society makes it difficult, two people of different belief systems and mind-sets can live together and share erotic love. The worth of each person goes beyond the belief systems and the values they create. Such people in love are able to let go endlessly, increasing the depth and intensity of their intimacy at the same time that their growing intimacy *increases* each one's sense of self!

When a woman passionately loves a man in this creative way, she has to find a courage stronger than any she has known. There was no difficulty in disengaging from what Psyche disliked; but to disengage from what seemed closest to her heart felt like tearing out her heart itself. Psyche loved Eros.

How very hard patriarchy makes this kind of sorting! On the one hand, a woman has a legitimate need for passionate masculine love (first to awaken her from her girlhood and then to fuel and refuel her spirit). It is hard to separate one's self from what one needs. On the other hand, society condemns such separating. Faceless and nameless, woman is expected to take her identity and direction from man. In a patriarchy, a woman's success *as a woman* is based on belonging to some man. Yet it is this very position of "success" that demotes her to an inferiority that only reinforces man's subjugation of her. She remains a second-class citizen in his sight as well as hers.

And patriarchal man is willing to be bored out of his mind to ensure that his wife is kept second-class and in the dark, unconscious of her identity. Further, he is willing to beat her into unconsciousness—verbally, silently, or physically—to keep her in her place as his commodity. It is impossible for a man who is stuck in a patriarchy to treat a woman as a person. No matter what he says or does, the real message is that she is, at best, an inferior (and, more often, a nonbeing) whose feelings and judgments are insignificant. He does not take her seriously. He simply does not think about her. And to a woman who is becoming more and more conscious, alive, and productive, unevolved man's message is "You are not the wife I wanted you to be." And, indeed, she is not; she is *not* his mother. A patriarchal male rages in disbelief when his wife becomes a wife.

So Psyche could not sort the seeds until she could bear the hurt and say: "I am what I am. This is what I have to give. You are free to want it or not." If a woman refuses to confront her lover on any of these issues for any reason, she forfeits the magnificence of her sexuality and the purity of her spirit. This is the price of conforming and leaving the seeds unsorted. When a woman accepts the patriarchal situation the way it is—at home or at work or in her chosen profession—she is making an active choice to remain a victim and leave the man in control.

However, Psyche needed to keep an open heart towards Eros and refuse to categorize men. If she should so deafen her ears and blind her eyes that she could not detect the least sign of change in Eros, then she would have to forfeit the passion of her womanhood and her right to self-development. Bigoted, sexist thinking prohibits sorting the seeds.

Psyche's sorting the seeds meant she would have to further differentiate her responsibility as an adult from the patriarchal picture of responsible woman. She was responsible only for herself. She was responsible for the fulfillment of her needs, the accomplishment of her tasks, and the creation of her self.

If Psyche assumed responsibility for her parents or her sisters or her friends or Eros, she would destroy her power to be and forsake her capacity for communion. She would replace her autonomy with a life of "have to's," "should's," and "don'ts," and her intimacy with taking care of people. (It is not possible to be intimate with unautonomous adults, adults who want you to be responsible for them.) If Psyche let herself be coerced into giving away the good feelings she had about her self as well as others, then sooner or later she would project the negative feelings caused by deserting her self onto Eros and their expected baby.

SORTING THE SEEDS
II

Poor Psyche, all of her brave determination gone, just sat with drooping head and folded hands. Then a little ant ran out from under a rock and, seeing Psyche's plight, called the whole army of ant people. They came for love's sweet sake and quickly separated the seeds, laying each kind by itself in neat piles. The ant people filled Psyche's heart with hope once more.

There were more seeds Psyche had to sort. She needed to find out why she accepted what was harmful to her, why she tolerated an uncreative job, why she felt dependent upon her man's approval when she was in fact a woman of independent means, and why she believed that an unhappy marriage was somehow sacred and that a divorce was a failure. And to do this she had to sort out the difference between the seeds of feelings, the seeds of thoughts, and the seeds of behavior—seeds which patriarchy keeps all mixed up.

Feelings are the most accurate and inexhaustible source of information a woman has about herself. They are her clues to what she needs and what is meaningful to her. If she tries to make herself fit the mold, she will never feel right about herself. When she knows about who she is, when she knows that her emotions are her own and cannot be judged by anyone else, she will start to feel good even if her feelings are negative ones.

In a patriarchy, however, man claims the authority to judge the feelings of others. He labels as wrong any feelings that displease him. He does not tolerate any powerful emotions. Any expression of passionate emotion is considered bad, whether it is sexual feeling or anger. Since most women do not know in their hearts that no one has the right to judge their feelings, they accept the harsh judgments of patriarchal authorities. As a result, women repress their feelings—their most unerring barometers of their well-being—until they become disconnected from them. They learn to doubt their own emotions.

A person's thoughts are also beyond judgment. But thoughts are more general than feelings. Feelings, after all, have names—sad or glad, helpless or hopeful, happy or disappointed, etc. Thoughts reflect people's beliefs and value systems, their mind-sets and impressions and perceptions. And it is these rather dimly lit, taken-for-granted thought processes that affect a person's feelings.

The good feelings that come from giving a gift are connected to self-affirmative thoughts: I like to make the people I love feel happy. I am a generous person. I like being kind. But these good feelings can turn sour in a flash if self-doubting, self-derogatory thoughts arise: maybe my friend won't like what I bought. I am a stupid person to think I could give a gift to someone who is so talented. These thoughts make a person feel uneasy, uptight, or anxious. The trick Psyche needed to learn was how to turn off negative thoughts before they could produce inaccurate feelings—feelings that would obstruct her self-determination and diminish her good feelings.

If Psyche had surrendered her right to determine her self, her identity would have belonged to the patriarchal complex—to her mother or father or group or phantom lover. She would remain incapable of existing independently. Only by knowing the truth of her thoughts and feelings, her needs and desires, could she become a self-governing person. Without moral independence and the power of self-government, Psyche would have been unable to recognize and connect with her innermost self.

Only from a position of some self-direction, freedom, and strength could she be enabled to recognize that she had a private zone of being, a secret place that was not open to any other person. Psyche had to grasp the fact that she did not have to tell anyone anything. There were parts of her she did not have to share. Communication was the result of a relationship, not its cause.

If Psyche could learn to sort the seeds of the innermost dimension of her being, she would be able to interact creatively with the reality of her inner life. Her innermost self was the principle character of the reality of her inner life. It both affected that reality and was affected by it. And a person's interaction with the reality of her or his inner life is what produces the contents of intimacy.

In other words, if a person has no consciousness of her or his inner life, then that person has nothing with which to be intimate. In addition, consciousness of the core self produces the entity that can operate a person's autonomy. Without consciousness of the reality of her inner life, Psyche would have remained incapable of autonomy as well as intimacy.

In order to experience this inner core, Psyche had to sort through the parts of herself that were living in the shadows. Though on the other side of consciousness, they nevertheless profoundly affected her feelings, thoughts, and behavior. Some of these parts were "good" and some were "bad," some were loving and some were not; some were mean and selfish rather than compassionate and sharing. And there were some that were really good but that Psyche had been told were bad.

It would seem that recognizing the good would be easy. But it was not. A lot of Psyche's loving, unselfish parts were labeled bad, stupid, illogical, promiscuous, or evil. Her compassion, which included caring about outcasts as well as the most acceptable members of society, was forbidden in a culture where compassion was limited. Nor was Psyche's ability to love more than one person at a time allowed in a system where love excluded those who were not on the approved list. In the value system of patriarchy the Supreme Being excluded from his heaven all those who did not meet his requirements and so did not fit on his approved list. This same value system called the vulnerability that opened Psyche's mind to reality, weakness. Her urge to achieve wholeness was called selfishness. And her many-sided vision was called emotional, unintelligible, garbled incoherence.

Nor was it easy to recognize all those parts of her self that violated the best she longed for. She had decided that she did not want to act out of blame or revenge; nevertheless, these emotions invaded her best intentions. And she had to deal with her memories and emotions. It was not easy to admit that she had not always acted or spoken or even thought according to the best that she knew. There was something in her that felt threatened by others' good fortune and something that rejoiced at others' bad luck. How hard it was to concede that she had probably demanded as much from Eros as he had demanded from her! It would take great courage to admit that she had not always acted like the kind, true, gentle, undemanding woman she had pictured herself to be.

Sorting the seeds of what she was taught to think were moral and ethical values from the seeds of what she found to be the real situation in the here and now, in the lives of real people whom she knew and loved, would force Psyche to change her values. Sorting the seeds of how she really felt about the people who did not live according to what she had been taught was right and good and holy would force her to further change her values. This whole process is extremely frightening because it shakes the foundations of self-identity. Who was she after all? And what was reality?

Psyche would have to change her deepest thoughts and feelings. She would have to cut herself loose from everything that had anchored her in the vast ocean of life. It is very hard for a woman to free herself from the idea that a Divine Love is pleased by a life of self-abnegation. The sign of sainthood for a patriarchal woman is abnegating herself, so that she can give to others every bit of her energy, every bit of her good cheer, every bit of her creativity. Like Psyche, most women believe that the world would somehow be better because of their suffering—as if their deprivation, hunger, and thirst would feed the poor, clothe the naked, and heal the sick. Psyche had to become aware, in the idea-changing part of her private self, that goodness is not more perfectly expressed through poverty than through abundance. And holiness is *not* more perfectly expressed through celibacy (or virginity) than through erotic love.

Psyche had to be able to contact that deepest, innermost self so that she could instruct her soul. For the truth was that the greater the abundance of every good thing in her life was, the more perfectly she would be serving the Divine Desire within her. She needed to develop the abundance of her self—including the abundance of sex and love, artistic and scientific creativity, the enrichment of the young, and the enhancement of the old! To counteract the lies of patriarchy, she had to instruct her soul every day.

Just as sorting the seeds would reveal difficulties, so it would unveil Psyche's talents and gifts. It would show her what it was she truly valued and what she wanted to be devoted to. When Psyche could encounter her private heart and face there all her unmentionables as well as her hopes and dreams, then she would experience simultaneously the uniqueness of her self and her kinship with all humanity. The uniqueness of the self is beyond thoughts and feelings, beyond values and wisdom. And the kinship of humanity is beyond religions and nationalities, beyond race and sex. And in the all-inclusive love of the Feminine that lies in the depths of every woman, Psyche would experience the goodness of Creation. She would taste the goodness of her own created, unrepeatable self.

If Psyche could get to this level of conscious self-identification, she would find a freedom and a force, a lightness and a spontaneity. By entering her inner world, she would be in communion with the life-giving, creative power of the Feminine. She would be in touch with the force that works intelligently within people to bring into fullness their individual uniqueness.

This kind of sorting takes acute awareness and time alone, not self-control and self-accusatory discipline. It takes focused attention and undistracted purpose. Above all it takes open-mindedness and the authority of love. A woman holds an unknown seed in the palm of her hand; she must direct her consciousness to it, opening her heart to its meaning.

Psyche had to learn to trust her heart. Her feelings, informed by her instincts, were her tools for evaluating reality. But since the authority that dictates what women should think and feel also acts as their judge (and finds them wanting), women are tempted to squelch their feelings. Patriarchal woman does not feel good about her instincts or her body. Her needs embarrass her; her body mortifies her. But by not accepting her needs and not loving her body, Psyche left her mind in charge of her needs and her ego in charge of her instincts. And then she had no accurate measuring rod against which to gauge the validity of her feelings and thoughts—and no means to separate her self from others.

Poor Psyche. You can bet all her brave determination had left her. This was a do-or-die task and she did not know how to do it. She had no reference point, in heaven or on earth, to which she could turn for help. She had no tools with which to define her self. She had developed no source of identity outside of her family, her group, her church, and her nation. She did not know how to discriminate her own feelings and thoughts from what she had been taught. Nor did she know how to distinguish her needs, wants, and desires from the unconscious, collective herd mentality.

What Psyche needed were the attributes of single-mindedness, undistracted purpose, focused attention, and directed consciousness. But these abilities did not lie in her primary mode of being, the Feminine Principle. Psyche could only find these self-identifying tools in the Masculine Principle, which constituted her secondary mode of being.

The Feminine Principle contains the ability to adapt to the many-sided nature of reality, the ability to see what is not yet seen, and the ability to keep track of many things at once but on different time and intensity levels. And above all, the Feminine Principle contains the ability to love many people at the same time—not equally, but individually and passionately. Such love brings personalities to life and gives people faces. But until Psyche had yielded consciousness of her self to be impregnated by her inner man with her inner man's masculine ability to focus attention and direct her consciousness, she would not be able to use the power inherent in her feminine wisdom. Her many-sided awareness would be poured like water upon the sand.

Many women faced with do-or-die tasks try to use the masculine traits of directed consciousness and focused attention as traits outside of themselves, traits they have tried to develop by self-discipline or self-control. But this approach does not work; it greatly hinders a woman's access to her irrational power and her feminine wisdom. Logic alone blocks her intuition. Rationality that excludes irrationality negates her gift of insight and forces her love into the patriarchal mold of exclusivity. Cut off from the irrational, women are cut off from erotic love. And out of erotic love they lose the feminine powers of tenderness, compassion, clear-sightedness, and appreciating individuals. Their authoritative hardheartedness turns into a masculinized superiority, a rigidity of seeing things only their way, and a belligerent attitude towards others.

If Psyche had tried to use masculine strengths by obeying patriarchal authority, she would have destroyed her contact with the nonpatriarchal masculine spirit that lived within her. Without consciousness of her inner man she could not integrate masculine strengths into her personality; therefore, Psyche could not define herself as fully and passionately female without some consciousness of her inner man. And without a sense of her inner woman Psyche could not have a sense of her inner man. Thus, by using patriarchal methods she would have surrendered the creative power of both her primary and her secondary modes of being! (This condition is just what patriarchal mind-sets and belief systems strive for, be they administered by the church, the synagogue, the mosque, the state, or a husband.)

How very hard this definition of self is! This separating from others would leave Psyche more visible than ever. By daring to differentiate her self, Psyche would be saying, "Here I am; I have a face. Because I am, I count." By making such a declaration of self, Psyche made others feel *other*. As she became more visible, no longer just one of the flock, she would become the accessible target of patriarchal condemnation. People find it much easier to condemn someone than to face what it means to be *other*.

Psyche wanted to weep; the task was too much to ask. But she had to see that regardless of the social and psychological pressure to obey, her need to be a person who was separate from all others was a life-or-death matter. The creative soul is the one who dares, the one who disobeys. Once again Psyche dared to disobey; she just sat and waited.

Then a little ant crawled out from under a rock. What was this ant? It was Psyche's sexual instinct. It saw Psyche's plight and called the whole army of ant people to come help Psyche for love's sweet sake. (The conscious reason for sexual desire is always "for love's sweet sake"!) And what were all these other ants? They represent our basic, earthy instincts, which people are so wary of trusting. Individuals only have to make contact with one of our instincts for all of the rest to rally to our defense. Since Psyche had not forsaken her erotic love, her consciousness of her sexual instinct could lead her to her inner man, where her instincts dwelt. So consciousness of her inner man brought forth a whole army of instincts to aid this woman (for love's sweet sake).

Instincts do not lie. They simply state what is: I need; I want; I desire; etc. They are absolutely trustworthy. For millions of years human instincts have guarded people's welfare, helped them feel good, and kept them healthy and strong. Instincts are never out of whack, but the patriarchal interpretation of them is usually so out of whack that instincts have a difficult time doing their job.

Those who have watched ants work know that the most obvious quality they display is undistracted purpose. If an obstacle is put in their path, they will go around it, over it, or under it—but they will continue to pursue their course. And if people try to distract their instincts, they will go around them, over them, and under them—but they will continue to pursue their course. This undistracted purpose and industry was just what Psyche needed in order to go around, over, and under all the distractions patriarchy put in her path.

Now in a focused state, Psyche could simply watch the ants mechanically doing what they did for her. Psyche's new consciousness of the goodness of her instincts put her in command of them. They had always been the sure and certain indicator of whether or not she was trying to force-feed herself proper, patriarchal emotions. Her instincts had made her feel uncomfortable, uneasy, and sort of sick whenever she tried to make herself fit the herd's patterns. And they made her feel good, strong, and optimistic when she felt her own feelings. But now she also *knew* what was happening. For the first time, Psyche had conscious use of her instincts.

Thus, Psyche was free to lead with her heart and could consciously use her feelings as her guide. Through them she could learn what she wanted to change in her values and her behavior; she could learn what traits, talents, and ideas she wanted to nurture in her self; and she could decide what to integrate into her personality from the Masculine. She did not confuse true masculinity with the patriarchal idea of man!

And so, *her masculine abilities integrated into her personality became like her instincts—ants that automatically did her work for her.* Focused attention, single-minded purpose, undistracted work, and directed consciousness were at her service the instant she called for them. (She did have to get used to calling for them, though.)

How effortless was the way in which Psyche gained the masculine traits she needed! No self-discipline, no obedience, no control. No master, no yogi, no guru, no teacher to tell her what she must do; no curriculum; no tests! Instead, Psyche used the way of intense giving and receiving that takes place between man and woman in sexual love. (Who knows who is the giver or receiver—both are giving and receiving at the same time.) By continuing to love erotically, Psyche had maintained her connection to the feminine way of yielding herself in love to the loving Masculine. And the passionate, masculine love living in her had impregnated her with whatever masculine traits she needed!

Thus, masculine traits were integrated into the fabric of her personality, enhancing her femininity and enriching her life. By staying powerfully in love, her consciousness of her instincts (which were now freed of patriarchal inhibitions) and her consciousness of her inner masculine strengths (which were now integrated into her feminine self) acted as an army to sort the seeds for her!

But Psyche's way is hard to initiate. The patriarchal mentality, which outlaws the sacredness of sexual desire, cuts people off from the saving health of their instincts. And this specifically prevents women from ever being able to consciously internalize the inner masculine strengths they need in order to become powerfully woman.

Psyche would soon need to dwell upon how it made her feel to have an "army" composed of her feminine instincts and the thinking processes of her inner masculine self. It was very different indeed from the way it felt when she sat alone and unarmed before the task! To have such an army composed of the irrational (her instincts) and the rational (the masculine traits) made her feel powerful and good about herself—strong and happy. But she had to consciously change her old habit of trying to use patriarchal means to sort whatever seeds were before her; she had to make a conscious effort to call upon her internal allies instead.

Turning off patriarchal judgment and turning Psyche's way of sorting the seeds into a habit takes a lot of practice— every day. Every woman has to cultivate the habit—in her car as she drives to work, or after the children are off to school, or as part of her planned quiet time. She must learn certain truths, even if she must write them out and paste them on her mirror. Whatever a woman who has sorted the seeds does for herself is good. It lets her feel cared for because she knows what it is she needs, wants, and desires. She must do whatever it takes for her to know that taking care of herself—taking time and money for herself, and acting in her own best interests—does *not* keep her from being a loving, caring, giving, unselfish woman.

Such a woman can rejoice in how nice it is to have her good feelings about herself be her guide!

SORTING THE SEEDS
III

Psyche let her instincts begin the lifelong job of separating the values and strengths inherent in the Feminine from all the patriarchal lies. Patriarchy believes that anything feminine is inferior, that everything masculine is superior, so that "God" is masculine. It states that women are evil, that women are the source of evil and death, that men are good, that men are the source of light and spirit, and that men are the conquerors and the redeemers of the inferior sex. Patriarchy even claims that creation is bad—that everyone is born in "original sin"! In the patriarchal value system knowledge is evil, birth is dirty, and sex is vile, etc., etc., etc.

Psyche's instincts, however, informed her of the reality of her self—that she was created good—and of the reality of her life—that it was good. When Psyche felt good inside herself, she could be pretty sure she was on the right track. But when she felt uneasy, empty, or anxious, she could be pretty sure that what she was encountering was a patriarchal trap. And her inner masculine virtues focused her attention on what she was doing. Becoming aware of her behavior became as easy as breathing in and out; there was no effort or judgment.

Oh, she thought. *I have been accepting blame. This makes me feel bad because I want my loved ones to be happy. I feel guilty over their unhappiness. And I have been apologizing too much, smiling through the grimmest of times. I have been watching every word I say and every gesture I make; I have been repressing my opinions, ideas, and feelings. I feel as if I've been walking on eggs. No wonder my muscles ache!* There was no self-blame, no "How could I have been so stupid?" Her instincts merely informed her that something was amiss. She did not get distracted from her main purpose, expanding her consciousness. So her question was this: What were the thoughts and feelings that had been going on inside her to make her feel that way? And her other ants—her masculine abilities to focus attention and direct consciousness—put into words the message of her instincts.

Being free to bypass the snares of using only logic and reason, Psyche became adept at using her intellectual processes to support, articulate, and interpret her intuition. This brought her the ability to remain attached to her feelings while she used her masculine resources to sort her thoughts from her emotions. Focused attention became the natural tool she used to monitor her own inner dialogue. And this clued her in to the negative thoughts, beliefs, and perceptions that provoked and sustained anxious feelings. It also allowed her to hear the voice of her inner man-self above the din of male domination.

Sometimes Psyche got tired and discouraged. She even wondered if what she was doing was worth the effort. But her directed consciousness informed her that she was tired because she had not slept well for several nights. She was not imagining her fatigue. Her instincts then urged her to take a nap. With her intelligence supporting her instincts, she took a nap and woke up feeling better. Now she could hear her inner man encouraging her: *I know, Psyche, that in the face of the monolithic structure of patriarchy it is hard not to be discouraged.* (Her appraisal of the situation was acknowledged.) *But every seed you sort, honey, brings you that much closer to the return of Eros and the liberation of yourself.* Her inner man-self gave her hope. He gave her a viable, realistic, alternate way of thinking. Psyche felt encouraged. She now saw how her fatigue and negative thinking had triggered her pessimistic feelings.

But she did not have to force herself to change. She had her "army" of instincts and integrated masculine abilities ready and waiting for her command. All she had to do was let them work for her. Changing her negative thoughts to positive ones required no self-discipline or denial. Thus, she was free to claim her feelings (whatever they were). Thus, they were beginning to belong to her self. Her feelings were no longer unconsciously regulated by patriarchal logic, nor was her thinking controlled by her unconscious emotions.

By becoming aware of her thoughts and emotions, Psyche became aware of how insidiously the patriarchal value system had been ingrained into the very basis of our mentality. She realized how she had accepted as true all the labels patriarchy sticks on women. And how women, seeking confirmation of their goodness, believe the labels and always try to do better.

She saw that passively waiting for change was not an objective virtue. In tune with her instincts and heartened by the loving support of her inner man, she found that she was letting go of the past. She was detaching her identity from places and people she had loved, and she was even relinquishing parts of herself. This gave her the freedom to enjoy whatever was enjoyable around her. She no longer had to depend on being with a particular person. She enjoyed being with her self alone. Psyche was thrilled, and not a little afraid, to find herself inviting change and moving forward.

She saw that security was no longer a meaningful attraction. She realized that she did not want it. She did not want to feel secure with Eros; she wanted love and excitement, challenge and new possibilities. Supported by the love of her inner man, she changed her opinion of uncertainty. She saw it as positive now instead of negative, as provocative and exciting instead of intimidating and fearful.

Of course she still wanted freedom from danger, deprivation, anxiety, and failure. Who doesn't? But she saw that confidence was something she had to cultivate in her self by accepting challenges, exploring new possibilities, and feeling the excitement that arose with self-discovery. Paradoxically, most women become less and less confident when they sell out for security. This is because of their increasing dependence on someone or something (such as a husband or a job) that is outside of themselves. By accepting the route of playing it safe, they actually encounter grave danger. They forfeit the positive belief in self every time they play it safe, because they demonstrate less and less trust in themselves.

Psyche began to see risk taking and decision making as traits she wanted to establish in her self. She found that by focusing on the benefits she could gain, the anxiety of risk taking began to lessen. Aided by her integrated masculine traits and abetted by her instincts, Psyche found decision making becoming easier and quicker. She chose between this seed and that one with very little hesitation.

Fortified by her expanded consciousness of her self and her inner masculine abilities, Psyche took the risk of investigating the reason for some of her negative feelings. Some of her pain came from believing the warnings of impending catastrophes and limiting herself to prescribed, play-it-safe behavior. Tummy cramps and a headache were the signal that she needed to say "I can" and do it. Pain in her neck and down her back and across her shoulders was the signal that she needed to say "I don't have to" and stop trying to do it.

By becoming aware of what was bothering her, as well as becoming aware of patriarchal lies, Psyche could change her attitude. She could offer herself affirmation instead of condemnation. She could exercise her "O.K." function! She imagined what it would feel like to be stronger and more alive, to acknowledge that she was good and competent and ready for the next adventure. And this process of imagining did make her feel good. By using her imagination she could contemplate how it would feel to ask her boss for a promotion or to confront a lover or to have a baby.

Playing out these imaginary scenarios to see where they might lead, Psyche gave her instincts free reign. And they let her know if she should take the risk or change her mind and find another way. Before she decided to take a risk she wanted to know whether or not it would implement her self-growth, accomplish what she wanted, and make her feel good, vibrant, and alive. And that was precisely what her instincts would tell her.

This seed-sorting woman was now ready to evaluate her stress level. This is probably one of the most important areas for modern Psyches to appraise. The patriarchal system wants people to believe that when a woman works in a position of power her stress level is raised and her health is adversely affected. Patriarchy wants people to believe that a woman feels happier, healthier, and less stressed out at home or in positions that require no exertion of authority. (As if raising children and running a house take no exertion of authority!) Society is led to believe that imitating the work lives of top executives is what has caused the increased smoking, drinking, and incidence of ulcers and heart trouble in women.

Women must understand these phenomena and differentiate the real issues from patriarchal propaganda. Alcohol is a dangerous drug and must be used with care. But what many people do not recognize is that a lot of women use it for more than just alleviating stress; a lot of women use it primarily to liberate themselves from male domination! To have to live in a world limited to rationality often feels like sheer hell. By putting herself into a comfortable state of creative irrationality, a woman can escape from man's self-limiting rationality and humiliating subjugation. She can feel her joy in being alive, she can delight in her own sense of humor, and she can luxuriate in living life in a body. And she can know when, where, and how much she wants to drink.

By carefully sorting the seeds, women will see that it is not responsibility or authority that have caused their health problems. In fact, it is the *lack* of any real authority as an adult woman that causes problems. Women have to deal with a social, economic, and political environment that was created by men for men. It is run by men, who invent the rules according to the power and money and sex they want to get. Women must compete (without the benefit of the authority and prestige men have just from being born male) in situations where the real decisions are often made before the issues are even open to discussion. Decisions are made on stag hunting and fishing trips, during men's golf games, and in their locker rooms—areas to which a woman has no access. She has the unmeasurable stress of being an outsider— an outsider who must always work harder, be more careful, and bear the brunt of male (and female) put-downs. Woman *is* the alien of aliens in a male-dominated world.

At home this professional—be she a secretary, an artist, a charitable volunteer, a president, a vice-president, or a chairman-of-the-board—performs (and is expected to perform) most of the domestic chores, child care, and cooking. (Even if she has servants to help, *she* is responsible.) She also has to deal with her husband, his career, his potential envy of her successes, and the guilt laid on her for being an "imperfect" wife, an "inefficient" housekeeper, and an "incompetent" mother.

Psyches of today need to see that their problems are related to man-made gender roles (many of which women have unconsciously internalized) and female sexuality (which can be a constant reminder to men at work of their problems at home). Women's problems with stress are not related to responsibility or work load or tough jobs. Nor are they related to a woman's "forsaking her proper roles."

Indeed, those women who stay at home and are dependent on their husbands for economic support, approval, and self definition are the very ones who experience the greatest levels of stress. The stress of self-repression, of trying not to contend in the world, and of being afraid to stick up for oneself is the most damaging kind of stress. Such women are less healthy and die at younger ages than women who work—even if the working women feel frayed at the edges by the demands of job, marriage, and children. Not only are women working healthier, they are also happier. Like Psyche, they are experiencing the power to determine who they will be.

Clearly Psyche's way of sorting the seeds gives women an option they do not have in patriarchy. Suppose a woman's husband barely tolerates her, only thinly veiling his contempt for the Feminine. In a patriarchy she has two choices: she can grin and bear it, relying on him for everything, or she can confront her husband, demanding a fair share and fair treatment. But even if she gets what she wants, she is still dependent on him for it.

Psyche's way gives women a third choice. A woman can get in touch with her instincts, reviving her sexual desire if she has repressed it. She can reestablish conscious contact with her inner man-self so that she can have a loving masculine presence who will impregnate her with the masculine strengths she needs. Thus equipped, she can start sorting the seeds.

First she evaluates her job situation: she does not have a job; she wants a job; she does not want a job; or the job she has is too unrewarding. At the same time, she starts doing whatever she must to feel beautiful and fit, healthy and strong. She educates herself in updated history, in finance, and in current laws. She exercises her mind and expands her consciousness so that she is so flexible she cannot be bent out of shape.

She uses her active, well-informed imagination to explore different possibilities. She imagines going through the steps of getting a divorce, finding out how it would feel and where it would leave her financially and socially. She can alter the scenario and see how it would feel if she and her husband went for counseling instead. How would she change? Would he change at all? Would it feel right if they were struggling together to improve their relationship? Or would she still feel dominated, unable to stand up for herself? Using her instincts to evaluate these situations takes very little time. Imagining and feeling can be almost instantaneous processes. By becoming actively aware, this woman is laying the groundwork for creative change. In this way she will be free, whether she stays or leaves.

This woman is no longer finding her identity, security, and guidance in other people, in the culture, in religion, in her social group, or in her husband (as she once did). Like

Psyche, she is beginning to find them inside of her self. She feels herself understood and defended by a loving inner masculine presence. Consciousness of her inner man-self helped Psyche outline the boundaries of her self in the world and sense the reality of who she was.

In this lifelong process of sorting her self from others and their expectations, Psyche had to sort through all of the old images she carried with her from patriarchy and all the feelings and thoughts they produced. In the process of sorting she automatically began to form new images that reflected the reality of her inner self—images that would support her new growth. Woman, as artist, stands at her easel and paints. Then the old domestic image of "good wife" appears, and the image is seductive: some day, it claims, the role of the "good wife" will pay off. But the woman's expanding consciousness of her inner man supports a new image of herself as artist.

When Psyche could recognize and feel the reality that she, herself, was not "daughter" or "sister" or even "wife," that her value lay in being *Psyche*, a joy she had never experienced flooded her whole being with new life. Though this joy was not constant, no one could take it from her; it came from inside her and was not dependent on any other person. In tune with all the good feelings that her instincts elicited, she had a sense of self so focused and directed that she could see and she could think, she could hear and she could feel. She could generate her own sense of self—a self that was mindful of the fact that she was different from and greater than any image or role or collection of them. Ah, that sweet taste of autonomy—it made her want to reach out and love others with a great, compassionate caring.

What was she going to do with all that good feeling and power? (For feeling good is powerful.) Psyche had to learn how to incorporate her good feelings into her sense of self. She had to recognize that her self *was* her good feelings and that any negative feelings were impostors. This meant accepting wholeheartedly the power of her sexuality and the purity of her spirit. She could be both sexual and independent, both spiritual and tough-minded. To make sure that she would not give away her good feelings (her self) to her man, her children, or her culture, Psyche had to learn how to root and ground these feelings in her body. She had to practice feeling them swelling her breasts and filling her solar plexus with gladness, feeling them moving down through her body and enlivening every nerve and every particle of flesh. That way she could claim what was her own. These were *her* good feelings, her self was *her* self. Regardless of what patriarchy said or did to the contrary, she had a right to exist, a right to be happy, and a right to rejoice in whatever and whoever increased her gladness.

Psyche now had a new mentality, and the questions she asked herself had changed. She was no longer concerned only with what she should do and how she could make others feel good. Now she also asked herself what she wanted to do, how she could make herself feel better, and how she could fulfill her adult need to become more and more autonomous and more and more capable of intimacy. Psyche had to practice asking these new questions over and over again in order to learn how to answer them.

As dusk approached and the seeds were sorted Psyche became aware of that deep, masculine love living in her. It was as if she heard the voice of her love praising her for a job well done. For a split second she felt overwhelming erotic love. It lit her face and she felt warm and soft. Psyche had to practice bringing awareness of her inner man's love for her into her heart and mind. And she had to practice it over and over again.

Consciousness of her inner man had restored Psyche, who represents the conscious Feminine, to her role as the sorter of the seeds. It was the resurrection of this very same feminine consciousness that would empower Psyche to complete her tasks and then to live her life. And Psyche had to practice being alive to her inner man-self over and over again so that she could experience over and over again the power of her feminine consciousness.

At the close of day Aphrodite came, garbed in the brilliant colors of sunset. She saw that Psyche had finished her task and, in haughty annoyance, threw her a crust of bread. She said She would return in the morning and set Psyche a much more difficult and dangerous task. Exhausted, Psyche fell asleep on the ground.

GATHERING
THE GOLDEN FLEECE
I

In the morning she woke up yearning for her lost love.

Disheveled from sleeping on the ground and hungry after only a crust of bread, Psyche yearned for Eros—for his smile and the sound of his laughter, for the way he smelled and the touch of his hands, for the feel of her body against his and the weight of his arm holding her.

In the cruel light of day she was fully conscious that she was alone and bereft of her love. Having sorted the seeds, she knew what she felt and what she thought. There was no postponing her heartache—no unconscious drifting into a never-never land, no latching onto another man, no promise of some automatic redemption that had once protected her from feeling the pain of imperfect human existence.

Though the temptation to try to *think* a way out of her feelings was intense, Psyche had to face her loss and accept her grief. All alone she had to hear Aphrodite out; alone she had to face the task; alone she had to find a door in the blank wall. Going into the unknown is hard indeed.

Aphrodite came in beauty adorned ...

Before Psyche could even comb her hair, Aphrodite arrived perfectly groomed and gowned. Shit. What chance did Psyche have? Very little, but enough. How easy to play the game with a guarantee to win; how hard to play when defeat hangs heavy overhead. So Psyche, with a gnawing at her heart and a knot in her throat, had to sit there on the ground and listen to Aphrodite's next impossible task.

Aphrodite arrogantly pointed to the river. On the opposite shore grazed the sun rams, whose wool was golden fleece. "Bring me some of that wool," She demanded.

Wool, that should be easy enough. But the wool Aphrodite wanted was the golden fleece from the sun rams. The "sun" in "sun rams" represents male-directed, male-oriented consciousness: the consciousness of daylight with no consciousness of the light that shines in the dark; the awareness of things that can be seen, heard, felt, or measured in some way; the absence of the irrational mode of apprehending reality. The rams represent masculinity that is undifferentiated from animal strength. The golden fleece represents wealth, and wealth is power.

Aphrodite wanted Psyche to get the golden fleece because Psyche, like everyone else, needed to sense the wealth of her self. This would empower her to aggressively assert her expanding selfhood. Only a woman's intimate knowledge of the great worth of her feminine self and all the strengths and virtues in the Feminine Principle can procure the personal power necessary for her to assert her self aggressively. That intimate knowledge was what Psyche would find in gathering the golden fleece.

Psyche could only accomplish the tasks Aphrodite set before her if she knew how to aggressively assert the value of the Feminine. She therefore seemed doomed to fail, because patriarchy had murdered the value of being woman. And underneath all the feminist bravado, all the hard work of real achievement, that is the way most women feel: doomed to fail. No matter how much they accomplish, no matter how creative they are, no matter how much they contribute to society, the culture in which they live does not value the Feminine.

It is not only patriarchal men who depreciate the contribution of women to corporate worth and cultural well-being. "Imitation men," women who despise the Feminine and idolize the Masculine, are also guilty of depreciating the Feminine. These women, in the arrogance of their artificial masculinity, are traitors. They betray not only themselves but also other hardworking women who make vital contributions to corporate, professional, and humanitarian institutions—contributions that cannot be measured by the patriarchal methods that the "imitation men" use. These neutered women also reveal themselves as the unravished brides they are.

What Aphrodite asked Psyche to do was something that no individual had ever done before. Aphrodite wanted Psyche to obtain the golden fleece by using feminine means. Up until then the quest for the golden fleece had been a manly quest, a great masculine adventure. In it men proved their courage, strength, and virility. In the male myth it took Phrixus's masculine strength to tackle the sun ram, shear off his precious wool, and then kill the animal in a sacrifice of thanksgiving. Undifferentiated man knows only one way to separate animal strength from male-directed, male-oriented consciousness, and that is by killing the beast.

Once the golden fleece had been shorn from the sun ram, the only way to get it was to steal it. After the golden fleece had been stolen by a foreign power, it took Jason and his whole group of friends to steal it back. In a patriarchy men have to have physical power or the power of a brotherhood to get the golden fleece. Therefore, man's sense of his self-worth is dependent on male physical power or the power of a brotherhood. The result of this dependence is that man can assert himself only through the power of his group or through the power of his physical strength.

Since patriarchal man has no personal sense of self-worth based on his individuality, he cannot assert the authority of his personal self. Consequently, what he asserts is only his interpretation of the rules, regulations, dogmas, and doctrines of his group and his physical strength. He is blind to any alternative to what he and his group consider right and good. He believes his group is "God's" chosen people, whether his group is the Hebrew people, the Roman Catholic Church, Jehovah's Witnesses, or the street gangs of Los Angeles.

Without a personal sense of the value of one's self, a person feels powerless. Feeling personally powerless, people feel a desperate need to exert control over others and dominate them. Patriarchal power is power *over* others. It is not power *for* others, and it certainly is not power for one's self.

Power over others corrupts. Absolute power over others corrupts absolutely; it corrupts both the powerless and the powerful. Lack of personal power, power for the self, corrupts one's personality. It seduces the self into submission to an ego that is inflated with pride and cramped with fear. And absolute personal powerlessness corrupts the very power to be.

Therefore, powerlessness breeds violent disruptions: riots in the streets and rebellions in the homes. The urge to fulfill the adult need for autonomy is relentless, like thirst or hunger. People want personal power to live their own lives (even though patriarchy has convinced most that obedience is the way to achieve selfhood). Consciousness of one's inner personal power generates power for the self, power for others, power for creativity and production, and power for our planet. Personal power for one's self releases the ego from being controlled by patriarchal images and frees the self from submission to the ego.

Aphrodite demanded that Psyche get the golden fleece all by herself—the same golden fleece that it had taken a whole group of men to steal. Then her self-worth and personal power would be free from the need for any group support (from her family and friends, her religion, or her cultural value systems) and free from the need for physical strength (the masculine strength of her dearest erotic lover or the might of her nation). She would be free to aggressively assert the authority of the passion of being woman. For a woman the gathering of the golden fleece is an individual, conscious affair.

In order to gather the golden fleece Psyche had to cross the river. The tangible wealth of the feminine self lives "across the river" from the feminine self, in her masculine mode of being. Across the river Psyche would find a true masculinity, uncorrupted by patriarchal values.

Only by becoming intimately aware of masculine passionate love for her self could Psyche find her personal sense of the value of her feminine self. But it took a masculine love that was freed of values that must despise the Feminine. Individual self-worth is always found in the love from the opposite sex. No matter how close and loving the relationship, a mother cannot give her daughter a sure sense of her adult self-worth. She cannot empower her to exert her self. Nor can any sister or friend give to another woman that intimate knowledge of the wealth of her self which is personal power. Only through a personal awareness of masculine erotic love for the Feminine can a woman find the basis for her self-activating self-esteem.

What a woman experiences when a man loves her erotically is her own erotic love. She loves her self erotically regardless of the circumstances life throws at her and despite the negative judgments of a patriarchal society. When a woman has experienced a man's erotic love for her, she has found the sure foundation upon which to build her passionate love for her self. Her self-love is the eternal source of her sense of the wealth of her self; it is personal power. Her self-love reflects her vision of the Eternal Love in the heart of the God/Goddesshead, which is revealed and made accessible to her in her experience of erotic love.

How lovely it is to find such love for one's self in a real, live man. But that experience is not necessary; a woman can know the erotic love of a man for a woman without it. For it is from the Feminine that the Masculine is created. Biology attests this psychological and spiritual truth: the female comes before the male. Thus, a woman can find the masculine love she needs in the Feminine Principle, which lies deep within every woman. For woman has created man for her self.

Psyche had to reexperience the feeling of erotic love that she had had the night before. Then she could come into contact with a masculinity that was not fettered by patriarchal standards—a masculinity she loved, one that loved her and honored the Feminine, one that reflected the value of her femininity to her and showed her a more complete picture of her goodness. The paradox is that although a woman's sense of self-worth comes from male erotic love for her, it does not come from an actual man. Her sense of self-worth comes from her inner man. She must cultivate her relationship with him and experience his erotic love for her. Otherwise she will remain forever dependent on the men in her life (who are, after all, only imperfect human beings) and the Masculine in the culture.

If Psyche could accomplish this second task, it would forge an expanded, conscious connection between her and her inner man. And the support and love from her inner man would encourage her to assert what she had discovered in sorting the seeds. Her increased consciousness of her inner man would also hearten and strengthen "him" to uphold her more and more. She and her inner man would follow the way of sexual love, which gives and receives intensely, passionately, and consciously. Without the experience of receiving masculine love, a woman will have a hard time receiving a real, live man's love for her.

Thus encouraged, strengthened, and upheld, Psyche could devote herself to changing the behavior that patriarchy had taught her. A person's behavior is what lets others know how much they can impose their wills on that person. This masculine task, done by a woman in a feminine way, would empower Psyche to aggressively assert the values and talents inherent in the Feminine and individualized in her.

Without support it is difficult, if not impossible, to change one's behavior. If Psyche refused the challenge to go inward and cross over to her masculine side, she would be left deeper than ever in her unconscious. She would have severed her direct connection to her inner man-self. She would hear her inner man only as a voice parroting the cultural voices that denied her; she would not hear the inner masculine as the voice of one who loved her and treasured the Feminine. A woman thus bereft of the consciousness of her inner man-self is also bereft of the power that comes from a consciousness of the value of the Feminine.

So Psyche had to get the golden fleece. But she knew that if she approached the sun rams directly they would kill her. She made no mistake: male-directed, male-oriented consciousness, unseparated from driving animal power, kills the Feminine. Man's corrupted, patriarchal sense of the Masculine can never give a woman a true sense of self-esteem. The patriarchal mentality is blind to man's greed to own women, his lust to possess them, his envy of the Feminine and arrogant pride in the Masculine, and his ferocity towards all who threaten his system of values. The patriarchal mentality can therefore do nothing but murder the Feminine even as it deforms the Masculine. There is no hope of evolution without redeeming the basic unit of society—man and woman—from patriarchal polarization.

Instead of fostering evolution, man's rationality and logic, devoid of the ameliorating power of the Feminine, turn driving animal strength into brute force. Brute force is the power behind the control in a patriarchy. It underlies all male-directed, male-oriented consciousness that is unenlightened by the irrational and unseparated from the collective animal strength of a masculine brotherhood. Man uses his rational power to justify the brute force that gathers his armies and the taxes to pay for them. And brute force is what empowers all his logical authority, ensuring control. Behind the negotiations of the superpowers lie billions of dollars invested in brute force. And behind the cooperation, consideration, and compatibility of patriarchal relationships, the threat of brute force is the specter that makes them work.

That is why the myth of masculine development required man to kill the animal as a sacrifice of thanksgiving. It was an attempt to keep the Feminine alive, that it might redeem the parts and regenerate the whole. It was an attempt to limit the rule of brute force. But patriarchal man does not even follow the safeguards of his own patriarchal myth. He does not sacrifice the animal in thanksgiving for its golden fleece, because he fears that if he kills the rams he will no longer have a source of wealth and power. Since man has gotten all the golden fleece he is going to get by dominating others, he has got to fight over it. The history of Western man has been the game of "Who's got the golden fleece?" and "How do we wrest it away from them?"

When a culture is devoid of the Feminine, the powerless are pitted against the powerful. The only way for the powerless to get power is to usurp it. And the only way for the powerful to stay powerful is to defend their power by increasing it. In polite society the "civilized" way to usurp power is to become a superperson and be associated with superpeople. Supermen have superwives. Superpeople raise superkids. Supernations compete against supernations while the powerless scheme for the wealth and power they do not have.

Since there is no Feminine Principle to value in a patriarchal culture, there is no magnanimous spirit or shared humanity to offer as an alternative to power over others.

Psyche had to find a new way to get the golden fleece. If she tried to accomplish this task like a man, she would end up like a man—dependent on brute force and rationality. But she did not have brute force at her disposal. Nor would reason work; logic was not the tool she needed. And killing the animal in a sacrifice of thanksgiving is the antithesis of the feminine way.

The power a woman would get by attempting to accomplish this task like a man is worse than worthless! Indeed, a woman loses her feminine power if she acquires the golden fleece in the masculine way. She becomes merely a stand-in for male power, an "imitation man." As a neutered woman she has no femininity with which to cross the river and gather the golden fleece in a feminine way. And without the precious wool she dies.

However, if Psyche had tried to use her feminine intuition to cross the river while still unpenetrated by the strengths and values of her inner Masculine, the sun rams would have killed her. Intuition that was unimpregnated by the Masculine would not have worked; nor would rationality that was unleavened by the Feminine. The sun rams would kill her if she tried to get some of their precious wool, and Aphrodite would kill her if she did not get it. Psyche faced a blank wall.

Once again Psyche went into a panic, knowing the rams would kill her. She made for the river to drown herself for sure this time.

Panic was the only way out. Face to face with a hopeless situation, drowning herself was the only rational course of action Psyche could think of. Water is a symbol for unconscious, oceanic femininity. Psyche was going to drown herself in the Unconscious Feminine. But unconscious femininity is also a woman's source of inner feminine wisdom, the wisdom with which she can find a way to gather the golden fleece. Irrationally, panicking got Psyche to the river. It got her back in touch with the wisdom of her inner femininity, which was beyond rationality and logic, and had no need for brute force.

The reeds that grew by the river's edge whispered encouragingly to Psyche to be still. "Do not go near the rams, for they are fiercest in the noonday heat." They told her to wait until the evening, when the day had cooled and the river song had lulled the rams to sleep. Then she could cross the river and pick all the wool she liked from the bushes, where the sheep had left it clinging.

The reeds, a symbol for the Feminine, represent the strength of the adaptable, bending, hiding nature of the Feminine. They were telling Psyche that she would have to accomplish this "masculine" task, but that she would have to do it in a feminine way if she were going to succeed. They advised her not to try to gather the wool directly from the sun rams but to wait, hidden in the reeds. What valuable advice! Don't engage in a death struggle with male-directed, male-oriented consciousness. It can twist the meaning of everything a woman says and does, deny the truth of her assertions, intimidate her, and blame her for everything. Women must remember that man is a master at rewriting history. Women do not win at the masculine game of logic and brute force. So the reeds told Psyche to bide her time instead, to hide in the Feminine and wait.

Biding one's time is different from passive patience, which waits until something is over. Biding one's time is active waiting: in the stillness one's eyes are ever watchful and one's ears ever attuned to the smallest change in conditions that might offer an opportunity to act.

Waiting is a feminine quality that includes the uncanny power of irrational timing, the ability to control time by slowing its pace or speeding up its tempo. The reeds advised Psyche to slow time down for this task. Then in the cool of evening, when the river song had lulled the rams to sleep, Psyche could speed time up and cross the river to the opposite side and there gather from the bushes all the golden fleece she could carry.

In order to gather the golden fleece Psyche had to consciously use her femininity to cross to the opposite side of the river, where her masculinity lived.

But Psyche would have had no power to use her femininity if she had not yielded these feminine traits to be impregnated by the passionate love of her inner man, which gave her the masculine ability to focus her attention and maintain a single-minded sense of purpose. Without consciousness of her inner man, a woman waits and waits until she turns into a toadstool and her life is over. Her faith, undiscriminated from the influence of patriarchal religions, cannot support her becoming consciously woman. Her flexibility and adaptability, unpenetrated by the masculine, become so purposeless that she loses all sense of her self. And her ruthlessness and cunning become mere meanness and game playing.

But the feminine way, impregnated by the masculine, becomes an invincible power. It is easy and light and does not hurt anyone. By consciously crossing over to her masculine side, Psyche found the sure and certain source of her self-worth. This feminine way of getting self-worth and personal power simply bypasses the need for physical strength and group support. Action in the Feminine Principle does not have to depend on a consensus or even a majority vote to act (and voting always divides people into winners and losers). In the Feminine there are no losers—everyone wins. Since Psyche did not have to use brute force, she did not have to sacrifice the animal. Instead she lulled it to sleep. In the feminine way the animal is allowed to live. And living, it is always there to provide her with its golden fleece.

So Psyche waited until the sun was low and the day had cooled. Then she crossed the river to pick the golden fleece, unnoticed by the rams, and returned with her arms full of the golden wool.

Psyche did as the reeds instructed her. She consciously used her femininity to cross over to the other side, where she found the unrestricted love of her *other*, the love of the Masculine for the Feminine. To this love of man for woman she unreservedly yielded her self.

In this process Psyche felt the love of her inner man for the woman she was, and she felt the passion of her love for man. And this gave her consciousness of the wealth and beauty of her priceless feminine self. Her inner man had *seen* her; he had known her with all her seeds sorted, and he loved her. He loved her whether she was fat or thin, with or without makeup, sad or cheerful. She felt completely acceptable to him as she was. He did not require that she be any other person than who she was or that she live up to any image or ideal.

What an incredibly good feeling this gave her about her self! Finally she was accepted as she was by her earthly *other.* Psyche's feet barely touched the ground as she gathered the golden fleece. She had regained consciousness of the value of the Feminine! She was free from the patriarchal masculine and from the Unconscious Feminine. All she had to do was root and ground that personal sense of the value of her unique feminine being into the very marrow of her bones and receive the benefits of masculine passionate love.

GATHERING
THE GOLDEN FLEECE
II

In response to the pure masculine love she had found, Psyche had asserted her feminine yielding nature. And in response to her asserted femininity, true masculinity could do nothing but receive her! From the storehouse of his masculine wealth, her inner man greeted her (as a man should) with cake and wine. And her glad reply was "I take them." The Masculine Principle in Psyche released all of its positive male energy to her, the one who had crossed the river and gathered the golden fleece all by herself.

Because Psyche had gained an awareness of her body and an acceptance of the goodness of her sexuality, she had a container that was strong enough to hold the energy generated by the exuberant masculinity living in her. Such a woman is able to receive into her body, as cake and wine, the goodness of masculine sexuality and the wildness of man's spirit, without guilt or shame!

So with great relish Psyche took masculine energy into her self *as part of her feminine personality.* She felt the masculine life-force throbbing through her heart and mind and senses, making her earthy and sensual and happy in her body. She felt an intensified desire to *do.* She wanted to experience herself, and she wanted to do it directly, without psychologiz-

ing or explaining. She wanted to experience the pleasure of
her mind working, focused and undistracted. She wanted to
feel the exertion of her muscles strengthening her body. And
she wanted to taste love sweetening her heart.

At the same time, she responded to her expanded capacity for spiritual ecstasy. As she had taken Eros into her
heart, so she took love into her soul. She felt it filling the
empty hole in her solar plexus, and it felt like filling her
belly with good food. And she felt her self being loved by
a Divine Other who shattered all judgments. Every time
Psyche reconnected with her feelings of erotic love, she reconnected with the Eternal Love of the Supreme Deity. The
power of love is the power to create and regenerate; Psyche
was re-created every time she experienced erotic love. She
was made new.

She felt the power of the untamed masculine spirit
within her yearning for freedom. Its passion sought ways to
burst the bonds that chain us to old, habitual patterns of
thought and invalid value systems. She was exhilarated by
the currents of creativity within her, which were inventing
positive new ways to think and feel and new things to do.
Her quest for knowledge was like a hunger she had to feed.
Psyche felt the power of the urge to seek truth. And in that
quest the focus of the hunter, that which allows the hunter
to hit the mark, became Psyche's. The animating power of
the masculine is goal-oriented and pursues its ambitions to
completion. It combines intellectual, physical, and spiritual
gifts in such a way they are synergized; they work together
as more than the sum of all the parts. And this was what
Psyche was experiencing.

Within Psyche, male energy found the conscious
Feminine that the Masculine needs to keep its energy positive.
The combination of male energy and female energy generates
that excitement which creates new mind-sets and modes of
behavior, giving people viable, individualized alternatives.
Positive personal power is power *for*, not power *over*. It has
nothing to do with dominance. Rather it expresses the life-
force and works for positive change.

Psyche now had that kind of power inside of her self. It automatically gave her choices that are not available to someone with a patriarchal mentality, a mentality that asserts there is no place for the Masculine in the Feminine or the Feminine in the Masculine and that sees power only as control over others (which is ultimately the power to destroy). And since Psyche had gotten this power for her self, she was not beholden to anyone for it. She was not dependent on any system to express it; she could assert this power herself.

She was free to aggressively assert her self—not an imitation man or an unconscious sex symbol, not a cause or an ethical principle. She had sorted the seeds and knew who she was. She had integrated into her personality the masculine abilities to discriminate, to direct her Feminine-oriented consciousness, and to maintain an undistracted purpose. With her arms full of the golden fleece, she was now conscious of her power to exert her self. Regardless of the hand fate dealt her, Psyche felt in charge of her own life, no longer the victim of an uncontrolled destiny.

Psyche saw clearly that she did not have to do anything to be equal to men. She was born equal; she was born a "good." She was not trying to compete in a masculine way. Nor did she have to usurp power from anyone: she had gathered the golden fleece all by herself. Therefore her assertiveness was legitimately aggressive. It was not adopted from someone else, it was the result of having gathered the golden fleece. Her assertiveness was her part of her feminine personality, not an acquired trait, and it possessed the higher qualities of human nature—qualities inherent in the Feminine Principle, such as kindliness and affection.

Asserting her self was no longer as frightening or fatiguing a job. She now had the masculine energy to execute her irrational methods, and she had her masculine abilities to work for her like ants. A woman's true aggressiveness is marked by an easy naturalness and a freedom from emotional dishonesty, artificiality, or exaggeration. It carries the authority of the Feminine Principle, which is the authority of love.

By accomplishing her first two tasks, Psyche took a stand on the issue of power in the Feminine Principle and the passion of being woman—but not the way patriarchal man does. The way patriarchal man takes a stand is to "ram" home his logic, beating his opponent to a bloody pulp. But Psyche did not "ram" anything home; she did not want to, and she did not have to. Understanding and valuing the Feminine Principle, she consciously used feminine methods to assert the power of her self. Having integrated the aggressive self-assertiveness of her inner Masculine into the fabric of her personality, Psyche's *feminine* attributes had become her power tools. When she was told she should confront, attack, or combat, she stopped and thought, "Is that the best thing I can do?" Though the Feminine can do battle, she does not make war.

Psyche used her feminine tough-mindedness to keep her instincts cleared of patriarchal pollution, her mind unshackled from its rationalizing, psychologizing, philosophizing bullshit, and her heart free from its fear-producing tendency to expect catastrophe. Such expectations sabotage a person's self-direction. Psyche asserted her ability to adapt to real-life situations and people's personalities. And her adaptability created alternatives to the tyranny of patriarchal belief systems, alternatives that expressed the worth of each individual.

Asserting her flexibility, she could slip under, around, or over the rigidity of patriarchy. She was not afraid to change horses in the middle of the stream—to get out of bad situations and leap for better ones. Nor was she afraid to use her anger. If she had to scream to get through patriarchal rationality, she screamed. She did not let the limitations of her job limit her. Nor did she let tradition bind her. She found creative new ways to express her expanding erotic love. Now that she was building her own house, she had a place to which to invite those whom she wanted to visit her. She was not bound to the traditional seven-days-and-seven-nights-a-week relationship in a man's house. She was no longer afraid to try new and different ways to keep her erotic love strong and vital, because she no longer equated acceptance with meeting someone else's expectations. If she got caught in a fracas over her actions or proposals, she could bend without giving in and let the male storm rage until it wore itself out.

Psyche used her cunning and guile to outwit her adversaries. Being cunning means knowing as much as possible about the adversary. Psyche knew three things about the sun rams: they were fiercest in the noonday heat; they slept; and they brushed against the bushes, leaving their golden fleece on the branches. Being guileful means being shrewd—crafty and wise. It means calculating risks and forming strategies based on knowing the opponent. So Psyche waited, hidden in the reeds. She used the sweetness of the river song to lull her enemies to sleep. She did not need to clobber them. Her ability to keep herself hidden was an aggressive tactic; it was very different from having to be invisible in order to survive. And it accomplished much more than the bulldozing approach of the Masculine did.

Her ability to wait, combined with her masculine ability to focus attention, became a powerful tool for timing. She could slow time down (her lovemaking felt eternal, whether it was fifteen or forty-five minutes or all day) or she could speed time up (sitting and chatting with her friend while her friend's husband underwent surgery sped up the time of waiting).

By appearing to be unthreatening, by keeping quiet about new ideas, inventions, and products, and by practicing her intentions without talking about them, she learned how to throw her weight around and her adversary off track. (A woman who is conscious automatically knows how to do this. After all, her baby is hidden until she gives birth to it. Then it comes out screaming and teeming with life.) Psyche used her wiles and feminine ways to disarm the adversary. She used her voice, she used words of endearment, she used her smile and her body language. She used her feminine tenderness to assert her tough love; she used her facial expressions and her power to sing the river song.

Because she could use the light of the Feminine that shines in the dark, Psyche could move about under cover of darkness. "Seeing in the dark" is more or less the same as using irrational abilities such as intuition and extrasensory perception. Intuition is like a light going on in the dark that reveals what otherwise would remain unknown. It is a perception of the truth that the light of reason and conscious attention cannot reveal. And extrasensory perception gives her a power that simply transcends the need for rational communication.

These irrational functions are primarily and essentially a faculty of women (but not exclusively; they are available to a man through his inner woman). By using her intuitive abilities Psyche could envision what was yet to be, she could see the many sides of reality, and she was not bound to consciously regulated processes (such as logic, reason, rationality, etc.). By using her irrational abilities Psyche could get around "in the dark" so that, unseen, she could gather the wealth she needed; unheard, she could muster her power. By relying on her extrasensory perception to "see" the facts, Psyche freed her intellectual processes for creative purposes.

Feeling passionately loved, Psyche declared by her actions as well as her words her right to exist as a free, independent, and sexual woman. She was not a possession man could enclose, a fenced-in field he owned and sowed with his "seed." Nor was her sexuality a vessel for his semen, a commodity he used for reproduction and relief. "She," the Feminine, was the creator.

As the Great Goddess was the primeval life-giving force, so a woman's genes are preeminent. They are there first. Nor is it by the process of "adding" a man's genes to a woman's that new life is produced. It is the prerogative of a woman's ovum to accept or reject a man's sperm. Further, it is from the substance of a woman's body that new life grows, and it is her labor that gives birth. The Great Goddess represents the exclusive power of the Feminine to create and produce life. A male is created out of his father's genes as well as his mother's, but his life substance grows out of the substance of his mother's female body and her labor gives him birth. Out of a woman's body by the strength of her labor is born the Holy Spirit in human flesh. A man cannot make a baby out of his body. Biologically, psychologically, and spiritually, it is *not* man's "seed" that perpetuates the human species and carries the Holy Spirit; it is woman who is the mother, it is the Feminine Principle who is the Creator of the human race as well as each individual.

As a woman conceives and gives birth to a man-child, so the Feminine conceived and gave birth to the Masculine. The Feminine perpetuates not only the Feminine but also the Masculine! *This is power!* It belongs to every woman. Furthermore, the Feminine contains the principle of regeneration. It is in the Feminine Principle that people find the power that transforms their death into new life. It was precisely because the Great Goddess had been worshiped and adored for Her potency, Her creativity, and Her perpetuation of Her Holy Spirit that patriarchy had to destroy Her. In an arrogance beyond imagination patriarchal man claimed the Feminine power to create and produce life as his own. And he made up the lie that women have no generative power, no power to perpetuate the species and no spiritual power. Man's appropriation of the power of the Feminine and his devaluation of women is the most despicable sin ever committed on this earth.

In the face of patriarchal devaluation of women, Psyche declared the uncreated goodness of the Feminine, which she had experienced in tasting the goodness of her own created self. Consciousness of the love and goodness in the Feminine (and in a woman) is the pearl of great price. For the uncorrupted goodness of the Feminine and her unconditional love, a wise man will sell all his lesser pearls: his ambition, his fame and glory, his armies, his patriarchal loyalties, his work ethic, his political power—anything that requires him to leave the worth of the Feminine behind (and betray a woman's erotic love). For only when a man has understood that the glory of his masculine heroism is a lesser glory, can he return home to the Feminine. Without "her" he is less than a man. But with "her" his ambition is turned into aspiration, his fame and glory into honor and thanksgiving, his work and political power into creativity and loving care of others. And with "her" the indignities of outrageous fortune that afflict all humans is made bearable, if not overcome.

By loving and valuing her feminine strengths, Psyche asserted the primacy of the Feminine Principle and the necessity of the Masculine Principle. (This has nothing to do with superiority or inferiority.) From her inner knowledge Psyche confirmed that the male was created to love the Feminine and to give pleasure to woman. He was created to affirm and strengthen the forces of the creative and active female, both in the culture and in the women in his life, as well as his own inner feminine self. The undistorted Masculine supports, articulates, and executes the creative design of the Feminine. By revering both Principles as *inseparable* symbols of exuberant life, Psyche affirmed the equivalence of the sexes and refuted the subordination of either one.

Psyche would no longer tolerate the patriarchal attitude towards woman. She refused to accept the shame patriarchy dumped on her for being woman. She—all of her—was loved by a Masculine that was freed of the patriarchal mentality. She regarded her body as the temple of the Holy Spirit, and she regarded her female parts as objects of beauty. Acknowledging and cherishing the irreplaceable joy of the body, she refused to bury her enjoyment of living life in her body.

She asserted her right to own her own body and decide her own reproductive destiny. Only woman has this authority. Man does not. Psyche also asserted her right to use her sensuous and erotic capacities directly, immediately, and concretely. She refused to postpone her sexual desires until the "right man" and the "right patriarchal moment" came along. She actively affirmed her right to be responsible for herself. She wanted to meet her own needs as best she could, without man's judgments.

And so Psyche refused to be treated as a subjugated, simpleminded inferior, incapable of resisting man. She was loved and highly valued by the Masculine on earth and by the Supreme Deity in heaven. Therefore she repudiated patriarchal man's behavior towards women. She refused to accept as "normal male behavior" man's possessiveness and jealousy, his questioning of her intelligence, his condemnation of her spirit, his self-righteous moral judgments, and his hatred towards the Feminine, or the dirty jokes that debase female sexuality. She slipped out from under his insistence on controlling her life, her thoughts, and her behavior. She refused to let him diminish her self-love with his unrelenting criticism or his withdrawal of love, money, approval, or sex whenever she displeased him. She would not let him get away with blaming others, or even himself, for whatever he did not like. She insisted that he take responsibility for taking care of himself. *And the way she maintained her self-esteem was by returning often to her inner masculine self to be renewed and heartened by erotic love.*

Psyche no longer gave in in silence, doing whatever patriarchal man (or the Masculine in his culture) wanted her to do. Instead she asserted what she thought, what she believed, what she wanted, and what she would or would not do. She stopped trying to justify, explain, or defend herself, her actions, and her values.

By insisting on her autonomy, she declared her right to respect, kindness, and support; her right to express her self, to be heard, and to be taken seriously; her right to hold her own beliefs, opinions, and values; and her right to act on her values. She refused to take responsibility for any other adult's problems or bad behavior, and she insisted on the right to protest unfair treatment or undue criticism. She maintained the right to change her mind. She demanded the right to hope and plan for a life-style that was meaningful to her, based on the value of the Feminine and the undistorted love from the Masculine.

These rights come with being an adult human being. Taking them into her being, Psyche began to assert the *privilege* of doing as she pleased. She had earned it: she had sorted the seeds, she knew who she was and what it was she needed, wanted, and desired, and she had gathered the golden fleece all by herself. The modern-day Psyche asserts the privilege of gladdening herself: she, too, has earned it. She may do anything to make herself feel good, beautiful, and fulfilled. She may work, marry, have children, not marry, not have children, make a home, or change her career. She can enjoy whatever she does. She can enjoy being a homemaker. Anything she does is enough to give her pleasure, because she does not let being a homemaker become more important than being herself. Alternatively, she can enjoy her job, career, or profession because she sees it as a job, a career, or a profession—not as who she is. She can become a mother and enjoy her motherhood because she does not confuse it with her selfhood. Nor does she confuse her children with her self.

A modern-day Psyche can use all these roles or any of them, in combination or singly to express her self, because she is conscious of who she is and what the roles are. But those who have not sorted the seeds of their selves had better not try to do as they please, because they do not even know who it is they are trying to please. And they certainly do not know what would please them.

The feminine consciousness is a both-and world, not the either-or world of patriarchy. By her life-style the modern Psyche affirms that it is O.K. to live alone and like it, and it is O.K. to like men and sex. It is O.K. to live in a family she loves, and it is also O.K. to desire solitude. It is O.K. to want the pleasure of the company of men, and it is O.K. to want the pleasure of the company of women. And she knows that in a patriarchal society it is practically impossible to enjoy the company of both at the same time.

By her blunders she confirms that it is O.K. to make mistakes, to fall down and get up again. No more Super-woman. No more picture-perfect home; no more magazine-perfect figure; no more well-adjusted, well-fed, exercised, and educated children; and no more catered-to, coddled, and protected mate. This woman is a real live person, and she wants to *live* with real live people.

By using her wit and sharp tongue the modern Psyche asserts her right to speak up and tell it like is—regardless of how hard-hearted, merciless, and uncompassionate it may make her sound. This lady does not confuse compassion with sentiment. The modern Psyche, like her sister of long ago, proclaims the royal authority of love, which rejoices in life and beholds the goodness of sexual desire and the holiness of erotic love.

By believing the best and refusing to think evil (which is different from not acknowledging the existence of evil) she accepts all creatures, as a mother hen tucks all her chicks under the protection of her wings. Her vision of the incarnation of the Holy Spirit in human flesh and of the goodness of creation stands in opposition to the celebration of death and the patriarchal concepts of the dirtiness of human sexuality, the evil of knowledge, and the need for a man and his god to redeem his messed-up creation. Like Psyche before her, evolving woman refuses to accept patriarchy's invented ideas of original sin, of the sinfulness of her body, and of the indecency of birth.

And she refuses the "redemption" patriarchy offers: belonging to a man, accepting his male god as the one and only true god, kowtowing to patriarchal values, and denying her self and the priceless treasure of the Feminine. If woman is to emancipate her self from patriarchy, she must realize that the system is such that her rights and freedoms are regulated by man. No matter how much women may have enlarged their field at certain times, man has always enclosed it and called it his own. With the rights won in the revolution of the sixties and seventies he simply widened the fence. No matter how far women may stretch the leash, man can always yank it. And no matter how hard an individual woman may have worked for her independence, *if she has not refused man's redemption*, he has the power to yank her in. Unconsciously undifferentiated, patriarchal man consumes the Feminine. Like an animal, he eats her whole.

When unevolved men and their unravished women see Psyche asserting her self, they think that she is trying to take man's power away from him. Undifferentiated and unconscious man feels that if women become his equals he will have to sacrifice some of his power. (But of course he doesn't have to sacrifice anything!) And this misbegotten mentality is as threatening to "imitation men" as it is to their submissive sisters; both depend on the patriarchal concept of unmitigated masculinity for their power.

Women who are dependent on men do not want their men's power diminished. As long as they are unconscious, women are unempowered—and justifiably terrified of having to act like men's equals. They have no power, no authority, and no knowledge of how to do such a thing. And "imitation men," being insecure, think they need unmitigated masculine power to clobber. It is the only way they know of keeping the positions that they have won by using masculine methods.

The only alternative to patriarchy that these people can see is a matriarchy—patriarchy in reverse. And in that case man would have to become the subjugated one. For man to be superior, his *other* has to be inferior. (Most people are ignorant of the fact that a matriarchy [as the reversal of a patriarchy] has never existed. We have no name for what did exist before patriarchy; the word has been wiped out of our language. Perhaps we could call it a gylany—the beautiful word coined by Riane Eisler to describe a society in which all men and women are partners without ranking or hierarchy. A fuller explanation of the term appears in Definitions at the end of this book.)

For the first time Psyche realized that Eros, in his mother's house, was absolutely blind to her. She beheld the patriarchal horror: Eros, in his "godhood," could never see her as his equal opposite. In patriarchy the opposite of man is not woman but a second-class, subhuman being. But worst of all, Psyche felt the destitution of not being visible to her lover. It was not the task of gathering the golden fleece that was so overwhelming; it was the fact that even now, after developing her self, the man she longed to be with still could not see *her*. She was face to face with the man she loved, she was open and available to him, but he was blind to her. It was as if she were not there. And it felt like the cold hand of death on her heart.

Psyche stood there and wept. But mixed in with her grief was an almighty anger. Eros had not been born blind. He *had chosen* not to see her. She knew the difference: she had chosen to see. She had chosen to see him, and she had chosen to see her self. She had lit her lamp in full knowledge of what she was doing. And she had seen truth—the truth of him, the truth of herself, and the truth of their erotic love.

But Eros had refused to see. He had chosen to cast her out. He had chosen to be cruel. He had chosen to hate her. He had chosen to reject his child. Instead of seeing and taking responsibility for his emotions and behavior, he had run home to his mother and, from the safety of patriarchy, he blamed Psyche, his once "innocent" wife, for all his woes. She had not cooked supper for him! He could not see that she, a flesh-and-blood human being, was worn out by a full day of honest work and exhausted from staying up half the night with a distressed child (or meeting her sales quota). All he could see was that his wife had neglected him. She had disobeyed their marriage contract. She could not be trusted: she was unreliable!

Psyche's anger at Eros's refusal to become a grown-up man and see her as the adult, sexual woman she was blazed in her heart. Not even the tears of her grief could water down, much less put out, the fire of her anger. Using whatever voice she felt like using, from a yell to a whisper, Psyche spoke in passionate anger. "God damn it, Eros! *See* me! I'm not trying to take your power or boss you around. I don't want your power; I have my own. I have gotten the golden fleece for myself. I don't want the power you think you can give me as your wife, or as the executive vice-president of your company. I don't want to be your superwoman—your super playmate, your super cook, maid, and errand runner! And I don't want to be a supermom to either you or your superkids. Eros, look at me: I am."

But until modern man can see his opposite as woman, eternally different from him and eternally primary, he cannot see at all. He cannot see himself as a man. He has no valued *other* to give him a sense of self-worth. Like woman, man derives his individual self-worth from the love he feels from the opposite sex. But how can anyone feel loved if it is by a grade B person?

Man's true self-esteem lies in feeling a woman's erotic love for him. He finds his true worth and power, which no man can steal from him, not in relation to an almighty brotherhood but in relationship to feminine erotic love. A man's real power lies not in his masculine-ordained authorities—his armies, his churches, his governments—but in his ability to awaken the Feminine. It lies in his ability to fuel and refuel the fires of the feminine spirit with his irrational erotic love.

The way he can become a man is to find out who he is by ravishing the woman he loves as his valued *other.* When he does so, a new "she" is brought to life: an adult woman whose spirit receives his sexual love as her body greets his masculine spirit.

Thus a new "she" is brought to life in man's consciousness, a "she" capable of ravishing him and knowing him as an adult man. Only such a "she" can save man from the painful irony of feeling sexual desire but being trapped in a patriarchal dependence on his mother. *When a man can cross the river to his feminine side, he will find the inexhaustible source of the power he seeks so ardently: the erotic love of an independent woman, a woman who is free from the curse of the devaluation of the Feminine.*

It is in a woman's erotic love, the love of his valued *other*, that a male discovers his self-worth as an individual man. He no longer needs animal strength or the power of an exclusive brotherhood. The Feminine in his heart restores his aggressive self-assertiveness to him, fully freed of unconscious, misdirected, driving animal strength. He can be angry without being afraid of his anger; he can be strong without being afraid his strength will clobber or kill; he can be soft and warm and cuddly without being afraid of being dominated! Finding the value of his masculine nature, he can afford to sacrifice brute force and an allegiance to the rules and regulations of a domineering brotherhood.

As the Masculine releases energy to the yielding Feminine, so the Feminine releases to the embracing Masculine the power to sustain feelings without the fear of being swallowed up by them. When a man experiences a woman's erotic love for him, he can comprehend the passionate love of the Feminine for the Masculine without feeling overwhelmed. He is no longer threatened by the primacy of the Feminine, for he has tasted and inwardly digested the necessity of the Masculine. He knows no woman wants an inferior male!

Feeling free, he relaxes in the Feminine and delights in his woman. It is his pleasure to bring her pleasure. Whatever he can do for her is what he does. Likewise, whatever she does is enough to please him, because he has become pleasable! Her work is his pride and her motherhood is his joy because he sees *her.* He sees not a mother or a worker or a housewife but a woman working or mothering or homemaking. He sees a woman playing tennis, not a tennis player. Whatever she does to please herself will please him, because she has sorted her seeds and gathered the golden fleece. And she has shown him an inner Feminine who will sort his seeds and gather the golden fleece for him—his own woman-self.

Since he does not have to wrestle with the ram anymore, his animal energy is free to make him young and lusty, strong and healthy, happy and playful. And since he does not have to belong to a brotherhood anymore, he is free of having to live by superimposed rules and dogmas. He is free to form real relationships with other evolving men and women. Regardless of his circumstances, his life feels pretty exciting. His joy level rises, and he is easily made happy. With his connection to his inner woman-self deepening, he becomes more and more glad to be alive as himself.

When a man has learned how to feel his feelings and gather the golden fleece the Feminine way, he too will have earned the privilege to do as he pleases. A self-gladdened man is pure joy to be around. Even if he is tired or angry or sad, his joy remains because he knows that he himself is not the fatigue or the anger or the sadness. That is why such a man can be a "boss" and not boss anyone around, or be a judge and not damn anyone. Such a man becomes more and more sure of his masculinity and grounded in the worth of his individuality.

If Eros could become man enough to see Psyche as she was, then everything would take care of itself: he would be transformed by loving the Feminine and by receiving her love for him. The intense giving and receiving that is generated by erotic love would connect him consciously and passionately with his own inner woman-self. And through his conscious connection to his *other* he would know that he could gather the golden fleece abundantly within his own feminine mode of being and so become powerfully male.

This is really very easy for man to do; it takes tremendous energy to keep it from happening. Just look at the energy it takes to keep a man depressed; he can hardly do anything else. But there was only one way Eros was ever going to comprehend that the Feminine is as essential as the Masculine, and that was for Psyche to continue the hard task of aggressively exerting her self. By honoring her feminine self-worth, Psyche gave Eros a chance to come into contact with the valued Feminine.

The history of Western culture that man forgot to write is the history of the Psyches throughout the ages. There have always been women who have had the courage to disobey and love erotically, the courage to sort the seeds, and the insight to know how to cross the river and gather the golden fleece. They are the ones who have known how to assert the saving grace that lies in the Feminine Principle. They are the reason there is still an earth upon which men and women can live.

GATHERING
THE GOLDEN FLEECE
III

How does a woman gather the golden fleece today? She develops her self by integrating her inner Masculine into the fabric of her personality. This means that when she speaks, for instance, she does not sound masculine at all. However, the strength of her inner man is heard. She discovers the love of the Masculine for the Feminine within herself, so that, as a woman and a man in love, they love and strengthen each other. They commune with each other.

This conscious communication is mandatory and it is difficult. It is difficult because nothing in our culture supports this inner relationship, much less tells a woman how to implement it. In fact, most people would think she was crazy—trying to commune with *what*??? But this communication is mandatory, because without (daily, even hourly) consciousness of her inner man's love for her a woman dies. She loses the source of her self-esteem and the power to aggressively exert her self.

Modern woman, like Psyche, must take the time to yield herself to the loving Masculine, to be alone with her inner man, so that she *feels* her erotic love. This intimate knowledge of herself (of her inner man and her erotic love) is the inexhaustible source of her power. She needs to breathe in his undistorted masculine love and breathe out the poison of patriarchal lies. A woman must *make* the time, therefore, to receive the true masculinity that willingly gives in to the yielding feminine or he cannot release to her his masculine energy—the energy she needs to fuel her poignant, passionate, joyous sexuality and her intense, dynamic, feminine spirituality.

To gather the golden fleece today a woman needs to accept the joy of receiving exuberant, single-minded, masculine sexuality into her self, realizing that it alone can enhance and empower her femininity. And she needs to root and ground it in her self by taking the time necessary to do so. Then she can recognize her feminine power, which is consciously supported by the eternal love of her inner man-self.

Taking the energy of masculine sexual love for her into her self, she aggressively wields her power—the power of her sexuality and the power of her spirituality. She wields the power of kindness, the power of her smile, the power of lamenting and rejoicing with others, the power of her endeavors to prevent or relieve suffering, the power of her joy in life, the power of her endeavors to promote forward the welfare of those around her, the power of her efforts to refine life by politeness and by bringing beauty into everyday living. And she wields the power of a feminine hero (a woman who can pick up the phone and call the sheriff on her own behalf) and the power of a masculine heroine (a woman who loves enough to kick her loved one out of her house and refuse food and shelter because of drug taking). This modern-day Psyche wields the power of her gentleness and her tough love, the power of her empathy and her hardheartedness. (She can feel the plight of others, yet refuse the unrealistic, sometimes sick demands they try to put on her.)

Psyche's gift to men was to discover how the powerless can get power without the need to usurp it—without the need for violence, riots, and rebellion. She gave men (as well as "imitation men") an alternative to the patriarchal games of "who's got the power" and "how do I get it (or keep it)." By accomplishing this task, Psyche showed that there is always plenty of golden fleece for anyone willing to cross the river and use the feminine method of gathering the precious wool.

Psyche's gift to women was the possibility of an effective sisterhood, effective because it would be composed of independent, self-governing women. Such a sisterhood is very different from the patriarchal brotherhood of men who are dependent on their group to obtain their share of golden fleece. Psyche's sisterhood is the sisterhood of ravished brides who, knowing the power of erotic love, have sorted their seeds and gathered their golden fleece. In the sisterhood of Psyches, each woman remains the unique person she was created to be. So not one of the women who come together is dependent on the others for her sense of self-worth. And being free of the group, they are free to love each other. They are friends.

The love and support among friends is free of power *over* others. Each woman experiences power *for* her self and her friends. And the signs of power *for* the self and others are abundant laughter and caring, a high intensity of living and loving, and a loyalty among peers. Such women can be loyal to each other because they are independent of the men in their lives (and the Masculine in the culture) for their sense of self-worth.

There is a fundamental difference between the brotherhood of men as it has been and the sisterhood of women as it is evolving. The sisterhood has an energetic Masculine incorporated into each individual, thus invigorating the whole; the brotherhood, however, is devoid of the Feminine. The Feminine is not allowed in the individual man or in the group. The creativity in the brotherhood of men is sterile, because there is no Feminine to mate with the Masculine and give birth to new life and ideas. The energy once generated by a group of men struggling to wrest their share of golden fleece from a driving animal strength has almost dissipated itself. And the new source of energy it needs is dammed up because the Feminine Principle is still not allowed in the masculine world.

The sisterhood that is becoming conscious is energized and inseminated by a consciously courted, wooed, and won

Masculine. The fact that the Masculine is consciously operative in Psyches reflects the power of the Masculine in the
Goddesshead. On earth this masculine power is manifested
in the power of masculine erotic love. The life-force in the
erotic love of both sexes is the only power that can oppose
the seduction of death (the fatal attraction of remaining
obediently unconscious, cradled forever in everlasting arms).
To respond to the full impact of erotic love is to feel the
power of being "touched by God," being transformed from
good into goodness, from helpless child into creative adult.

The potential driving force of a sisterhood composed
of seed-sorting, fleece-gathering women who love each other
is just now entering our society's consciousness. Nothing can
hold these women down—except memories of their past
enslavement. Such memories are what can destroy a woman's
self-love and so wreck the sisterhood of women, just as they
sabotage any new relationship with an evolving man.

Like Psyche, her sister of today must somehow be
empowered to forget the destructive memories of patriarchal
values—all the ought-to's and should's that she has been
taught, which goad her by day and haunt her at night and
corrupt her decision-making power. And she must be empowered to forget her own personal memories of man's subjugation. Still-hurting memories of past pain erode her sense of
the power of her self; they chip away at her self-esteem. And
they undermine any personal relationship with a man.

So once again Aphrodite must come to the aid of all
those women who want to go on, who desire more life, more
autonomy, and more intensified intimacy in their relationships. If a woman truly values her self, rest assured that her
deep inner feminine core will provoke her and challenge her
and demand that the next task be accomplished.

FILLING
THE CRYSTAL VESSEL
I

W*hen Aphrodite came and saw that Psyche had collected the golden fleece, Her anger knew no bounds. Furious, She gave the instructions for the third task: "Take this crystal vessel and fill it with the waters from the Fountain of Forgetfulness."*

Aphrodite knew that Psyche had to keep on expanding her consciousness. Part of Psyche was still unconscious, and that put her in grave danger—the danger of unwittingly remembering her past enslavement, which could undermine her self-love. The Goddess could not relent. Psyche needed to find a way to reconnect with the power of the feminine spirit that was freed from patriarchal rule. She needed its power in order to expand her consciousness in the face of the inevitable, ongoing struggle between her urge to grow and the pressure to conform.

The degree of consciousness she had gained by sorting the seeds and gathering the golden fleece was not enough. It could not protect her from her unconscious reaction to the fact that she had differentiated her self from the collective value system. She had no protection from the voices of patriarchal images, which tried to rob her of her feminine spirit. "You are wrong, Psyche! You are not respectful or respected.

You are sacrilegious and unfaithful. You are not wanted. You had better change your ways." Of course they were right: Psyche had to change her ways. But the change she had to make was a radical break with patriarchy.

Psyche did not yet see that patriarchy offered no meaningful avenue of expression for her increasingly passionate sexuality and no activity for the expression of her increasingly powerful spirit. She did not recognize the cause of her acute pain: she was still unconsciously waiting for the patriarchal system to give her the life and love she so desired. Having been schooled in patriarchal philosophy, patriarchal theology, and patriarchal psychology, her mental, spiritual, emotional, and physical survival had depended upon staying within the system. She did not know of any other way.

Unless Psyche could recognize the trap she was in, she would regress to the inaction of unconscious obedience—regardless of how busy she was. She would then become bored, depressed, and impotent. In order to extricate herself from the web patriarchy spins, Psyche needed to consciously forget her attachment to patriarchal values. She needed to abandon her faith that somehow all would work out for the best, her false hope that all her pain would be gloriously rewarded by the system that had caused it, and her belief that her love and loyalty would somehow be recognized and honored by the same authority that had degraded her.

The expression of spiritual power is not found in remembering—no matter how glorious patriarchy claims the past was, no matter how holy the traditional beliefs are said to be. Spiritual power is found in freedom from unconsciously remembering, in the ability to consciously forget. And so is sexual power.

Consciously forgetting is not the same as being unable to remember. Nor is unconscious remembering the same as being able to remember what one chooses to remember. Unconscious remembering, the inability to consciously forget, is what holds us prisoner to the past and robs us of creativity.

Remembering is a tricky business. What we tend to remember are constellations of feelings about past events;

the reality of those events is shadowed by our reactions to it. Unconscious remembering snookered Psyche into returning to the past. It seduced her into categorizing all her feelings according to male-ordained authorities and judging all her behavior by a system that dulled her capacity to differentiate. Psyche had been asserting her self against the blank wall of patriarchy, wasting her masculine energy in a futile contest. Patriarchy encourages such wastes of energy; it does not want women to have the power to initiate independent action based on their new standards. Better to have women get all riled up about their rights than to have them disobey and free themselves from patriarchy's lies.

Listening to remembered voices scrambled all the seeds Psyche had sorted. It made her confuse what *she* wanted to do with what the culture told her she ought to do. (For instance: if a lot of her friends were getting married, she thought that was the thing to do; if enough were getting divorced, then that was what she found reasons to do.) Remembering past mind-sets devalued the golden fleece she had gathered. She had inadvertently let the old patriarchal picture cloud the identity of her inner femininity, and that dimmed the intensity of her self-love. Being seduced into remembering meant that Psyche was stripped of her new power to be Psyche, and she lost the excitement of becoming the person she was yet to be.

When a woman starts unconsciously remembering, she stops living; she stops growing; she stops changing. And she stops loving—first herself and then others. She becomes unconscious of what she is doing. She does not realize she is only repeating the past. This causes her to feel an unnamed destitution; she does not know she is losing her self, sacrificing her spirit. Hungrily, she searches for answers in astrology, yoga, transcendental meditation, and weekend seminars. But they are inadequate. She has no patriarchal way to recognize her inherent faculty for connecting to the Divine energy that lies in the Feminine Principle, her primary mode of being. And so she has no consciousness of her ability to perceive transcendent experiences. She has no conscious container to hold her spiritual energy. Because woman is the religious outcast as well as the political outcast, she has no way to express her innate talent for ritual—a talent which would root and ground her in an easy connection to the Divine.

All that she remembered was like a dead weight that pulled her down into submission to patriarchy. Psyche felt the weight of remembered values as the unrelenting pressure to conform. Expanding her consciousness brought her into direct conflict with this pressure. On the one hand, she was no longer able to obey the old code of behavior. On the other hand, she felt helpless to sustain the process of her individuation. For Psyche, as for a lot of women today, trying to adapt once again to the old commandments felt like suffocating. She experienced a frightening loss of vitality and creativity. A heaviness settled in, dulling all the colors of life.

At the same time, Psyche was frightened of taking an unknown path. It was dark out there. She was intimidated by the unknown work of developing her self. She did not know where her increased autonomy and her broadened ability to connect intimately with others would take her. Who would she become, and with whom would she connect—or disconnect?

What Psyche did not know was that she had not reclaimed her spirit. She had given it away to everything and everyone except her self. She had given it to her family and friends, to her religion, and to all the good causes that demanded her time and energy. Without her spirit, her body was poverty-stricken. That was why she felt so tired most of the time.

Once again, what she needed was an expanded awareness of her inner man. By filling the crystal chalice with the water of forgetfulness, she would be able to further differentiate her inner man from her unconscious projections and from the unconsciously remembered masculine of patriarchy. Then her inner man's love for her, his masculine power dwelling in her, could bring her into a more conscious relationship with her feminine spiritual power.

She needed her inner man to hold high her light so that she could recognize all the externals to which she had unknowingly given her spirit. And she needed his ability to exclude so that she could claim the exclusive right to her own spirit. She needed her inner man-self to become her torchbearer and light whatever path she chose to take. Only by intensifying her internal experience of erotic love could Psyche increase her consciousness of her inner man-self as the real Masculine that supports and endorses the Feminine, loving her and carrying the torch for her.

But to do this Psyche had to be empowered to consciously forget an insidiously ingrained tradition whenever it came to mind. Without the awakened ability to consciously forget, Psyche was left grounded in a sterile field. So Aphrodite in Her feminine wisdom set out the task for Psyche. Psyche must fill the Goddess's crystal chalice with the waters from the Fountain of Forgetfulness or she would be without the means to forget obedience.

This fountain—with its twin, the Fountain of Remembrance—was at the top of a very high mountain, higher than any man could climb. The two fountains gushed forth from two huge rocks and joined in the valley below to form the River of Life.

The ancient wisdom was that one must drink from both fountains in order to drink from the River of Life, but one must drink from the Fountain of Forgetfulness first. The ancient wisdom is irrational. Forgetfulness, a symbol for unconsciousness, must inform remembering, a symbol for consciousness. Forgetfulness must enlighten the remembrance of things past with the reality of the here and now. But if one were to drink directly from the Fountain of Forgetfulness—from the moving, chaotic waters of the unconscious—one would forget everything. Therefore the water of forgetfulness must be contained. The patriarchal lie is that only the Masculine can contain the power of the spirit; only men can translate the language of the irrational into meaningful terms.

In a patriarchy the "spirit" is supposed to be the sole property of man. The Masculine Principle is "spiritual"; the Feminine Principle is "earthy," "dark and dank." The father contains the spirit, the life-force, of the family, of the country, of religion. The patriarchal institutions of state, law, religion, and medicine contain the power of the irrational spirit. Only through obedience to their authority can healing and renewal, life and its meaning, be found. If woman is even capable of having a "spirit," she will get it only by being obedient to the authority that contains "masculine spirit" and by commitment to some "holy work."

But patriarchy is wrong about all of this. Rationality cannot contain irrationality. Reason does not get rid of the ghosts that haunt a person in unbidden memories. Nor does logic get rid of demons that taunt a person with threats of future catastrophe. Obedience does not lead to life. Nor can "spirit" be found in institutions.

Only in the Feminine Principle, for which the crystal vessel is a symbol, can the waters be contained. Only irrationality can contain both consciousness and unconsciousness, because it transcends the rational. The light of the Feminine is the light that does not obliterate darkness; it allows both light and dark to exist together as two parts of one whole. When the water of forgetfulness was contained, then Psyche could drink thereof and be empowered to consciously forget whatever pulled her back into an unconscious inertia. Then she could consciously remember whatever took her forward into her individuation. So the container for these waters is vitally important.

A chalice—or any container—is a symbol for the Feminine, representing the ability of the womb to hold and generate new life. Crystal is clear and represents consciousness, but it also refracts the blinding light of the sun into all the colors of the rainbow. A "female vessel" (a woman's body) is irrationally made out of "crystal"—it is transparent consciousness sparkling with the bright, many-colored spirit of the Feminine. Psyche had to fill it with the waters of the Fountain of Forgetfulness, or consciousness of the feminine spirit would die. So Psyche took the crystal vessel from the hand of the Goddess.

The myth tells us that the fountain was at the top of a mountain that was higher than any man could climb. Masculine rationality, logic, and reason can go only so high. The masculine spirit alone cannot reach all the heights of which human consciousness is capable. It is not rational to reach for experience which is beyond one's control. But the irrationality of the feminine spirit can see the whole universe in a star; it can see the Holy Spirit incarnate in human flesh; it loves the whole of humankind in each individual; and it administers healing grace by taking part in life. Only the irrationality of the feminine spirit can endow a person with the power to climb so high a mountain.

In order to climb this mountain Psyche was going to have to forsake the old, rational order. Only by acknowledging and shedding patriarchal values, as a snake sheds its skin, would she be able to reconnect with the power of the spirit of the Feminine.

Unconscious of her spiritual plight, Psyche went to sleep with the crystal chalice at her side. Before daylight broke, she awoke and began her climb. Why was it so difficult to climb this mountain? What was the matter? Why didn't she feel more alive? She did not know that it was higher than any man could climb or that she was still carrying the weight of patriarchy on her back.

Psyche began to ponder. Why wasn't she getting the results she wanted from asserting her self? Why didn't the seeds she had picked and planted grow better? Somehow she was stymied. She felt as if all her work had been in vain. She had sorted the seeds of her self and gathered the golden fleece, but she felt as if she had been put back into a boxed-in life where she married Eros all over again. Once more she had experienced the delight of being ravished, and now there was nothing. Back home Eros went to work every morning and came home when it got dark. On the weekends he played golf or went hunting or worked. He could be the ravishing hero, but he could not be anything else. He could not seem to grow up. There was no evolving relationship here. And the scenario was virtually the same at her work; there was no evolving challenge there.

Patriarchal man seems to be less afraid of curtailing his growth and living death than he is of having to deal with an avalanche of alive feelings should he remove his controls. He seems to think he will be annihilated by the abundance of life urging him to live. He is afraid of his sexuality, of the exuberant power of his sexual desires, and of the intensity of his erotic love. He is afraid of spiritual power that would attune him to his unconscious processes and his nurturing and healing abilities. And above all he is afraid of his power to awaken the Feminine, his power to fuel and refuel the fires of the feminine spirit with his passionate masculine love! (The same symptoms of disease are true of women whose inner man-selves are as underdeveloped as unevolved patriarchal men are.)

Tuning in to her instincts, Psyche found her pressing desire. She admitted she was hungry for powerful male-female relationships. She wanted a man who could grow with her and penetrate her with his growth, challenging her to grow even more. She wanted laughter and joy, play and passionate caring. She was sick and tired of worshiping wimps and boring brutes—whether at home or in the marketplace. All they could do was mouth the litany of patriarchal principles, because they were afraid to live! They convinced themselves that all the doom and gloom their Feminine-starved minds were broadcasting was going to happen any minute. They thought being discreet was somehow dishonest and being loving was somehow promiscuous. They were afraid of Eros, afraid of disobedience, and afraid above all of being challenged by a conscious woman.

Psyche wanted a man who was free enough to declare the royal authority of love and put all else under it. She was sick and tired of having men relate to her according to the roles she was supposed to play rather than the person she was. Being penetrated as a role—whether wife or mistress, secretary or boss—is tasteless. It leaves a woman with an aching void. (And so, too, with an evolving man: he finds it tasteless to penetrate a role. It leaves him with an aching void.)

Psyche wanted someone who could live life with her from the inside of their hearts outward. She wanted a man who did not need her, a man who had embraced the Feminine he needed inside of himself. Such a man would be capable of being embraced by the Feminine and by the woman who chose to embrace him. Psyche wanted men who were not afraid to meet her on new territory and who relished the electricity generated by the meeting of the opposites.

But patriarchy forbids women from having deep, personal relationships with men, thus denying men the single most important connection in their lives. The only deep relationship with a man a woman is supposed to have (or want) is the relationship she has with her husband. The only other profound kind of relationship she is allowed to have with men is the kind she might have with "professionals" or "ministers of God." In such relationships she is the "sick," the "helpless," the "needy," and the "ignorant" (i.e., the inferior) and the "professional" or "minister" is the "healer," the "rescuer," the "counselor," and the "knower" (i.e., the superior) for whose services she pays. And even these kinds of extramarital relationships are suspect.

What Psyche had to see was that her desire for a profound relationship with the opposite sex was legitimate but its primary purpose was to make her see the need for radical change. She needed to change from relationships based on need to relationships based on want and desire. But such a change was very scary. Without need, who would want her? And who was there for her to want if she did not need a male? But if she could not stop conforming to patriarchal standards, Psyche would stop growing and actually regress. Both her sexuality and her spirituality would grow weak and die.

Dawn began to color the sky. As she looked at the delicate light, Psyche's heart was heavy with the knowledge that in a patriarchy Eros could never love her. He could not see her. He could not want her. Sure, he wanted her back— but only as his version of the adoring, unconscious girl she once had been. Her heavy heart began to pound as she realized that she would not go back. She would not go back to needing and being needed, she would not go back to obeying other people's commands. She could only go on.

As she put one foot in front of the other, Psyche was forced to look inside herself to see what was going on. And, holy shit, she found that she was doing the same thing she accused Eros of doing—not changing. For all the seeds she had sorted and all the golden fleece she had gathered, she was just as stuck in the old mentality as he was. She had to admit that the problem was hers, that her bad feelings arose inside of her. The problem was not that Eros was stuck, or that she lacked the erotic love she wanted in her life. The problem was that she had not admitted that most of all she wanted herself.

Psyche saw how she had been betraying her self. She had been trying to make her newfound abilities fit into the old value system. She had been doing to herself what patriarchy does: she had been denying her feelings, doubting the worth of her new values, and questioning the validity of her own assertions. She had been analyzing all her new data according to the same old value system. In spite of her self-assertion, she had not declared that her values had become radically different from the old commandments and that therefore whatever she was doing could not be contained and measured by old mind-sets and value systems. She had not been able to sacrifice her need to be right, to be accepted, and to be respected. Instead she had sacrificed her spirit and her sexuality.

When Psyche first broke out of her role as the "good wife" who was obedient to her husband/god, all holy hell had broken loose. But since that time she had been acting as though she had not been ravished, as though she was not an erotic being, as though she had not become conscious, as though she had never disobeyed.

She had been trying to squeeze her expanding self back into the mold of patriarchy's "good woman," and she was feeling pinched. She had fallen into the trap of trying to make her assertiveness "respectable," trying to make her intuition fit into logical molds. She found she was back in the rational world, trying to juggle her wants, needs, and desires to make everyone else happy.

And rationalizing her new self so that it would fit into patriarchal misconceptions was not working very well. Indeed, all of her analyzing only blocked her flow of intuition and cut her off from the guidance of her instincts. Instead of rational processes serving her irrationality, Psyche had tried to make her irrationality serve them. She had put the cart before the horse, and she was not going anywhere.

So in order to climb this mountain Psyche needed the fire of the irrational feminine spirit, the fire that transforms and illuminates as well as gives warmth. Like the fire that transforms grain and water into bread, the heat of the feminine spirit transforms human sexuality from animal instinct into conscious pleasure which feeds the soul. It is the fire of a woman's passionate spirit and the heat of her loving body that warm a cold pallet and turn it into a bed. And it is the fire of the feminine spirit that burns like an incinerator, turning the garbage of patriarchy into ash. The love in the feminine spirit transforms the raw power of brute force into a force that seeks to protect the weak and encourage the good. The mysterious knowledge of the feminine spirit in a woman's body transforms an egg and the sperm it has chosen into an embryo. It is the patience of the feminine spirit (and the power of a woman's body) that allows an embryo to become a living spirit, a baby, symbol for the renewal of life and the perpetuation of humanity. It is the feminine ability to envision the unknown that allows the caterpillar to become a butterfly, symbol for resurrection and regeneration.

The light of the feminine spirit, which rationality cannot comprehend, is the light that darkness cannot put out. For those who would see, it illumines the unconscious that would otherwise seduce a person into living in darkness. But the light of the Feminine, which allows darkness to coexist with light, illumines the unconscious without destroying the obscure power of the unconscious to heal and inspire.

The illuminating, transforming power of the feminine spirit is permeated by feminine love, which cherishes each individual face. The power of the Feminine is the diffused warmth of a nonjudgmental force that encourages the personal growth of each individual. In the feminine spirit is found the power to love even the unlovable. And this feminine spirit is what patriarchal man calls "dark and dank?" (Is he blind or deaf or just insane? For without consciousness of of the power and glory of the feminine spirit he surely will live death).

Psyche had to reclaim the power in the feminine spirit and liberate it from patriarchal exploitation. Therefore she had to recover her spirit from all the externals to which she had given it, and she had to recover her sexuality from all the old ideas of what was appropriate. She had to take back her spirit from everything to which she had given it—even from the most worthy cause, even from her dearest love. And recovering it, she had to root and ground the power of her spirit/love in her body.

Spirit is incarnated, regardless of patriarchy's claims that it is intangible. Thus, Psyche had to reclaim the authority of her sexuality, which was the expression of her spirit. She could no longer abdicate the power of her sexuality or give away the energy of her spirit. Spirit connects a person to the authority of the humanity of the self.

To recover the magnificence of her sexuality, Psyche needed to be able to consciously forget everything patriarchy had taught her about male-female relationships. Then she could choose to remember the goodness of her spirit, which she had found in erotic love. She had to consciously forget the patriarchal idea that sex and birth are dirty and need a rite of purification; she also had to forget the idea that love is exclusive and should be permanent. She did not belong to a man, and she did not have an obligation to him. Nor did she have any right, marital or otherwise, to demand commitment from him; he did not belong to her, either. She had to consciously turn her back on the Ten Commandments and such words as "commitment," "adultery," and "infidelity"—words that patriarchy had created to control the sexuality of both sexes.

To reclaim the purity of her spirit and realize her vision of love, Psyche had to choose to remember the elation of her soul that she felt through erotic love. She had to consciously forget what patriarchy had taught her about the dichotomy between sexuality and spirituality. The truth is that you cannot have one without the other!

Patriarchy twists the truth about the relationship of sex to spirit and presents the corrupted concept of woman as goddess or whore. But there is a goddess in every whore, and a whore in every goddess. In his arrogance man claims to make a woman a goddess by giving her his godlike spirit, his life-force (which she may use by obeying his personal authority and the authority of his male-centered institutions).

Woman, according to the patriarchal mentality, makes herself a whore. And it has nothing to do with man casting her out on the streets because she displeases him, so claims this godly man. In actuality, however, patriarchally bound man makes most women prostitutes by morally and legally subjugating them. They sell their sexual services in order to survive—in the home as well as on the street—just as they give away the power of their spirit by obeying.

But woman does not find her spirit through obedience to outside authorities that require denial of the flesh and denouncement of sexuality. Spiritual "pleasure" is not separate from or superior to sensual delight. Nor does she find her spirit through self-sacrificing commitment to "good works" that are sanctified by patriarchal authority.

Woman finds Spirit in her body, by the power of erotic love. For it is erotic love that reveals the very Love that moves the stars in their courses. And man finds Spirit not in obedience either, but in a woman's body! It is in the power of erotic love that men and women find the creative spirit of the Supreme Deity, which manifests itself to people as a feminine spirit and a masculine spirit. Each needs the other in order to become active and effective.

Erotic love reveals to man and woman alike the spirit in the Feminine Principle as well as the spirit in the Masculine Principle. The life-force in the feminine spirit generates the power to envision and conceive, to nourish and mother, to originate and initiate, to invent and design, to animate and give life, to illuminate and transform. The might in the masculine spirit generates the power to love and embrace, impregnate and enrich, abet and advance, nurture and promote, encourage and enhance the creative spirit of the Feminine. This means that the Feminine envisions what is yet to be, and the Masculine constructs the vision. The Feminine hears, and the Masculine composes. The Feminine dreams, and the Masculine fulfills the dream. The Feminine loves, and the Masculine protects and nurtures the loved ones.

But in a patriarchy man has consumed feminine power, eaten the whole, and become fat on the energy of the Feminine it has devoured. The filth that comes out of such greed has polluted the whole wide earth. We watch in horror as species after species becomes extinct, as our sparkling waters become international garbage dumps, as our air, our very breath of life, is poisoned with the exhaust fumes from factories, automobiles, and airplanes. Acid rain falls from the sky. Our good earth, our very bread of life, fights a losing battle against the toxic waste we dump upon her. As deadly radiation streams in through the holes we have carelessly made in the ozone layer, the incidence of cancer rises and the polar ice caps keep on melting. And as South American, Australian, and Hawaiian rain forests disappear, no one knows how to replace nature's great balancing act. No longer is it safe for man, woman, or child to move about on city streets, to love freely, or to eat without fear of being poisoned. And no one sees the connection of such horror with the patriarchal murder of the Feminine!

By appropriating the power of the Feminine as his own, patriarchal man has turned our world upside-down. He calls what is good, evil; he labels any autonomous, intimate woman a whore, a harlot, or a bitch; and he demands obedience to a code of ethics that insists upon the superiority of man and the subjugation of woman. Until recently, when science proved otherwise, not even the power to mother was left to woman. Woman was thought to be no more than a nurse to the newly planted seed that grew within her womb! Thus, by obliterating any trace of the value and power of the Feminine, patriarchy has done more than unbalance the relationship between woman and man, the basic unit of society. It has destroyed the possibility of any unity at all. Without erotic love between man and woman, there is no sure foundation, no fundamental cornerstone, upon which to build a peaceful, prosperous, glad-hearted world.

Male and female are the two halves of being human. And the way a culture structures the relations between them inevitably affects the entire social system; it governs the way the society functions—from the bonding of mother and child to the forming of international relations. If the relationship of man and woman is unbalanced, so will every other relationship be unbalanced. If man devalues one half of the human race, so will his half be devalued. If man usurps the power of the Feminine as his own, that power will be corrupted because he does not know how to use it, and his own power will also be corrupted because he has forgotten what it means to be man. No socioeconomic, political, or theological reforms can abolish the patriarchally produced evils that threaten all of humankind. Reforms have been tried over and over again, but patriarchy has always reemerged in some form.

The central disease that infects all of civilization is the diabolical split between the sexes. The two sexes have pulled away from each other, destroying the identity of each and the unity of the whole. In a patriarchal system there is no way to balance the relationship between women and men. Only by forgetting patriarchal values can the relationship between woman and man, the primary unit of social organization, be righted.

Man and woman must overcome the patriarchally taught fear of the mutual attraction between the sexes. They must learn to consciously forget what patriarchy has taught them about the value of sexuality, the role of procreation, and the purpose of erotic love. They must learn to rejoice in the pleasure sexuality gives and give thanks to the Giver of all life for their humanness. Then they will want the holiness of erotic love and they will value the worth of the Feminine. Only then will they be able to develop their individual personalities and their unity as a couple.

When the whole culture sees and values both the Masculine and the Feminine as the necessary and different parts of one whole, then society can be transformed so that men and women can come together, drawn by the natural affinity between the sexes, which easily balances the two aspects of being human. When the sexes stop warring, so will the rest of the world.

The bleeding wound in the heart of the relationship between man and woman (the primary unit of human society) is what causes the split and hate between nations, between religions, and between races. And it is this wound that causes the split and self-loathing in individual human personalities. This wound will heal itself when what is good is called good—when human sexuality is as honored as human spirituality, when sexual desire is respected as the avenue to the discovery of the self in relation to the *other*, and when erotic love is revered as the manifestation on earth of the Supreme Love in heaven. For when love is reestablished as the supreme value and human sexual desire as a virtue to be nurtured, then the Feminine will once again be valued as primary and the Masculine as necessary. With the primary unit of society restored to its natural balance, the wealth of nations will go into enhancing and enriching life—not into building bigger bombs—and men and women can live together, freely united as couples by the power of erotic love.

FILLING
THE CRYSTAL VESSEL
II

It was imperative that Psyche fill the crystal chalice with the waters from the Fountain of Forgetfulness. If she failed (if she did not reach the top of the mountain or if she could not get to the fountain) not only was she doomed to die in patriarchy but all of humankind with her. Without the power to consciously forget the diabolic values of patriarchy that have torn the sexes apart and turned reality into a lie, there is no way to heal the split between woman and man. There is no way to restore the primary unit of life, formed by man and woman, the Feminine Principle and the Masculine Principle—to a healthy, joy-producing balance. There is no way to stop war, murder, and rape and turn destruction into the enhancement of life.

So Psyche had to reclaim the power of the feminine spirit for her self; for without that power there was no way she could climb this mountain that was higher than any man could climb. This meant she had to leave behind the life-destroying values of patriarchy and experience not the struggle to change patriarchal ways (which is futile) but the very death of the masculine world she had known—the death of her father, the death of her husband/lover, the death of anything patriarchal in her family, the death of the patriarchal religion she had been taught to love, and the death of the patriarchal state she had been taught to revere. And she had to experience her own death. The person she had been in patriarchy had to die; otherwise she could never escape living death. Her grief was real; Psyche felt alone and afraid in her sorrow. She was sad and depressed. But she had to accept her grief so she could pass through to the other side. She had to rely on her tears, not inhibit them, so that they could cleanse the wounds and heal the hurts.

No matter how cruelly patriarchy condemned her, no matter how much Eros hated her, Psyche had to retract her loyalty from all to whom she had pledged it and be loyal only to herself. This is not easy to do. All of the people and good causes to whom she had given her loyalty would not like this; they would try to ostracize her. And fidelity to self exacts yet another price. Retracting her spirit from old mind-sets and behavior patterns shook up Psyche's relationship to the world around her. She had to bear the anxiety of transition—that period between leaving the old and constructing the new.

A woman's faithfulness to her self and others means living out her allegiance to her self in spite of the fact that it contradicts everything in patriarchy—the current vogue as well as the traditional idea of a woman's loyalty. (According to patriarchal tradition a woman's first loyalty should be to man and his authorities, and according to the current vogue her first loyalty should be to the *idea* of woman as defined by her group or cause.) It means being condemned by both the left and the right. Psyche was not acceptable to *any* idea in patriarchy.

Each step that Psyche took beyond the limits of patriarchal beliefs and roles created almost unbearable tension and an intense sense of aloneness. No one in this culture was going to support her trying to reclaim her spirit, not even her seed-sorting and fleece-gathering sisters. Reclaiming her spirit meant she was also reinstating her authority over her own sexuality—an absolute taboo in patriarchy. If a woman's sexuality does not belong to a man, then it must at least conform to his value systems and mind-sets. And if a woman's sexuality does not belong to a man, then it must at least conform to his value systems and mind-sets. And if a woman's sexuality does not conform, it is proof she is bad. Psyche was going to find herself ridiculed for trying to climb a mountain that was too high for any man to climb. (It was not seemly, it was not womanly, it was not faithful, kind, or true; and it certainly wasn't obedient.) And when she succeeded she was going to find herself hated by all those who had failed.

Everyone would judge her by the old standards and find her guilty. Even her best friend. Even Eros. They would call her sacrilegious; they would call her a slut and a whore; they would accuse her of being an unfaithful, adulterous wife who was unfit to be a mother. Does anyone know how much this hurts? But Psyche could do nothing. No amount of explaining would change their minds, and no amount of justifying would free her from their condemnation.

By going up the mountain, shedding her old allegiances, throwing off patriarchal mind-sets, and reclaiming her spirit, Psyche found, however, she had transcended their mentality! By casting off the old, she gave herself a chance to find the illuminating, transforming life-force of her spirit. And because she knew and valued her body, she felt her spirit secure in it. From high on the mountain she could look down and see that their condemnation was meaningless. Though the effects of their ignorance hurt, Psyche was outside of their judgment. She was even outside the judgment of her beloved.

With no one to support her, it was the strength of her faith in her vision of erotic love (and the expanded consciousness of her inner man that it gave her) that helped Psyche trust her feminine way and assert the fact that all-inclusive, individualistic love is the highest good. She had aligned her spirit with the irrational power of the Spirit, and *she did not stop loving.* Though her world condemned her as evil, she did not stop loving the goodness of her self.

Anyone can love those who love in return; the difficulty is in loving those who hate you. Psyche's spirit was in agony as she thought of Eros hating her. "I love you," she thought.

"And I do not know what to do. You hate me. You get so angry. I feel as if you could kill me. The way you are treating me is breaking my heart. But I love you, even though you would not cry if I died."

As she went through this ordeal, Psyche needed the support of her inner man's love even more than she ever had before. And she discovered a double paradox: the more she tossed off patriarchal masculine values, the more she experienced love from her inner masculine, and the more she experienced love from her inner masculine, the more she experienced the strength of her own femininity. And it was the power of this feminine spirit that could withstand being hated. It was the power that would get Psyche to the top of the mountain.

Thus, reconnected more profoundly to her inner man, she had a conscious and passionate ally. He could hold high her lamp and expose the lies in all the rational reasons for her to give up this task. Patriarchal voices were telling her not to climb the mountain. "This is no mountain for a woman to climb. Return to masculine authority and be saved; outside of it you are immoral, evil, and damned. You want those you love to be unhurt by your new knowledge? Return to where they are and wait for them to grow up before you go on." Even the gushing waters yelled at her to flee from them. But with her inner man-self encouraging her to mount higher, the mountain was getting easier to climb!

At last Psyche was almost at the top of the mountain. Her heart beat with joyful anticipation. Then to her horror she saw the two monsters who lived in the caves on either side of the headwaters of the River of Life. Their screeching was almost deafening. Most women would have turned and run! And not too many men would have stuck around either. But Psyche stood glued to the spot, trying not to believe the terror welling up in her throat.

In the west cave there danced about a she-witch of overwhelming ugliness. Her dirty, unkempt hair was an insult to her sex. Half her teeth were gone, and her mouth gaped in on itself between her screeches of filthy curses. She was naked to the waist, and her breasts were long and skinny, sagging to her navel. Below her ragged skirt her feet stank with a crust of filth that was like webbing between her toes.

Then, hoping for some relief, Psyche turned her head to the east cave. Ogodalmighty! There, leering at her, stood a huge, naked giant—twenty feet tall. Psyche looked and was paralyzed by fear and horror. His genitalia were green and orange and purple, like some baboon's grotesquely colored rear. His arms were long and hairy, bulging with monstrous muscles. His bald head glistened with secreted oils.

His eyes fastened on the she-witch with terrible hate, and he leveled her with a logic laced with overwhelming malice. The she-witch was reduced to a weeping wretchedness, clawing at her pathetic breasts with her malformed nails until blood ran from the self-inflicted wounds. Then all of a sudden the she-witch became inflamed with rage and lashed out at the giant, screaming at him about how horrible he was. Psyche watched as the giant shrank to the size of a midget with no balls at all and only a dangling purple penis.

And so patriarchy polarizes the sexes—they stand on either side of the source of life. They rage at each other and vilify each other with the power that only erotic love turned to hate can generate. Psyche's screams of horror joined the damnation chorus. But there was no one to hear.

Then, before her very eyes, the monsters changed. In place of the ugly witch stood an elegantly groomed and gowned lady, her jewels sparkling in the sunlight. And in the giant's place stood a distinguished gentleman garbed in rich array. Psyche looked in nauseated amazement. Her parents!

As she looked closer she saw that the ruby necklace around her mother's throat was not made of precious stones; it was blood! Psyche looked in horror at her smiling father; he had her mother's vocal chords hanging around his neck on a golden chain. When next she looked at her mother, the lovely lady parted her skirt and Psyche saw that she had no genitalia. Her vaginal lips had been sewn together by a system that taboos erotic love. What was made to be touched and loved, penetrated and brought to vibrating life in order to reveal to her the power of Divine Love, was sealed shut. Psyche was frozen with repulsion.

And all the while her father had been lecturing her mother about what he expected from his good wife. With a sadistic cruelty he criticized her, scorned her pathetic, malnourished values, and outlined the details of her servitude to him. And as his toga became transparent Psyche saw that his genitalia had withered up and turned grey.

"No, no," screamed Psyche, "I can't see any more!" But she knew what she was going to see even before she looked. She saw herself standing in her mother's place and looked across to see Eros in her father's. "Oh Eros, Eros!" she sobbed. But there was no way he could rescue her now. Nor could she reach out to touch him. "Oh god," she thought. "There is no way to get to the Fountain of Forgetfulness. I am going to die." And at that point she hoped she would.

Thus has patriarchy sealed the fate of man and woman by outlawing erotic love and destroying consciousness of the value of the Feminine. Envy, hatred, and malice are super-imposed on compassion, competence, and sharing. Jealousy and spite, greed and lust, reveal the hardness of a heart unpenetrated by the spirit/love in the Feminine. Psyche could not move.

As Psyche stood paralyzed by fear and hopelessness, Zeus sent his eagle to help her. The eagle was his chief agent, for the eagle was stronger and could fly higher than any other bird. When the eagle had landed, he told Psyche to come and spread her arms out over his wings and lay her head upon his neck. So, with her heart in her mouth, Psyche knelt down behind the great bird and did as she was told.

Then he bore her up on his eagle wings and soared her to the Fountain of Forgetfulness. With powerful grace, he dipped his wing over the gushing fountain. There he hovered while Psyche reached out with the hand that once had held the knife, and filled the crystal vessel with the gushing waters. Then he bore her back safe and sound and set her down on the mountainside, where Psyche stood up with the crystal vessel filled with the healing waters.

Psyche had flown on eagle wings! She had filled the crystal chalice with the empowering waters. And her joy in the freedom to forget felt boundless. But in order to complete the third task Psyche had needed the power of the great father archetype to lift her out of the grip of historical inertia and bear her up and over the polarization of the sexes. The power of the great father archetype is the power to aid and abet whatever will allow further evolution.

Being a noncondemning judge of character and conditions, and representing competence and authentic know-how, the father power knows how to act in complex situations. Represented by lightning and the thunderbolt, the father power is also the power to intervene and initiate independent action. It is the power to concentrate on what is central in order to create and produce. Such concentration does not destroy relationships; it does not seek to dominate. Instead it seeks a Self-dominated ego that furthers the autonomy which is necessary for intimacy.

Zeus had decided to come openly to the aid of his son (not Psyche). He had gotten tired of Aphrodite's anger and jealousy. The same power of unconscious feminine anger that stirs every human heart stirred also the heart of father Zeus and provoked him to action. And, of course, this was the purpose of the anger of Aphrodite, the Goddess of Love. Her anger exists to provoke both humans and gods to do something, so that love may abound.

So Zeus sent his eagle to help Psyche. He put his power at Psyche's disposal because he loved his son. He knew that Eros needed to be free to love the Feminine. The only way Zeus could help Eros was to help the woman Eros loved to free her spirit/love from patriarchal rule.

By helping Psyche to get to the Fountain of Forgetfulness, father Zeus offered his son what he needed. Only a free-spirited, sexual woman can empower the man who will accept her to accomplish his hardest task: to "kill" (forget) his mother. Only then can he find the feminine sexuality he needs to become a man. Then he is free to sexually love a woman with all the power of his passionate masculinity. In his freedom to erotically love the Feminine, wholeheartedly receiving the magnificence of her sexuality and the purity of her spirit as part of himself, man finds the freedom to love his own masculinity.

If Psyche had succumbed to hating Eros (despising the Masculine), or if she had tried to become like patriarchal man (despising the Feminine), Zeus would not have bothered with her. He sent his eagle power to her because she passionately loved man with all the heat of her desire, even as she loved her self. She valued the Masculine with all the intensity of her discerning intellect, even as she treasured the Feminine. Having faced the horror of patriarchy, she viewed all women with compassion. And she viewed all men with a merciful understanding born of the knowledge of what the patriarchal mentality does to the male.

Psyche never stopped loving consciously, passionately, and sexually. And that is why she became the first person to have the great force of the father archetype, freed from bondage to patriarchal authority, at her conscious disposal. This meant that she was endowed with the moral strength of a father-god to uphold and express the values inherent in the Feminine. The energy of the father archetype empowered her to stand up for what she believed, giving her the power to move others. Consciousness of the power of the father archetype equipped her with an inner strength so powerful that wild animals lay down before her.

The power of the father archetype, active in Psyche now as part of her feminine personality, gave her a force of character, a penetrating mind, and a buoyant way of dealing with the world. The energy of the father archetype gave her the power to lift her self up and bear her own weight. She could soar as on eagle wings. She could run and not be weary; she could walk in the noonday heat and not faint.

But to avail herself of that power Psyche had had to climb higher than any man; she had had to shed the patriarchal values that make monsters out of men and women but which still judged her; and she had had to risk her life, daring to fly.

The power of erotic love between a man and a woman is what frees the energy of the great father archetype from bondage to patriarchal values that exact deadly obedience. Zeus sent his power directly to Psyche because she had sustained her erotic love for his son.

The father power can be sent to man only indirectly. It is made available to man when he values the Feminine with his whole heart and consciously and passionately loves a woman. And this can only happen when he has freed his love from his patriarchal images of what a woman should be. The power of the father (freed from obedience, authority, and controls) came straight to the aid of Psyche, the conscious Feminine. She could then make it available to the man who dared to value the Feminine, who dared to love woman erotically, and who loved his own masculinity.

The particular power that a woman's erotic love gives to the man who erotically loves her is the power of the father's love for his son (freed of patriarchal values by the power of erotic love). When a father can love his son in such a way, the father's love generates a nonjudgmental force for growth in which a man can mature. By filling the crystal chalice with the water of forgetfulness and offering it to the man who will receive it from her, a woman gives a man the power to forget. He is enabled to leave behind the patriarchal values that hinder his growth—the superiority of the male and inferiority of the female, the heroism of war and conquest, the glories of political power, and the passion for making a name for himself. And he is enabled to forget his mother (and all her substitutes). He no longer projects her image onto the women in his life. Nor does he need to consume the Feminine. *He has the power of his father's love to nurture him!*

Such a man is free to love a woman for who she is, and he is free to love her with all the passion of his powerful masculinity. (And he loves his inner feminine self in the same way.) He is now able to fuel and refuel the fires of her spirit with his erotic love. And when this happens the spirit of the Feminine can enliven his daily life, transforming everyday activities into the glories of living. The spirit of the Feminine, consciously reclaimed from all externals and emancipated from patriarchal values, protects him from despair and gives meaning to his old age, sanctifying the process of his life.

How wonderful it is when the sexes can desire each other, love each other erotically and give each other the pleasure only man can give woman and only woman can give man. What wonderful things happen in the whole world when this possibility comes true.

FILLING
THE CRYSTAL VESSEL
III

Psyche had the crystal goblet filled with the water of forget-fulness. She had faced the monsters and found the power of Zeus at her disposal. She had risked her life to fly and had soared on eagle wings. And she had accomplished what no other human being had ever done before. What a calling to be woman! With the irrational power to consciously forget firmly entrenched in the conscious Feminine, Psyche could reclaim the gifts of the feminine spirit for her self—the gifts she had sacrificed to patriarchal control and exploitation—the gift of nurturing, the gift of an increased abundance of the life-force and feeling intensively, the gift of spirituality sparkl-ing through her sexuality, the gift of laughter, and the gift of time.

Consciously forgetting what she had been taught, she was able to detach her self from the pressure of patriarchal obligations and consciously let her feminine spirit take over on her own behalf. She used her feminine power to nourish herself with the benefits of the nurturing masculine love that lived in her, as well as her life-giving inner femininity. Every-thing she did for herself helped her to feel cared for. She used the love that is at the heart of the Feminine to nurture her soul and instruct her in the wisdom she needed to live her life fully.

Instead of using the feminine spirit as an escape from the everyday world, she let its power penetrate the unnamed emotions of her hidden self, which opened her to an abundance of the life-force and an increased intensity of feelings in the depth of her being. She was no longer afraid to satisfy the awakened depths of her sexuality, which patriarchy had sought to keep dormant.

Consciousness of the depths of her sexuality opened her to the heights of her spirituality. The life-nurturing love she communicated to her self illumined the spiritual functions of her sexuality. Her sexuality served to convey to her the goodness of her being woman and the goodness of the *otherness* of man; it served to reveal to her the mystery of the Holy Marriage. The two become one without losing their individual identities. And above all her sexuality and enjoyment of sex served to show her how wonderful heaven was. She never had to be afraid of dying again.

Now she could let her love operate directly. She no longer needed to unconsciously manipulate. This meant she could continue to grow and work and enjoy life. She could experience freely and abundantly the pleasures of human enterprise, intellectual activity, and spiritual development. She no longer had to burden them with the demand to repay her for her renunciation of sexual pleasure.

To her great delight Psyche reclaimed her gift of laughter. With her spirit lodged firmly inside of her self, she found she was back in tune with her ability to laugh at life, at herself, and at the impossible. Her joy—released from the control of masculine authorities and their life-restricting values—bubbled up inside of her, making her young and playful. Instead of struggling to combat the lies of patriarchy, she could laugh in the face of patriarchy. She laughed not with ridicule but with the joy of one who knows the truth. As much as possible she used her sense of humor to expose the lies in patriarchy by revealing the truth that sets people free from rigid obedience—obedience to values that curtail the movement of life and love. With gladness she reclaimed the gift of the absurd, which freed her from taking everything so literally. She needed the absurd as another window from which to see life—and so did Eros. Claiming the reality of what she irrationally felt freed Psyche from trying to fit her feminine power into the restricted forms of patriarchal logic and values.

Thus freed, Psyche regained her sense of time. She valued each moment as eternity intersecting time and sanctifying experience. If she felt depressed, at least she was feeling! By climbing it, her mountain had been made low. The power of her feminine spirit pulled pleasure out of the future and out of the past and put it into the present.

Psyche rescued her knowledge of Divine Love as something that is incarnated in people, freeing it from abstract theories. And she insisted on the boundless mystery of sexual intimacy. In spite of the reality of death, the power of the feminine spirit encouraged her to embody the reality of eternal love in her mortal, time-bound flesh.

By accomplishing this task, Psyche proclaimed her personhood. Her life was not just a continuation of the past. Her life was a new process, unfolding new meaning for the here and now and a new hope for the future. But the changes she made were not a denial of who she had been. She, Psyche, was a changeless person experiencing change. Now whenever the old patriarchal values started to judge her, she had the power to consciously forget all the patriarchal concepts of right and wrong, good and bad, sane and crazy. She could stop judging men and holding the Masculine responsible for her happiness as well as her misery.

And she could consciously forget everything she had been taught about the Feminine that denied her her right to the dignity of being woman. That meant she stopped demeaning herself. At the same time she called a halt to patriarchal debasement of the Feminine and criticisms of women. By consciously forgetting all the hurts and rejections and put-downs of patriarchal subjugation, Psyche freed herself from the destructive memories of her past enslavement; she stopped reacting to unevolved patriarchal culture. She stopped repeating the past. She was free to continue to expand her consciousness. (It is highly advisable for modern-day Psyches to carry a flask of the water of forgetfulness so they can take a swig whenever they start feeling the guilt and pressure of patriarchal judgments!)

With her spirit secured in her body, Psyche cast off other people's mind-sets about the reality of the world. She cast off their ideas about who she was and how she ought to think, feel, and act. She stopped letting other people's belief systems control her life. Instead she relied on the power of the Feminine Principle to guide her to the truth about each person and each situation.

A modern Psyche investigating the increase in recent times of love affairs ("marital infidelity") among married women would let her feminine spirit guide her to the truth of the matter. First of all, she would cast aside the old terminology. She would recognize the source of words like "adultery," "infidelity," and "commitment" and realize that they were not appropriate. All they did was lock any search for truth in the old, patriarchal value system.

She would see the hypocrisy in the patriarchal mind-sets that encourages all sorts of affairs to abound except one. It is good to have all the business affairs, legal affairs, medical affairs, and affairs of state one wants. The only affair that is forbidden is a love affair. Although some business affairs are unethical, some legal affairs illegal, some professional affairs unprofessional, they are not called by derogatory names. But a love affair is called adultery—an ugly name—whether or not it adulterates love. She would recognize that the concept of "cheating" on a husband (or a wife) could only be thought up in the context of relationships based on contracts. After all, having another child is not considered cheating on the first child.

Drinking from the water of forgetfulness, she would ask different questions. Could it be that these women, having loved the unlovable, had increased their capacity to love? Could it also be that such women have integrated into their personalities their own valued and loved feminine selves? Could they therefore have found the capacity to love many individually—a capacity that lies in the heart of the God/

Goddesshead—in their hearts also? Having opened her self to love and loving, is it strange that a woman would be "touched by God"—shot by an arrow from the god of love—more than once? And loving more than one person erotically, was she supposed to feel guilty for loving? Was she supposed to stop loving her husband because she also loved another?

Only in the context of love as a limited emotion can the idea exist that one takes love away from one person in order to give it to another. Love is individualistic; it has as its object a unique person *for whom no substitution is possible*! Only in role-playing can one person substitute for another! People, being unique beings, cannot be loved except uniquely.

But individualistic love is not the way of patriarchy. People are terrified of their loved ones loving someone else. And they themselves must keep a tight rein on their loving, lest their loving too many should threaten the ones they love.

This creates a most schizophrenic way to love. I cannot love you because I love A. You are you, not A, so I cannot love you. But inside me what I feel is love—not the same love I feel for A, but love for you. Patriarchy demands that I cut off my love for you because you are not A. And it insists that I cannot receive love from you if you love B. This either makes people crazy or it makes them into zombies. If I have to deny the reality of my love for you because I love A, or renounce my love for A in order to love you, I must suppress so much love that I stop loving and go mad. Or I will make myself so numb that all I am is a zombie and all I can see are zombies around me.

Loving others is not being disloyal to the people who are primary in our lives. Most of the women who have expanded their capacities to love do not want additional husbands; they love the ones they have. They are devoted, loyal, loving wives. They just want to be able to love whomever they love and experience the joy of being vitally alive human beings! They do not use other relationships to hurt or punish those they love.

A modern Psyche, at this stage of the game, knows that what is required is discretion—the ability to combine the art of understanding others with the science of discrimination. Until collective values have changed more, this means a conscious woman must move silently, under cover of darkness, as a thief in the night. For it has taken patriarchy thousands of years to get people to think that the goodness of human sexuality is an evil and that sexual love is a sin.

The great commandment is to love. But the institutions of man issue other commandments. The state commands people to hate (and kill if necessary) whoever are the state's designated enemies, and religious institutions command them to judge and condemn whoever are the designated unbelievers. The righteous ones are those who obey, those who judge and hate. Those who love and embrace the designated enemy and the designated unbeliever are the unrighteous according to the laws of the state and the courts of the patriarchal god. So perverted is the patriarchal notion of love and sex that the whole concept of erotic love is contaminated. It has been totally divorced from procreation. Procreation is the only excuse for man and woman having sex, according to a large majority of today's religions. Making babies is O.K., making love is not. And so too many babies are made who must live in a loveless world.

How long will mankind insist on a world turned upside down by his patriarchal ways? What is good he calls evil. He calls love treason and betrayal; he calls consciousness insubordination; he calls individuation selfishness; he calls knowledge evil. And what is evil he calls good. He calls hate love; he calls death life; he calls cruelty kindness; he calls exploitation everything from justice to education; he calls the fear of a Supreme Being faith; he calls despair hope. Will he continue until he blows us off the face of the earth? Or will there be enough Psyches who accomplish the four tasks? Will they be able to free enough men so that together they can become a force strong enough to turn reality right side up again? Will humankind ever be able to get on with the business of evolution?

But at least one woman reclaimed the power of the feminine spirit, the power of illumination and transformation, the power of love and regeneration. To every man and every woman she offers the chance to drink from the cup that holds the water of life. But the chance is not free. Every person who wants the freedom to consciously forget must also climb the mountain. They too must shed the dead-end values of patriarchy and face the monsters alone. They must reclaim and cherish the spirit in the Feminine Principle.

It is feminine values—that which patriarchy calls weakness, dependence, and immorality—that are our hope. Psyche had found great strength in being vulnerable. She was willing to be exposed, to let others affect her, to feel intensely and to trust love enough to get emotionally involved. She had stood alone and unarmed before the monsters, and Zeus had sent her his eagle. She now knew that her greatest defense was simply being who she was. Allowing herself to be vulnerable, she was free to refashion her self into the real Psyche—the Psyche who had never before existed. Her greatest gift to her self—and to Eros and to their child—was her ability to become more Psyche. This is the meaning of "transfiguration."

Asserting her vulnerability, Psyche was free to be emotionally honest. This takes great courage because she must face and feel what she has let life in a patriarchy do to her. Though she was highly responsive to others and their feelings, she stopped trying to be nice so everyone would like her. She admitted that she was different; in fact, she was special. At the same time, she recognized that what she wanted from life was what everyone wants: to be happy, to have a sense of self-fulfillment, to have children who would love her, and to have a spouse who would cherish her and leave her free.

Being able to consciously forget patriarchal values that judge and condemn released the power of her compassion for all humanity. She felt the common bond everyone shares. Feeling at home in the universe, she felt like a friend to all the people on earth. And so Psyche transcended nationality, race, creed, and sex. There were still a lot of women who felt resentful and bitter, who wanted her to join their cause. But Psyche had found a higher calling: the calling to be human!

Her humanity, freed of false notions of an unattainable perfection, lifted her level of consciousness, especially her level of awareness of her humanness. Her humanity also had the power to lift other people's levels of consciousness as well. By reclaiming her spirit and realigning it with the Spirit from on high, Psyche had found the means to sanctify—to make holy—her own personhood. She had found a way to heal the hurts of the past and remain true to her feelings. She had found a way to so plant her personality in the power of the Feminine Principle that she was free to take on her full sexual and spiritual identity.

And her inner man-self supported her and defended the sanctification of her identity with his erotic love. Before, her sexuality had been her hiding place, but it now became the instrument through which her femininity played. Just as the human spirit works through the mechanisms of the human brain, so it also uses every cell of the body to express itself as life! And Psyche had found the real meaning of and power in the great father archetype. She could fly on eagle wings!

By the power of the spirit she had recalled, she was able to initiate a bonding of the human spirit with the Holy Spirit. Psyche was not some Great Out There; she was here and now. One could touch her and love her, because she allowed herself to become touchable and lovable. She never became a spiritual essence or a religious teacher. And today she offers us a way to blaze our own trails—not an example to follow. She had overcome the monsters by loving consciously and passionately, not by following rules and obeying dogma.

But before she could be transformed she had had to accept the diabolical reality of her patriarchal self—the fact that when she was undifferentiated from patriarchal values she had fragmented relationships rather than drawing people together. She had split the truth, trying to make the pieces fit the patriarchal molds. She had had to be nailed to the cross-purposes in her being before they could be reconciled. And she understood intimately the amount of courage it takes to bear these realities.

Understanding the paradox of twoness in oneness, Psyche embraced the communion of the flesh and the spirit. She integrated the mystery of this bond into her own being. Psyche found the power of Love/Spirit—not by breaking her will and abnegating her self to serve some transpersonal power—but in a relationship of mutual creative involvement and understanding. She found the power of Love/Spirit in the nearness as well as the distance between the human and the Divine. This was symbolized by the relation of her self to her Self, the relation of her self to the image of the Divine Being within her. All of life became a sacrament: the outward, visible, and material things symbolized the inward, invisible, and spiritual grace. A kiss was the symbol of her love.

The mysterious spiritual activity and unconditional creative power of the Feminine became visible in Psyche. Freed of the dead weight of the past, she could choose to remember the good—the good of her and the good of Eros. And she could forget the rest. All blaming automatically ceased. Bitterness and resentment vanished. She felt light-hearted and enthusiastic even when the problems of earthly life seemed heavy.

Psyche's personal power was now enhanced by the irrational power to consciously forget and enriched by the power of the father energy. Such personal power, enhanced and enriched, enabled her to initiate new and independent action—not in league with men nor in league with women—but in league with passionate, individuated human beings. And regardless of the forms her new action took, they had a ring of authority and the sound of joy!

Psyche was alive! She was free! Her spirit was hers! And the whole wide earth rejoiced; it too was free from the condemnation of man.

In joyful radiance, Psyche skipped down the mountain that was higher than any man could climb, which in the dawn's light she had labored up.

THE DESCENT
INTO HELL

Psyche went happily to Aphrodite with the crystal vessel full of the water from the Fountain of Forgetfulness, just knowing the Goddess would be pleased.

Psyche was elated: she had soared on eagle wings, and she had filled the crystal chalice with the waters from the Fountain of Forgetfulness! The spirit/love she had reclaimed shone through her, making her radiantly beautiful. In the happiness born of being able to consciously forget, she went to Aphrodite. She just knew the Goddess would be pleased. What else could She possibly want?

Psyche's death!

In a life of consciousness expansion there is no retreat. One can either go onward and die to the old order or be dead, as in buried. Aphrodite was determined that the last vestiges of the patriarchal girl-woman would die so that Psyche could be born into the fullness of the mystery at the heart of the Feminine. For that was the only way that Psyche was going to live. But, of course, Psyche did not know that.

But Aphrodite was not pleased. She was angrier than ever and determined to destroy the hated woman once and for all. The fourth task She devised was almost foolproof. She gave Psyche a small pot with a tight-fitting lid and told her that she must descend into the dark underworld. There she must obtain from the hand of Persephone some of her immortal beauty ointment and deliver it to Aphrodite unopened.

When Psyche heard this, she knew beyond doubt that Aphrodite meant her utter destruction.

"Oh god," thought Psyche. "If Aphrodite wants me to die, what chance have I got? Why should I even attempt this task? Why should I descend into the depths where even Aphrodite won't go? If she wants Persephone's immortal beauty ointment, let her get it herself!" Psyche was tempted to regress into unconsciousness. Who wants to face those unseen powers in the depths of self that fight against the urge to wholeness? And the more a person has already differentiated the self from the unconscious, the harder the unconscious fights and the greater the temptation is to regress. "Why me? Why should I have to do this?" are the questions of temptation.

Then Psyche remembered why. She wanted her self, and she loved and wanted Eros. The only question left was how. This time no helpers appeared—no ants, no eagles. Nor was there any place to hide so she could wait until the danger had passed. Psyche despaired. She knew of only one way to enter the world of the dead, and that was to die. So, putting the little pot in her pocket, she rationally climbed a tower so she could throw herself off. But when Psyche did this an irrational thing happened: the very stones cried out to her.

"Psyche, Psyche! Stop. Listen. From yonder dark chasm, choked with thorns, a path leads down into the underworld. Put two coins in your mouth and take two pieces of barley bread in your hands, then follow this rough path. Refuse to help a lame donkey driver who will ask you to pick up some kindling wood. When you come to the river Styx, Charon will ferry you over for one of your coins. Refuse the groping hand of a dying man as he reaches up out of the water begging you to save him. Pass by and do not assist three women weaving the threads of fate and fantasy. Toss one of your pieces of barley bread to Cerberus, the three-headed dog, who stands guard at

the entrance to hell. While the three heads are fighting over the one piece of bread, enter the palace of Hades where Persephone is queen. She will give you a portion of her immortal beauty ointment, shutting it into the pot with a tight-fitting lid. Then repeat the whole process in reverse on the way back up. And remember, you must deliver the pot unopened."

Unlike the other tasks, which were accomplished by irrational means, this task required a conscious plan in order to plumb the deepest depths of irrationality. Only a woman who has climbed the mountain that is higher than any man can climb and who has been transfigured can use such a conscious plan. Without the ability to consciously forget the lie of the supremacy of reason, a woman would get caught in all the ifs, whys, and buts of rationality. Logic would block access to her instinctive wisdom and intuitive knowledge, which automatically know how to use a conscious plan.

Psyche stopped from throwing herself off the tower and listened intently to the instructions the stones gave her. She put two coins between her lips and took two pieces of barley bread in her hands. Holding the coins in her mouth, she could not talk or eat; and holding the bread in her hands, she could not help others.

Coins in the mouth and pieces of bread in the hands! What significant symbols for our age of transition! Today noise abounds while silence is almost unknown, and the welfare dole dehumanizes the receiver. Welfare fails to stimulate talents, it renders people unproductive, and it aggrandizes the giver with an inflated sense of doing good.

Coins are things of value. By successfully completing the last three tasks, Psyche had increased her self-worth immeasurably. She had gained a consciousness that far exceeded what was possible in a patriarchy. To avoid misspending the value of her self, Psyche had to hold the treasure of her self in silence. If she talked, the coins would drop out of her mouth and she would lose the riches she had earned.

In patriarchal cultures, talk has assumed the role of a saving grace. There are talk shows, talk therapy, international talks, talking teachers, and talking preachers. Talk, talk,

talk. If we just keep talking enough, maybe the witch that lurks in the silence won't get us. The devouring ogre of our patriarchal age is the Great Mother gone crazy, going to eat her children. It is she (and the unacknowledged Feminine in a man) who prowls the silence.

The fury and the hurt caused by the dehumanizing effects of patriarchy, which degrade woman's spirit, flesh, and mind, turn the mother into a child-eating witch. Worse than the degradation is the fact that patriarchal man's passion, aborted by his control and obedience, cannot meet the passion of woman. *Nor can he connect with her on her level of awareness.* He has no power to expand his consciousness without passion. He has no increasing self-love to sustain him as he faces his patriarchal death.

Woman comes to an adult, male-female, erotic relationship with passionate devotion. But she is asked only to serve man, to listen to his complaints, to keep a clean house, and to raise respectable children. He wants her to send him off in the morning with a kiss as he goes to work, and he wants her to welcome him home in the evening with a kiss. He expects his dinner to be cooked and his children to be quiet. And while he waits to be served he criticizes his wife for all she has done or not done and berates his children. Or he ignores them all, barricaded behind his newspaper or incommunicado in front of his television.

Such a relationship is too devastating to a passionate woman; there is no life or joy or playfulness, no challenge, no stimulation to grow and think and feel. (An evolving man faces the same dilemma. He comes to the relationship passionately devoted and hoping for an increase of intimacy that nourishes his autonomy. But he finds a patriarchal woman who is paralyzed by her fear of breaking taboos, a woman who cannot contend in the world or make a house a home.) It is not serving a man or being rejected by him that produces the fury. It is the fact that the man's passion is so puny. The mother gone crazy from lack of stimulation from her mate devours her children, digests them, and then excretes them.

The neglected and despised Feminine (in both sexes) is swollen with the energies of the unconscious, undirected,

and frustrated passion of suffocated womanhood. This sickness
is in our culture. And no one escapes the volcanic fury that
erupts from the abhorred and scorned Feminine. Whether
the eruption is inward or outward, it is the unavoidable price
every human pays for the devaluation of the Feminine and
the subjugation of women. Male or female, we cannot keep
quiet; the silence is too threatening. For we have not only
dropped the coins out of our mouths, we have spit the
treasure of the Feminine out and we are finally bankrupt.

Silence is very hard to find. It is out of vogue. Our
culture has become an endless bombardment of sounds. Tele-
visions blare twenty-four hours a day. Radios hang around
people's necks with earphones that inject noise directly into
the brain. The never-ending sound of traffic and jackhammers
battering away at old concrete pollutes the air as much as
auto fumes and stale smoke. Out of style, silence has become
highly suspect. It is black when it is feared and white when
its noiselessness is perceived as a void no person can fill. Few
can see the brilliant colors sparkling in silence; few can hear
the inaudible music of our universe. We must have something, even if it is silent work, to kill the noise of silence.
Otherwise the No Thing, the silenced Feminine, assumes
gigantic proportions, looming like a monster to devour.

But the irreplaceable value of the human soul cannot
be found in noise. Nor can it flourish without time alone in
silence. It is only by keeping quiet that a person's conscious
can commune with the unconscious in an ongoing movement
of self-learning and self-growth. In silence the body has time
to breathe. And breathing, the self gains strength to set the
soul free to dance to the music of the stars.

Two coins in the mouth. Treasure in silence and fasting.
But fasting is about as fashionable as silence. What a crazy
irony: diets abound like noise. There are diets for everything—hair, skin, sex, brains, energy, weight loss, and
weight gain. The patriarchal mentality has taught us to view
the body as a thing to be worked on, a thing to exercise, a
thing which must be purged of its impurities. The idea of
living in our bodies has been replaced by the idea that bodies,
being less than spirit, need to be whipped into shape. People

even go to classes to learn how to fast. But fasting is not purging the body. It is praying. Fasting lets the body pray. Praying and fasting, the body becomes so attuned to the rhythm of life that it can respond to every breath of the Spirit.

The fruit of fasting is feeling good—very good and very alive. It allows individuals to experience their own power to increase their self-worth. The other side of fasting is feasting. Feasting expresses a heart overflowing with thanksgiving for life in the body—for food that nourishes the body and tastes good on the tongue, and for wine that makes glad the heart. To feast is to enjoy the fruits of our labor, delighting in the abundance that we have produced. Both fasting and feasting gratify the soul as they intensify the pleasure of the body.

But in a patriarchy people are not supposed to feel good; patriarchal values do not want them to experience their own worth. They are supposed to feel guilty for their prosperity. And if they don't feel guilty before "God," then the "holy community"—all the "righteous," law-abiding men (and their women)—will *make* them feel guilty. Feeling good is considered dangerous; our society cautions us against it. So fasting is definitely out. It would make us feel too good. But without fasting there can be no feasting. Both are children of the Spirit. So in her descent into the depths, Psyche practiced both fasting and silence. And what an increase in her sense of the treasure of her self! Coins in the mouth.

And bread in the hands. If Psyche stopped to pick up sticks for the lame donkey driver, she would lose one piece of bread. And if she stopped to pull the dying man out of the river, she would lose the other. She would have no way to get past the three-headed dog on her way down into the darkest depths or on her way out into the light of day.

Cerberus, the three-headed dog standing guard at the entrance to the palace of Hades, represents a distorted and overgrown masculine "head-ego." This aberration can exist in men and women alike, and it destroys the driving power of both the "heart-ego" and the "head-ego."

A healthy head-ego drives the self by thinking. It responds to the person by setting the self apart from the unconscious, and it *thinks* the person into a distinct and independent being. The process of thinking includes analyzing, classifying, categorizing, and comparing. The heart-ego, in both men and women, drives the self by feeling. It responds to a person by connecting the self directly to the feeling that comes from a person's sexuality and spirituality. The process of feeling thrusts the contents of the heart into consciousness. This evokes a spontaneous evaluation as well as stimulates behavior that is responsive to feeling. The heart-ego humanizes men and actualizes women. A distorted and overgrown head-ego in a man or a woman discounts the validity of the heart-ego and prevents a person from coming into contact with the function (process) of feeling.

An overgrown head-ego, instead of separating feelings and thoughts from the control of the unconscious, divorces itself from the unconscious altogether. It elevates the rational process of thinking while it denies the irrational process of intuitive feeling. A distorted head-ego exalts the class, category, and profession of the self it identifies with and it degrades everyone else. It drives the self by vanity (or despair).

Having disposed of the authority of the self, an overgrown head-ego does not consider the seat of consciousness to be the integration of Masculine and Feminine, rational and irrational, into one unified person. Instead it considers man and the Masculine to be the seat of consciousness, the organized interpreter of conscious reality. It exalts the Masculine as the sole life-force in the world, and it excludes the Feminine. It drives the self by an overweening admiration for the male sex (or by a false humility). Distorted and overgrown head-egos view power as power over others—that kind of power which only the power to destroy can give.

Such a power-ridden head-ego in a woman is deadly. A distorted masculine head-ego in a woman depreciates her feminine ideas and objective inquisitiveness. It also depreciates her feelings, calling them nothing more than feminine sentiments. It depreciates her thinking, calling it nothing more than imitations of masculine rationality. It is hard to beat the destructive power of the patriarchal judgment: "You are nothing but a woman."

Such depreciations spur a woman to scrutinize all of her motives and judge all she does harshly and negatively. A distorted masculine head-ego stifles a woman's initiative and increases her sense of inborn inferiority. An overgrown head-ego will drive a woman to use power instead of love to accomplish what she wants. Instead of yielding to the power of her love, she tries to dominate. She believes she must forsake her Feminine in order to deal with her relationships and her subjugation both at home and at work.

But power without feminine love does not increase her effectiveness. It merely isolates her from her effectiveness and disrupts the relationships she seeks, especially the relationship of her self to her Self. It drives people apart instead of bringing them together.

Women must get past the three-headed dog—that is, past the patriarchal masculine experience of having an exalted ego that is separated from the unconscious. Without doing that, no woman can reach the depths of her own unconscious, where her life-giving, life-renewing femininity dwells. Only in her depths, past the lure of analytical procedures, can a woman come into the fullness of her feeling, thinking, touching, and intuitive knowledge-gaining processes. In her depths she encounters the raptures and ecstasies of her own sexuality. And the heat of her sexuality fires her spirit and her love, melting them into an inseparable compound that courses through her body, giving life to every cell.

The only way Psyche could fulfill herself was to develop the full potential of the three components of her compound nature: her sexuality, her spirituality, and her intelligence. Only in the depths, undisturbed by a distorted, overgrown, patriarchal head-ego, could Psyche understand that love is above and beyond any law. No law can ever generate love or fulfill it or increase it. Love is Spirit and the Spirit blows where it wills.

But Psyche had not reached the depths yet, and the way down was loaded with temptations. One mistake in hell and you don't get out! The stones' instructions were specific: she must pass by the lame donkey driver who begged for her help, she must say no to the dying man, and she must pass by the three women weaving fate and fantasy. The myth leaves no doubt. Psyche had to stop serving others.

If she continued to serve others, Psyche would lose her opportunity to get past the three-headed dog. She would remain trapped in the hell created by a distorted head-ego. A distorted head-ego, overgrown with patriarchal values, would invisibly disconnect her from the value of the heart-ego. And she would have to surrender the feminine spirit she had so arduously reclaimed.

Service has nothing to do with the ministering spirit in the Feminine. What makes this fourth task so dangerous is that, unlike any of the other tasks, it prohibits actions that are extremely "do-able." For a woman who is not conscious enough, it is illogical and immoral not to pick up the sticks of the lame donkey driver and it is damnable not to haul the dying man out of the river. To help these poor people seems natural and logical to a patriarchal woman.

Patriarchy teaches people that her service is all a woman has to give. She is packaged, advertised, and sold by the service she should give—as chief cook and bottle washer, efficient secretary and switchboard operator, diaper changer, laundress, nurse, teacher, housekeeper, or the perfectly groomed woman who is ready to serve her man, filling all his needs and fitting into his picture of what she should be. And if she is *not* all these things, she is considered less than feminine! Any successful (money-producing) woman in a patriarchy— from Scarlett O'Hara to television's female tycoons—is denigrated and portrayed as an immoral, self-seeking bitch.

Not being conscious enough to see that it is a lie, patriarchal woman believes that her service is all she has to offer. She listens to her distorted head-ego and gives in to the pressure to conform and "do good." She gives her service to her husband/lover, her children, her job, her church, her community, her aging parents, and her sisters in their miserable marriages. Patriarchal woman gives and gives and gives until she is blue in the face, drained of her life-giving, life-renewing, life-transforming energies.

How many sticks she has picked up already! How many dying moments and dying relationships she has hauled out of the river! Thus, she has unknowingly kept alive the old ways of relating to others and the old ways of relating to her self. She is not free to follow a new and authentic love or to deepen the intimacy of an old love. She gives away her good feelings by serving others, and she gets nothing in return. She does not know that she did not get her good feelings for nothing. She earned her good feelings; they are her coins! And she gives them away as if they were free.

To stop serving others Psyche had to throw away the idea that living for others was the way to happiness. She had to admit that taking care of others was not the way to self-fulfillment. It was the way to depletion and exhaustion! If service is all a woman is allowed, then she ceases to exist as an individual. She seeks out somebody or something she can serve, thinking this will give her value. But there is nothing of real value to be earned by service; the coins a woman receives for her service are hollow ones. And sacrificing her self for others does not help them find fulfillment or self-worth either. It only keeps them prisoners in an overgrown childhood. Service stinks.

Rejecting service, Psyche had to get in tune with the rhythm of her ministering spirit. She had to become conscious of the difference between her ministering spirit (which is not for naught) and her service (for which she does not get paid). Service is heavy-laden; it is laden with commitment and burdened by a sense of duty and obligation. It makes a woman feel diminished, somehow bad about her self. Service is a betrayal of the Feminine; it is a sorry imitation of her ministering spirit. Instead of creating a bond, it creates a conflict between her self and those whom she is supposed to serve. It makes her feel irritable, resentful, and spiteful, and it makes the served feel guilty and limited.

The ministering spirit embedded in the Feminine is easy and light. It is free of any sense of obligation or duty. Psyche found that it flowed naturally from the erotic love within her. And just as naturally, it required a real response from others. Though it demanded her full participation, it did not deplete her. Instead, dispensing her ministering spirit filled Psyche with vibrant life. Whatever forms it took, it gave her a sense of deep fulfillment, peace, and joy.

The ministering spirit of the Feminine expresses the innate goodness of the Feminine that in adulthood blossoms forth as the love that draws people together. Those who receive a woman's ministering spirit also feel good about themselves, because she is giving them something they can respond to. By responding to the ministering spirit in the Feminine Principle, a person gains a sense of self, a sense of being loved and valued as a unique person. Such an expression of giving and receiving is diametrically opposed to commitment.

Men and women make commitments because of some exterior agreement—marriage vows, motherhood, or some other "holy" work—but not because of anything a person does or does not do. People with commitments are assigned duties. Commitment is not an honest response to reality. It burdens people with obligations, regardless of what anyone else does.

The ministering spirit of the Feminine is not free. It demands an answer, because it is a real response to real people. One must be conscious to exercise it, and one must be conscious to receive it. She who dispenses it finds no blanket reasons for giving, no single cure for all situations. The ministering spirit has nothing to do with fulfilling an obligation or obeying an authority. Nor has it anything to do with being fair (life is not fair) or treating people equally (people are not born equal). The ministering spirit is a two-way street that demands a conscious response from the receiver. And its benefits are beyond the imagination of the patriarchal head-ego.

Conscious femininity knows that what the lame donkey driver does *not* need is someone picking up his sticks; he needs to get well. And what the dying man needs is the dignity to die. But we seem to be unable to let the dying die and let the dead bury the dead. We do not know the difference between service and the ministering spirit, between sentimentality and tough love, a love that can prioritize its giving so that maximum effectiveness can be attained. In a patriarchy our daily bread is given to us, but we drop it on our way to do our "good works." And then we have no way to get past the three-headed dog.

Because the value of the Feminine has been shoved underground, feminine compassion is left in the unconscious and ruled by a misbegotten heart-ego and an overgrown head-ego. Therefore, the ministering spirit of the Feminine in both sexes is out of whack. Unconscious feminine compassion is not the answer to the ills patriarchy creates. Indeed, such misguided compassion is deforming the very society it seeks to help.

If consciousness of the value of the Feminine were encouraged, then the force of the feminine spirit could be consciously directed. Conscious compassion knows it is not rational to penalize the producers in society in order to give free help (reward) to the nonproducers. But according to patriarchal compassion it is "rational" for responsive, nonviolent citizens to live behind locked doors and for criminals to go free. It is "rational" for the creators of jobs and the producers of goods and services to be taxed out of business. Such "rational" compassion limits the freedom, safety, and productivity of responsive citizens while it gives the oppressed no power and no means of acquiring productive labor. It sabotages the right of individuals to self-determination, and it limits their choices of ways to make a living.

In a patriarchy the mark of "true goodness" requires that sane, productive people forfeit their freedom, their wealth, their health, and their good feelings for the insane, the incurably ill, the criminal, and the unproductive poor! When consciousness of the value of the Feminine is restored, such thinking will be regarded as utter nonsense. When the value of the Feminine is consciously honored, compassion will be served rationally by making the nonproducers productive, healing the sick, imprisoning the criminals, requiring social work from the law-breakers, and letting the dying die. In the meantime we have heads full of knowledge galore but we lack hearts of wisdom. Our society needs the feminine virtues of compassion, caring, and nurturing that are well grounded in consciousness of the Feminine Principle, and it needs the strengths of the Masculine that is informed of the soul. So Psyche had to hold the bread in her hands and refuse to serve others.

Next she came upon the three women weaving fate and fantasy, who called out to her to come help them. Here again the temptation is so deadly because it seems so innocent. How natural for Psyche to want to involve herself in other people's lives. She has sorted the seeds; she knows the difference between reality and patriarchal counterfacts. She has gathered the golden fleece and has the power of her self-worth at her disposal. She has filled the crystal chalice with water from the Fountain of Forgetfulness, and the power of her spirit is free and clear of patriarchal values. How tempting to use her knowledge and her power to help others! Weaving fate and fantasy seems like a mere extension of her natural desire to participate in relationships, to nurture and care for people. It also fulfills the masculine need in both sexes to be the rescuer and hero.

But weaving fate and fantasy is messing around in other people's lives. It is not nurturing, nor is it self-fulfilling. Rather, it masks a woman's legitimate need for autonomy and intimacy. It cloaks her desire for a passionate connection with the Masculine. And it covers up the lack of stimulation from her mate, from the men in her life, and from the Masculine in the culture.

Psyche must not let herself be deluded. Weaving fate feels like being involved. It feels like being autonomous. It feels as though she is doing something, as though she is in control. But it is only an easy escape from facing her need to strengthen her autonomy. It feels like intense intimacy, but getting involved in other people's problems does not constitute true intimacy.

Spinning fantasy—spiritual fantasy, sexual fantasy, or material fantasy—seems to give some meaning to a woman's existence and some excitement to her stifled life. But by fantasizing she has merely projected the life of her passionate soul onto her fantasies while the unbearable blankness of her patriarchal existence remains unchanged. She has forsaken her self in a retreat from a life that demands living.

It is hard for women to resist this temptation. This is because in a patriarchy a woman has to give up her ability to penetrate directly with her passionate love to get what she wants. And what she wants is the growth of her self in a passionate connection with man and the Masculine. Patriarchal woman does not use her love to accomplish what she wants. Instead, she misuses her feminine wiles and guiles weaving fate and fantasy, desperately trying to augment her autonomy and realize an intimate, passionate relationship.

What happens in patriarchal relationships between men and women is that once the rescuing and ravishing are over, any passionate connection fades because man fails to relate to the woman he has awakened. He simply does not know what to do with a wide-awake woman who loves him erotically. He sort of voids himself into relational nothingness. He uses the same rules of behavior that he uses at work. And of course those rules do not work in personal relationships. His attitude is unconsciously patriarchal: he is superior, he has rescued woman from her plight (where would she be without him?), and she is therefore obligated to him. All he knows he wants is her service. He has no idea that he hungers and thirsts for more.

Being unaware of the value of the Feminine has left man bereft of any consciousness of his inner woman, but she grows fat on his unfelt feelings and his undifferentiated emotions. And this inner woman-self, grown so grossly out of proportion, threatens to overwhelm him. Having forfeited his connection to his feelings, he has no way to differentiate one emotion from another. So if a woman offers him love and the ministrations of her spirit (instead of service), he is confused at best and more often infuriated. He feels abandoned and betrayed. And he is, but not necessarily by any flesh-and-blood woman. It is his own forsaken inner woman-self who has abandoned and betrayed him.

And abandoned (without any consciousness of the value of his inner feminine self), man has no energy to animate him. He has no power to penetrate, no passionate masculine love for a Psyche to connect with. The problem is not just the assumption that she will serve but also the fact that her passion is not met with corresponding masculine passion. (And the same is true for a man who is evolving, who hungers and thirsts for more, but who is mated to a patriarchal woman who only offers him her service. His masculine passion is not met with corresponding feminine passion.)

So Psyche passed by the three women weaving fate and fantasy. Holding the bread in her hands and the coins in her mouth, she pursued instead the path of her own individuation. She did not desert her self; she had the courage to be. Psyche offered no explanations and no justifications, and she could not apologize with two coins in her mouth.

So on her descent to the underworld Psyche practiced silence and fasting, the fruit of which is feeling good and feeling one's self-worth. And how she was going to need all that good feeling of self in order to sustain her in the world of the dead! For plumbing the depths required that she consciously remember and confront her past.

IN HELL

Psyche came to the river Styx, that boundary between the living and the dead, with coins in her mouth and bread in her hands. She paid Charon one of her coins, and he rowed her across the river. To live, she refused to help the dying man who reached up to her and begged her to pull him out of the river. On the banks of hell she threw Cerberus one of the pieces of bread and watched in fascination as the three heads fought over the one piece. Then she remembered—she'd better run while she could and enter the palace of the dead.

She was greeted by the beautiful Queen Persephone, who ushered Psyche into her palace. The queen began to lead her through the rooms of the palace. These rooms represent the rooms of remembrance and confrontation. Though Psyche had attained the power to consciously forget, now she had to sip from the cup of remembrance and confront the past in full consciousness. In each room Psyche had to face the evil of good unused and the demonic waste of love unloved. And in each room she had to assume responsibility for not opposing those evils.

Arm in arm, Persephone and Psyche entered the room of dear, dead hopes and desires. Here Psyche had to face the pain of what could have been. She had to recognize all the times she had not stood up for her self and her evolving values. She had to face all the times she had refused to recognize love and had turned away from it, believing she was doing the right thing. She had wandered from the truth of her love, which excluded nothing in the universe; she had tried to contain it within the man-made limits of patriarchy's distorted beliefs. She had betrayed the identity of her eternal self!

She had sought false phantoms of the good in perverted values that promised joy and life everlasting. But in reality they denied life and exalted death, and thus could never ever fulfill their promises. Now Psyche had to pay the price for not admitting that what she had found in the depths of her heart was radically different from what she had been taught was the truth. All that Psyche had refused to let die, all that she had refused to forget, had robbed her of the truth about herself and cheated her out of new and renewed love.

If Psyche had been more conscious of the supreme power of love, she would not have let her desires be buried by false values and the fears they generate. But she had let the promises of patriarchy's man-made values seduce her into believing they were the god-given truth. Now she must stand alone on the other side of love. The love for which she had longed was the love she had unwittingly sacrificed to the patriarchal belief system. She had blinded herself. Now she had to admit her blindness and say good-bye to what now could never be. The depth of Psyche's pain was beyond belief, beyond fury or tears, and her sorrow was beyond description.

Next Persephone guided Psyche to the room of sacrifices to false gods. Here Psyche faced the fact that she too had sacrificed herself, her love, and her talents to the wrong gods. She had sacrificed her ministering spirit to male rationality and had gotten only endless service as her reward. She had sacrificed her time to a waiting game—the false hope that one day Eros would sit down with her at the table she had laid for them. Under the pressure to conform she had sacrificed the intensity of her erotic love, turning to her children and to her religious causes and social duties to fill the void of lack of passion. And she had found her bed empty. She had sacrificed her feminine, all-inclusive, individualistic love by obeying false gods (and their false values). And she had found only meaninglessness and despair.

In spite of all the seeds she had sorted and all the golden fleece she had gathered, in spite of being able to consciously forget, she had on some deeper level sacrificed her life and loves to a male-ordained authority—an authority that murdered any consciousness of the value of the Feminine and mutilated the meaning of erotic love. And all the time Psyche had passed up the loves she could have had.

Psyche had to face the terrible hurt that serving the wrong gods had caused: she had not known how to love herself enough, so she had not known how to receive fully the masculine love that was offered to her. She had not known how to love Eros all by herself. She had needed some belief system to bridle her passion and curb the masculine love she yearned for but could not completely receive. Denying the reality of the whole of herself, she had left the man she loved all confused. She had loved him as the pieces of himself—one minute a god, the next minute a man, and the next a beast. He had had no feminine mirror in which to see his masculine self. Psyche had given him only pieces of her self and gotten only pieces of him in return. She had not known how to love him and receive his love all at once.

Conscious of their crushed possibilities, Psyche's heart broke for Eros and the man he could have developed into. They had entered their relationship with such high hopes. Eros had been so loving and caring, concerned about her daily welfare and little happinesses. But inevitably the patriarchal way had aborted the promise of such passionate masculinity maturing into the full stature of manhood. Eros had changed the object of his passion. He stopped thinking about Psyche and started focusing on his ambition and his work, the only acceptable object of passion for patriarchal man (except for sports). And Psyche had substituted service for her passionate ministering spirit. Maybe enough service would bring her his recognition, but denying herself and trying to fit the patriarchal picture had not changed him. He did not love her any more or less than he wanted to.

Each had forsaken the erotic love that had drawn them together. And so they were divided and alienated from each
other. Psyche wept. How could she ever overcome the alienation, the disunity, and the death of herself and her love?

Because Psyche had shown the courage to face the
unfaceable and accept the unacceptable without offering any
excuses or explanations, Persephone could now show her the
way to overcome. Psyche needed to have the courage of the
now—the now of winter and the now of spring. Persephone
introduced Psyche to the fact that the eternal is in the now,
or it never is at all. The now was where Psyche must start
from. But it was also where she would find the eternal—not
as a whole but in the bits and pieces that began to make
the whole. The bits and pieces contain the eternal, so she
had had a glimpse of the whole even as she struggled towards
it. Do not despise the bits and pieces, Psyche, but taste and
savor the eternal love they contain.

Persephone could now reveal to Psyche the mystery of
the Feminine. So she led her to the room of demons—all
the demons of her dear dead hopes and lost loves that tor-
mented her soul, and all the demons whose energy she had
been taught to fear. She had been taught that the might of
sexual desire was evil, that the force of inclusive love was
promiscuous, that erotic love was sinful and led to damnation.
The power of the vulnerability of being human was called
weakness. The might of instincts was called bad. And most
important, the energy of the body was called dirty. Patriarchy
makes monsters out of these powers, some of which are
neither good nor evil but all of whose forces can be used for
enhancing or destroying life. According to patriarchy all
demons must be "made good" (that is, disempowered) by
the authority of man-made laws or the commandments of
"God." Otherwise they must be considered evil and avoided
at all costs. But there is no escape from them. It is the fear
of these "monsters," and the fear that our "evil" will be found
out that gives us nightmares in the dark and free-floating
anxiety in the light of day.

So in this room full of demons Persephone revealed to
Psyche the mystery of the Feminine: the power to transform.

In the Feminine Principle is the power to change the bitterness of tears into champagne bubbles, bring success out of failure, heal the brokenhearted, set the captive free, and turn the bits and pieces in which eternal love dwells into one united whole. In the Feminine Principle is the power to bring new life out of death. Just as a woman's body mysteriously brings to life a new being out of the death of the ovum as an ovum and the death of a sperm as a sperm, so the spirit in the Feminine Principle brings to life a new reality, a new creation, a new person out of the death of the old. The now of winter becomes the now of spring.

It is this mysterious power of the Feminine that alone can make a woman a queen. No man can make a woman a queen. She is crowned queen in the depths of her feminine soul by her consciousness of her power to transform and regenerate.

A queen is different from a king. She is the one whose subjects gladly obey her commands. She needs no police force or armies. Her subjects gladly obey their queen, the one who knows how to make things better, how to bring life out of death. They obey her out of desire, not out of fear. Persephone revealed to Psyche that, as Queen of the Dead, all the demons of hell were her subjects. But she was also the Queen of Spring who could plant those demons in her feminine love. When she commanded them to love and bring forth fruit, they automatically obeyed their queen. So in the springtime the demons of winter come up as flowers that will bear much fruit.

Persephone explained that Psyche too, having plumbed the depths, had been crowned queen by the power that worked within her. She no longer had to be afraid or sorrowful, because she too had command over all her demons. All she had to do was plant them in the good soil of her heart and tell them to love and bear much fruit. And they would do it!

So Psyche accepted the "evils" and the hurts and the losses, and the power of the unknown to destroy. She embraced all that she had rejected. She held and cradled in her arms what she had thought were the ugly, mean, sinful parts of her self. She bent down and kissed the deformed faces. With tenderness and great gladness Psyche welcomed into herself her dear dead parts and all the powers that had made her afraid. She planted them in her heart, commanding all of them to love and bear fruit.

What she had rejected was now acceptable to her, and she was acceptable to what she had rejected. Not only did she love what she had cast out, but *she was also loved by what she had despised.* Psyche accepted their forgiveness. In full consciousness, stripped of all pride, Psyche had learned to love the totality of her self. And in that loving, Psyche restored love as the supreme, indestructible value.

In the room of demons Psyche asked their queen about the demons that pursued Eros. Persephone smiled and told Psyche that the great secret was that only a queen, only a conscious, sexual, spiritual woman, had command over demons. The demons that haunted her beloved could not be commanded by a man, not even a king or a god. But when a man gives his demons to his inner woman, the Feminine he consciously loves will command them to bring forth good fruit. And in the spring they will come up for the man, as the desires of his heart, bursting forth as the flowers and fruit of *his* garden.

Persephone then instructed Psyche in the lost art of loving according to the way of the Feminine Principle. Persephone showed her that love must love. If she tried to curb her love, and limit herself to just one flavor of love, not only would she limit her love for that person but she would deprive the very heart of the God/Goddesshead of the possibility of more love. And the God/Goddesshead has no other purpose than love. Persephone told Psyche that to be a queen—not a stand-in for a king, but a queen in her own right—she must love freely and trust her vision that the Divine Love in heaven is manifested on earth and made accessible to humans in the experience of erotic love between man and woman. In the darkest depths of hell Persephone showed Psyche the great light that shines when erotic love is allowed full rein. It fills man and woman with love and caring and tenderness. It overflows to all of creation—not one blade of grass nor one sparrow goes unnoticed. Each creature is loved consciously and passionately, and the whole wide earth rejoices in being loved.

Then Persephone took Aphrodite's pot and filled it with her immortal beauty ointment. Smiling her radiant, queenly smile, she handed Psyche the tightly shut pot.

For the sake of her love, Psyche had entered the world of the dead where she met death head-on. However, she was no stranger to death. She had experienced the agony of her own death when she died to the old, patriarchal ways of relating. She had experienced the death of Eros, her beloved, and the death of the Masculine, her earthly *other*, as they are defined by patriarchy. Now she had also drunk the sorrow of the death of her most intimate hopes. And she had seen, as though painted in bold strokes, how she had murdered them. Psyche accepted the irrevocability of death. And in her acceptance of that which is not humanly acceptable, she achieved her full stature as the mediatrix of death—the go-between between the desires of the human heart and the reality of death.

But in the realm of death Psyche had found the power of transformation and new life. There in the depths of hell her sexual "I am" and her spiritual "I am" were fused into an inseparable self. This self was separate from all others yet able to connect consciously and passionately with any who would respond. (She had grounded the power of her "I am" in the mystery of her own femininity, just as man must ground the power of his "I am" in his love of his own masculinity. And in that grounding she had freed her self of any unconscious ties to the Great Mother or the Spiritual Father or the Redeemer Son or the Phantom Lover.) It was this new "I am" that was not overwhelmed by death; the gates of hell did *not* prevail. Psyche prevailed.

She is. Life is. Love is. Eros is. So Psyche, a mortal, flesh-and-blood woman, stands for all time not only as mediatrix of the reality of death but, higher still, as Queen of Life. She was smiling as she consciously began her ascent.

THE GREAT
DISOBEDIENCE

At last Psyche was safely back on earth. All she had to do was deliver the pot of immortal beauty ointment unopened to Aphrodite, and Aphrodite would have to deliver Eros back to her and let her live. But her sufferings had been so great and her longing for her love so intense that she knew her beauty was nearly gone.

All Psyche had to do was obey the Goddess and she would be home free, delivered from her death. Just give Aphrodite the pot of immortal beauty ointment unopened, and She would have to give Eros back. What more could Psyche ask for? So she started towards the Goddess's temple.

Unbeknownst to Psyche, however, Aphrodite sat in Her Ocean Queendom of primordial femininity feeling something akin to terror. She waited with Her eyes squeezed shut and Her hands over Her ears, lest She hear Psyche's knock and see the woman who would not be a woman. Then what task would the Goddess be able to dream up to get Psyche to act on her own?

Up until now, Psyche had been obedient to the Goddess. She had done what Aphrodite had demanded in order to save her life and win Eros back. Though she had succeeded at each task, expanding her consciousness and intensifying her erotic love, though she had integrated her inner masculine self into her personality and become conscious of the value of being woman, Psyche still had not done anything on her own. She had initiated no action on her own behalf. Her womanhood still did not belong solely to her. (And the evolutionary power for all humankind was at a standstill.)

She had not yet claimed as her own that aspect of the Feminine which is strong and mighty in battle and in love. She had not taken into her self the power of the Feminine to destroy the indestructible, to move the unmovable, and to aggressively assert her sexual desires, the power of her love, and the power of her healing grace. She had not used the feminine, irrational, decision-making power on her own behalf. The very channels she needed to express the force of her passionate emotions and the might of her spirit were branded as evil by the patriarchal mind-set. (And they still are today.)

But Psyche had a choice: she could be a victorious "good girl" and do what Aphrodite had told her to do, or she could be her own woman and disobey the Goddess. If she decided to return the pot unopened to Aphrodite, she would get a "good girl's" reward. Her life would be restored— but within a patriarchy. She would get back a mother's "good boy," not a full-grown man in charge of his own masculinity. But if she disobeyed the Goddess and used the beauty ointment, she would get a woman's reward—the right and the responsibility to use the power of the Feminine. She would have to respond consciously and decisively to her power to generate beauty for her self—the power to move mountains and aggressively assert the goodness of the womanhood she had achieved.

But if Psyche obeyed, she would be consecrating the anonymous feminine of patriarchy—the faceless woman. She would be saying that the way to be holy is to be another obedient, unconscious, eternal virgin or another obedient, unconscious, holy mother—another unravished bride. Psyche's obedience would exalt undifferentiated, oceanic femininity rather than an individualized self. It would confirm the devaluation of the Feminine Principle, the authority of a patriarchal masculine, and the degradation of erotic love.

And Aphrodite would lose Her chance to restore the psychological and spiritual impact of erotic love.

But if Psyche used the beauty ointment for herself, perhaps she would learn the secret it held.

On her way back to the Goddess, Psyche passed by a clear, still pond. She stopped to look at her reflection. This was not vanity but the need to know. Psyche looked and saw her beauty ravaged. But what she saw was not the ugliness of aging or of suffering but the ugliness of obeying! The lines inscribed about her mouth and on her chin told the story of her hard determination, her willpower, and her battle fatigue. Standing by the pond, Psyche weighed the ugliness she saw against the pot of immortal beauty oil in her hand. If she gave Aphrodite the pot unopened, she would be assured of seeing Eros again. Her heart pounded at the thought. But whom would Eros be seeing? An obedient old woman?

So Psyche decided. She chose her self. If she were going to live she had to really live life, not just obediently exist. If Eros ever returned to her it would be because he really saw and loved *her*, not because she had obeyed his mother. For Psyche to regain his love for her based upon her obedience to Aphrodite, or even based upon her own accomplishments, was meaningless to her.

Thus, in a declaration of independence requiring the utmost courage, Psyche risked her heart's desire and her life itself. She disobeyed the Goddess!

She opened the pot to use just a bit of the immortal beauty ointment for herself—to be beautiful for Eros.

Psyche could not obey and be beautiful. She could not obey and be strong and mighty. She could not obey and be Psyche! There is no way to be in patriarchy and out of it at the same time! When she disobeyed, she became beautiful and good again. Now her soul was free to dance, and dancing, generate all the energy and beauty she needed. The purity of her spirit shone radiantly from her face. She was more magnificently sexual than she had ever been. When she disobeyed and used the beauty ointment for her self, Psyche took the mighty strength of the Feminine into her soul. She became a warrior strong in battle and mighty in love.

Single-handedly, Psyche changed the rules. The old rules maintained that in order to be spiritual one's body must be denied. A person could not be sexual and spiritual at the same time. According to patriarchal values suffering, limiting love, and pinching life are signs of being spiritual and good. The patriarchal mentality maintains that in order to be good a person must kill the appetites of the flesh, kill any sexual desire that has not been legalized or sanitized by state or religion, kill any urge to know the truth, and certainly kill any love for anyone outside of one's legalized and sanitized relationships.

Everyone still stuck in the old, judgmental value system wants the safety of obeying rules. All patriarchal religions and their values, which are ingrained into the collective unconscious, teach that if all the right rules are obeyed then a person can become perfect, a person can be saved! But obeying is what makes people mean and ugly. To want to be safe, to want to be righteous, to want to be saved, instead of wanting to live life *is* ugliness and meanness. Feeling good and being secure do not go together. Had Psyche obeyed the Goddess, she would have enforced the false goodness of patriarchal values. She would have endorsed the lie that obedience leads to life, to love, and to fulfilled relationships. But obedience does not enrich life or practice love, indeed it cannot; obedience leads to death.

In the mentality that celebrates death, beauty ointment had become the sacred oil for anointing the dead. (Observe today the prosperous funeral business and note that there is a whole service—whether religious or secular—accompanied by ritual to celebrate a funeral but there is none to give thanks and celebrate a birth.) But now, as the Queen of Life, Psyche changed that. She reclaimed the beauty ointment, using it to anoint the living and affirm the reign of life—especially the living Feminine and the reign of *her* life.

This is not as easy as it sounds. The sovereignty of life is the sovereignty of the Feminine. Each one flows from the deep, mysterious ground of being, which is the source of both terror and beauty, both aversion and desire. The Feminine demands of everyone who would live life fully, the acceptance of the ugly along with the beautiful, the dark along with the light, death along with life. In fact, the Feminine demands not only that they be accepted but also that they be responded to! By claiming the sacred oil for her self, Psyche responded to the sacredness of her life.

What Psyche's disobedience did was enforce a new reality: the truth that to rejoice in life, to feel exuberantly happy, sexy, and full of love, is the sign that the Holy Spirit lives in human flesh. Real goodness comes straight from a happy heart. And a happy heart lights a woman's face with an immortal beauty. Such radiance reverses the aging process.

By taking the immortal beauty ointment for her self, Psyche developed a new level of consciousness, one that allowed her to be both in her body and fully conscious of the Infinite at the same time! She could feel the goodness of her sexuality, the power of her spirit, and the total *Otherness* of Divine Goodness simultaneously. Being true to her self (using the beauty ointment) enhanced not only Psyche's life but also the lives of those around her, because it made her eternally beautiful and good. A soul of beauty is a joy forever.

Fully woman, Psyche took the immortal beauty ointment of the Queen of Spring for herself, as her right—a right she had earned by bringing the beauty ointment out of the depths of her own unconsciousness. In her descent into hell she had had to give up any last vestiges of a virginal or maternal way of relating. And there was no going back. In the bright, white light of the Feminine that had shone into the darkest recesses of her soul Psyche had had to see and confront who she had become. Plumbing the depths of her unconscious, she had had to recognize and accept the consequences of her experience (and nonexperience) as well as the consequences of her ignorance and false knowledge.

And in that confrontation Psyche had severed any last bond that tied her consciousness of her self to an oceanic, all-engulfing, feminine mentality—or to a domineering, demanding, masculine one. She had forsaken patriarchal values and the degrading picture of the Feminine they painted.

At the same time she had made a clean break from any last unconscious connection to any man or image born of masculine "superiority." She recognized that any lingering dislike she had for men or for any particular man was just her own feelings trying to get her to end an unhealthy, unconscious way of relating to men and to her self. By opening the pot of beauty ointment for her self Psyche declared the great "I am" of her self as she had found it in her depths. She declared her own uniqueness of spirit and her own wholeness as the fully sexual person she was.

This Great Disobedience restored the authority of a consciousness that is oriented towards the Feminine Principle. Feminine-oriented consciousness contains the ability to see the many layers of reality, to envision new ways of relating, to decide, and to act. Psyche's Disobedience made real the supreme value of the all-inclusive love of the Feminine, the final authority to love oneself. And it confirmed the way of freedom, the freedom to become more and more the person one was created to be. Without such freedom erotic love cannot grow and create. Her Disobedience resanctified the love of woman for man. Loving herself, she was consciously beautiful. She viewed herself as desirable and was therefore desirable; she was so in tune with her inner feminine self that her natural feminine radiance lit up her whole being. And being consciously beautiful became her new way of relating to Eros. The sanctification of her womanhood thereby consecrated the mystery of *Otherness* and the holiness of erotic love.

By her disobedience Psyche initiated her own independent action; she began to live. Taking the beauty ointment signified the end of tasks and the beginning of living. The doing and being were over; she had accomplished her tasks. Using the beauty ointment is what to do after one has learned the feminine way to sort the seeds and gather the golden fleece, after one has filled the crystal vessel with the water of forgetfulness, and after one has learned how to descend into hell and survive. Doing and being are merely processes which can be known: there is a beginning, a middle, and an end. But living cannot be known: it has no beginning, no middle, and no end. Living life means penetrating the unknown.

Whatever opens up or penetrates the unknown is beauty ointment. So it can be almost any pursuit that reconnects a woman with her creative ground, the part of her that is yet unknown—writing or singing or dancing or sculpting or playing the flute or taking a vacation by herself or with her husband or with her friends. By claiming her right to Persephone's immortal beauty ointment, Psyche could begin to live her life, *rooted and grounded in her consciousness of the value of her own feminine being.*

Psyche had planned to use just a bit of Persephone's immortal beauty ointment for her self. But she had had to take the whole package. She could not live by trying to live just a little. Beauty potions open wide the door into the unknown, and once opened it cannot be closed very easily.

THE SECOND
AWAKENING

But alas and alack, a strange, invisible vapor rushed from the opened pot. Overpowered, Psyche fell into a sleep so deep that she dropped to the ground as if dead.

This sleep was not a punishment for Psyche's disobedience. Aphrodite did not even know about it yet. The myth makes this clear: it was the fumes from the beauty ointment that caused Psyche's sleep. Aphrodite wanted Psyche to take the ointment and use it for herself. She wanted Psyche to affirm her passionately conscious, individuated womanhood and the power of her imperfect human love.

Obviously, the sleep that overcame Psyche represents death. Psyche had completed her tasks; her work was finished, and from this sleep she would enter heaven. But Psyche's sleep also represents the regenerative power of the kind of sleep that results from bringing the immortal beauty ointment up from the depths of the Feminine.

Through regeneration everything changes, and everything is changed (though everything may look the same). A whole new reality is born, not just a new insight or perspective. The sleep of renewal would transform Psyche into a new person. When she awoke she would experience her self as a new being—not constantly and consistently, but nevertheless as the reality of her self. First and foremost she would experience her new being as love: not as love for someone else, not even as love for her self, and not as being loved (although all these emotions were included), but simply as love. Instead of striving for righteousness, she would feel her imperfect human self accepted! She had no wish to present her self to the Supreme Being as acceptable by her own merits. She had deserted the ranks of the obedient ones, the guardians of the law and religion. The state of her mind, the ecstasy of her heart, and the freedom of her soul had shown her that something had happened to her. She had entered a new reality—the reality of acceptance. When she awoke she would be a new creation. The old state of affairs had died and a new state of affairs was arising.

In this new state of affairs Psyche would use the love that is at the heart of the Feminine to nurture her soul and instruct her in the wisdom of living her life. She would use the power of this love to penetrate the unknown emotions in her hidden self with the light of the Feminine. This loving light would reveal to her an abundance of the life-force and an intensity of heightened feelings in the depth of her being. And being regenerated, Psyche would have a strengthened and enlightened self that could contain such an increase of feelings and life-force without being ruptured by their power. Experiencing her new being as love, Psyche could sustain the impact of living life in multiple dimensions.

Being regenerated, Psyche would experience her new being as freedom—freedom from the habit patterns that held her emotionally obligated to the patriarchally designated *others*: her mother and father, her siblings, her aunts and uncles and cousins, her husband and children and the family they would form. She would be free to see and think, to hear and feel. She would be free to act according to her own inner authority, which is the authority of a self who is governed by love. She would be free to experience uncertainty and faith and to let faith arise from fear. She would be free to experience despair and find hope in the great abyss. She would be free to question, free to ask what truth was. She would be free to use the wisdom of the world, because she would be free from any ties to religions or philosophies or psychological doctrines that claimed a monopoly on truth.

As a new being, she would be free to immerse herself in science and not get lost in its passionate theories, free to immerse herself in the beauty and the execution of art and not burn up in its excitement. She could plunge into politics and not get killed in its dangerous use of power, or plunge into economics and not let its mental discipline stifle her creativity. She could study and not let the stimulation of thinking replace doing. Psyche would be free to enjoy eating and drinking and being sociable without becoming addicted or seduced by ritual. She would be free to enjoy the ecstasies of sexual love, the warmth and comfort of family life, and the intimacy only friendship offers, because she would not lose her self or mistake her self for the role she was consciously playing.

The wisdom and power of this world is in all these things—and all these things, with their wisdom and power, would belong to Psyche when she awoke. She would not be afraid to accept what was given to her—all the world—along with its beauty and wisdom, its riches and power. She would not try to escape the abundance of life by behaving as if she were a pauper and stupid! And all the world could belong to her, because she would have become a new being. She would enter a new reality in which she would be vitally aware that however great the wisdom of the world in all its forms might be, it could not know love. And all the power of the world with all its means could not reach love. Only a person who is not afraid to fail, who is willing to lose, to be broken, even to die, can begin to know and reach love.

And so when Love awakened Psyche, she would experience her new being as fulfillment—as heaven itself. She had learned that the eternal was present in time, in this moment of experience. The minutes pass, but the eternal remains. Minutes are not merely replaced by other minutes. Time is not in vain. Through regeneration the power of anxiety is broken; though Psyche would still feel its peculiar pain, it could not diminish or destroy her. It could not sap her energy. As a new being, Psyche could be deeply concerned about very profound issues and not be anxious or worried or worn out by them; she would know that, no matter how profound or high or noble their purpose, they were not her ultimate concern. Their fulfillment was not the fulfillment of her self, regardless of how wonderful and healing and helpful they might be for all humankind. Not even manifesting and broadcasting the love of the Supreme Being could be her ultimate concern or the fulfillment of her self. Her ultimate concern would be, as it always had been, her journey towards love, and the fulfillment of her self would come about through her union with love—the eternal individuation of her self, the eternal becoming more and more who she was created to be. From Life she was born and to Life she would return, eternally being regenerated, eternally being made new.

This new creation—Psyche's new being—and the new reality in which she would find herself had become possible because she had developed a self strong enough and solid enough to be transformed. Any woman who tries to use the beauty ointment for her self before she has completed all the preceding tasks can never be awakened from the sleep it induces; there simply is not enough conscious woman to awaken. There is not enough self to transform.

There is another kind of sleep, too, which results not from the powerful fumes of an immortal beauty ointment but from having finished the tasks, having transcended patriarchal values, and then not having anything else to do. This sleep results from the awful horror of having grown in truth and stature by completing the tasks and then coming up against the hard fact that there is nothing in a patriarchal culture with which to anoint the queenliness of one's womanhood, no music to celebrate the life one has found. The terrible pain of finding one's self and then having absolutely no way to express this love-filled self is almost beyond endurance. How can a woman experience her new being as love when love is denied her by an emasculated, deformed Masculine? How can she experience her new being as freedom when she is subjugated by the culture in which she lives? How can she experience her new being as fulfillment when her primary mode of being—the Feminine Principle—is debased or worshipped out of existence? To drift into the sleep of nothingness is often the only relief from pain that a woman can find. It can take a very long time for a woman to awaken from this drifting kind of sleep.

But Psyche's sleep was a sleep of renewal. It was not, however, the sleep of a Snow White or a Sleeping Beauty. It was not the sleep of youth. It was the sleep of a full-grown woman, ripe and sweet with her own personal femininity and individualized by an integrated, strong, and sexual inner man-self. The handsome prince awakening the innocent girl would no longer do. It would take much more than an eternally rescuing hero, a macho male, or a self-righteous know-it-all to awaken Psyche from this sleep. (By the same token, no Snow White could free Eros from his mother.) Psyche needed a king. She had become a queen. Only the passionate, sexual love of a man who was secure in the exuberance of his masculinity, who was made a person conscious of his self by his own well-loved, inner feminine self, could awaken her now.

Psyche needed a man who could consciously desire a passionate woman and who was not afraid of the power of the Feminine. She wanted a man who had let his inner woman-self integrate his maleness, his animalness, and his godness into a whole of powerful masculinity. She did not want a man who was domesticated, tamed, diluted, made safe and stingy, or molded in any way. She wanted a man who was not afraid of his positive male sexuality, who had fully accepted the invisible and untamable spirit of the Masculine as his birthright, and who delighted in the Feminine. (And she wanted a man who also knew that his dick was not going to fall off if he did dishes, vacuumed, or took out the garbage!)

When Psyche had fallen in love with Eros, a drop of hot oil from her lamp had burned him awake. Awake, he had seen. And in that seeing he had been penetrated by the magnitude of Psyche's passionate, conscious, erotic love. And he had hated it. Because he had not developed his masculinity enough, he was unable to respond to her with passionate love. He could not receive the magnitude of a woman's love.

So he had flown back home to Mama where he had nursed his tiny burn and his wounded ego.

But there comes a time in every male's life when he has to grow up or shut up, when he has to love a woman as a free, conscious human being or get out of her face and stop fooling around with her life. And Eros, as a man, was no exception. At some time, somewhere in the depths of his being, he had to respond to Psyche as Psyche. Otherwise he would never become a man at all. Sooner or later Eros had to face the ugliness within himself, which his obedience to patriarchal values had caused. He had to inwardly confront the meanness of his self-righteousness, which upheld his subjugation of Psyche and his right to control her. He had to accept responsibility for having cast the Feminine out of his existence and out of his culture. If he did not want to remain in his mother's house forever, a little prick of a bully dependent on the Unconscious Feminine, he had to take responsibility for loving Psyche.

Eros had to face the fact that the excluding possessiveness that patriarchy calls love cannot even recognize love. Indeed, it is incapable of knowing love. When it excludes the Feminine, "love" is unfocused in the universe. It is abstracted. It is love of humanity rather than love of a particular person. So, loving universally, loving humanity, loving ideas, man tries to use exclusiveness in order to bring his love back down to earth. And it simply does not work.

Loving a particular woman because she is *his* wife does not work. Loving a particular boy and girl because they are *his* children does not work. He loves these particular people because they are members of his family, his tribe, his church, his club. He cannot see them as the individuals they are. And his expectations of them are based on his insecurities and neurotic need to have his family and friends fit the proper patriarchal picture. In essence, he has substituted loyalty to his own kind (and their standards) for love. His "love" is therefore dependent on the source of his identity. He has no relationships. He hangs on, with all his strength, to the woman he despises—and he despises her because in casting the Feminine out he renders himself dependent on her (and once again he feels the helplessness of a baby boy).

When the passions of being human are excluded, love cannot be love. Without the activity of relating to each person individually and sexually, love becomes so spiritualized that it becomes love of souls instead of love of people. Devoid of the spirit of the Feminine and stripped of human sexuality, love becomes love of ideas and principles. Man then believes he must live by his principles. But a life lived according to principles is no life lived at all!

The result of respecting human sexuality, honoring sexual desire as the basis of consciousness, and regarding erotic love as holy would be a culture based on celebrating life and feeling good. However, this truth has been thoroughly wiped out of our thinking by patriarchal thought; it is beaten out of the realm of our imagination.

The exclusiveness in the masculine mode of being is useful only for evaluating things and determining causes and effects; when applied to love or to relationships it has proved destructive beyond belief. We have reaped the harvest of a masculine-dominated culture that utterly denigrates any possible value in the Feminine, and we receive a bitter crop of arms races, a destructive worldwide economy, and a rampant greed that has raped the environment of this, the only planet known to bear life. The Masculine must embrace and be embraced by the ameliorating capacity for inclusive love found in the Feminine Principle. The restoration of the value of the Feminine is vital for the evolution of humankind: it is vital for personal relationships; it is vital for international relationships; it is vital for the survival of our planet.

So if Eros wanted Psyche, if he wanted to experience the joy of his manhood, he would have to assume responsibility for himself, his thoughts, his emotions, and his actions and go to her. Psyche could not go to Eros in a patriarchy. It was Eros, not Psyche (patriarchal man, not woman), who had been judgmental and unloving. And the judgmental and unloving part of a woman is her tortured, unintegrated inner man, whom she has left in the hellhole of patriarchal values. Eros had to go to Psyche conscious that he had to free his ability to respond to her from every last loyalty to patriarchal beliefs—beliefs that perpetuated his suspicion and hate.

Psyche offered Eros a way out: the gift of the Feminine. The gift Psyche offered to Eros was the goodness of her sexuality, the treasure of her spirit, the riches of her feminine way of feeling and thinking, and the divinity in her all-inclusive, imperfect human love.

Eros was free to accept or reject it; the choice was his. If he accepted Psyche's gift, then he had to be prepared to accept the consequences as well. At the same time that Psyche was the liberator, she was also the destroyer—for consciousness of the value of the Feminine destroys the rule of patriarchy. It does not liberalize the existing patriarchal values; it inaugurates radically different ones.

Eros had to be willing also to enter a new reality. He had to be willing to be transformed into a new being. It was not enough to adjust or adapt to the evolving Psyche. He had to internalize and integrate into his very person the reality that both sex and spirit are to love with, that they are inseparable, and that they do not wait for or want perfection. This reality is not something one adds to the totality of being human; it is the very essence of what it means to be human. There is no quality that takes precedence over loving passionately.

He had to recognize the goodness of sexual desire and the holiness of erotic love; he had to know in his heart that every expression of human love was the manifestation of Divine Love on earth. If Eros wanted erotic love, then he had to admit that love begets love. He had to understand and inwardly digest the fact that loving is the antithesis of possessing. And he had to take a risk and embrace the Feminine way of loving inclusively. He had to see people as the unique individuals they were. Then, paradoxically, he would be free to love with all the power of his masculinity because he had learned to love the feminine way.

But in order to love with all the irrational power of the Masculine, he had to leave his mother's house (where all he could see was the distorted reflection of himself as a perfect god who felt betrayed by disobedient women. And how miserable this state of affairs makes a man feel is attested to by the depth of his depressions.) Eros had to see himself as

Psyche had seen him, as a man in whose animalness, maleness, and godness the Holy Spirit was incarnated. He had to see that Psyche's disobedience was not a betrayal of him but a courageous expression of her irrepressible love.

Instead of casting her out and degrading the Feminine, he had to allow himself to be moved and touched by Psyche, a mortal woman, as well as by the irrational Feminine she represented. He had to accept her invitation to live life from the depths of his being. And he had to grow in consciousness of himself enough to see and to know in the depths of his heart that no matter how many people she had relationships with, no matter how many men she loved, he was the center and focus of her erotic love. He had to understand that no matter how hard he had tried to cast himself out of her heart, he had not succeeded. No matter how his jealousy, his false accusations, his hatred, and his resentments had hurt her, they were not strong enough to cast him out of her heart. She loved.

As a woman, Psyche had sent Eros into the depths of himself. And he had experienced it as hell. He had tried to escape by running home to mother. But he could not escape his experience of falling in love with her, falling into a love which had opened his heart to that joy which excludes nothing in the universe.

Only in the experience of contrition, in which pride is ground to powder, could he become man enough to see again the one whom he truly loved with his whole heart.

The myth does not describe the specifics of his struggle towards consciousness, but Eros reenters the story as a man—a man strong in his masculinity and sure in his love of the Feminine, a man who could make people laugh and sing, dance and celebrate the joyful holiness of life. He had become a man who had received into himself the untamable spirit in the masculine sexual presence and who rejoiced in the wild abandon of his own caring and tenderness.

Eros, healed of his wounds and walking about, heard the thud of her fall. He flew to her and, dropping to his knees, felt the soft current of her breath on his face. Eros took Psyche by the shoulders and shook her awake.

But no man had better try to shake a woman awake until he has learned to love and value the feminine mode of being as he values his own. Rest assured that no man who is without the treasure of the Feminine passionately alive in him can ever awaken a fully adult woman.

Eros, now fully man, came to Psyche.

"Psyche, Psyche! Wake up. I love you and in love there are no endings, only beginnings."

Psyche blinked her eyes open and saw the face of her beloved. Her joy exploded! In rapture, they beheld each other, their love overflowing. And the love that moves the universe knew no boundaries in their bodies; spirit joined with spirit in high rejoicing; two bodies united, yet two wholes remained. So gladness came to be her handmaiden and mirth her companion.

In their freedom to be and to love as the individuals they had become, Psyche and Eros reconnected the passion of their sexual desires to the uncontrollable Spirit of the Holy. Thus they restored the true meaning of conscious, passionate sexual love: to experience the holy extravagance of heaven on earth, to grow in love and consciousness (of self and of the *other*), and to respect life and personhood. In their passion Psyche led Eros, as he led her, into the deepest places of Paradise in their bodies to experience there the ecstasy of their souls.

IMMORTALITY

Afterwards, Eros wiped the beauty ointment off Psyche's face and slipped it back into the pot, slapping the lid on tight. He gave it to Psyche and told her to take it to his mother; She would never know the difference. Then he flew to Mount Olympus to plead Psyche's case for immortality before his father, Zeus.

Of course, there was no case to plead, for the king of the gods readily agreed. He sent Hermes to bring Psyche immediately up to Mount Olympus. In the meantime, all the goddesses and gods assembled for a great feast. Then, with all gathered together, Zeus himself handed to this mortal woman the cup of nectar that imparted immortality.

Psyche reached out and took the cup from Zeus's hand. But before she drank she turned and looked at Aphrodite. There stood the most radiant Goddess of all, smiling at her with tears like diamonds on her cheeks. And Psyche knew. She comprehended that what was almighty was the everlasting strength of the Goddess's love. With human tears wet upon her face, she smiled back at Aphrodite. Then she drank, and straightaway two beautiful butterfly wings sprang from her shoulders. Though she became immortal like the gods, Psyche remained forever human.

In her "failure" to obey Aphrodite, Psyche won! By remaining faithful to her vision of love, Psyche reestablished within her self, within Eros, and within the gods themselves the value of the Feminine Principle, in which each unique, unrepeatable, individual self is held sacred. And by remaining faithful to her self, Psyche restored the supreme authority of love, the authority to love one's self. Single-handedly she turned reality right side up again. And so Eros won, and Zeus won, and Aphrodite surely won! There were no losers. Disobeying the Divine for the sake of the imperfect human made winners of everyone—immortals and mortals alike!

Thus did Psyche, the representative of the human soul in both men and women, win for all humankind the possibility of individual immortality. The consciously developed feminine self in each sex is what saves the Masculine as well as the Feminine and allows a person to enter heaven.

The beauty that Psyche had claimed for herself was the beauty of autonomy. And autonomy is eternal! Being autonomous means consciously and freely choosing to be one's self. It means placing a value on oneself that no one, not even one considered divine, can disqualify. Regardless of what Eros might or might not do, regardless of what Zeus might or might not do, regardless of what Aphrodite might or might not do, Psyche had chosen her self. She was capable of existing independently, beyond morals and duties. She was sexually and spiritually autonomous. She was her own self-governor and her inner voice was her authority.

Psyche's entrance into heaven was not the result of her striving or of having completed the tasks or of some god's redemption. It was her victory over obedience and success! In her last task she failed: she did not complete it. Moreover, she used for her self what was meant for the Goddesses alone. Her disobedience was radical! She did not just neglect to finish the task; she decided to choose freedom. She decided to choose her self. She chose to become a new being. She was willing to die so that she could become a new creation— the Psyche she was created to be.

Although she became like the Immortals, Psyche remained *who she was*. She never became a goddess. She remained consciously and passionately woman. Her new being in no way negated her humanity. On the contrary, it enhanced her humanness; she had never been such a vitally alive woman. And so do all of us remain forever who we are. Though worms destroy our bodies, it is in our flesh—in our humanity, in our individual personalities—that we shall enter Heaven. For it is from Life that we are made, and it is to Life more abundant we shall return!

The beauty of autonomy then bestowed upon Psyche the beauty to be fully and wholeheartedly intimate. And intimacy is eternal. Though naked we are born and naked we must return to Life, we take our relationships (or the lack of them) with us. Psyche had created the individual who she had become, and so there was a real, live person who could be intimate with those who chose to be intimate with her—and intimate eternally. But to make a personal connection with Psyche, others had to respond to her by changing and growing up. They too had to become autonomous.

So Eros could see this new Psyche and say, "Ah, there is someone who can be intimate." But if he wanted that someone, then he, too, had to be autonomous. He had to become a self-governing person, capable of exercising self-directed freedom and moral independence. He had to be conscious of his self in order to connect with another conscious self.

And Zeus could say, "There is someone I am related to—what is required of me before I can be intimate with her?" What he had to do was forsake what patriarchy had told him, that the disobedient deserve to die. In fact, Zeus himself had to disobey! And he did. He initiated independent, *disobedient* action. He handed to Psyche (the disobedient woman) the cup of immortality, knowing that if Psyche accepted she would become immortal, even as he was!

When Psyche dared to claim what was her own, then Eros could claim (and be intimate with) the Feminine that was his own. And Zeus, representing patriarchy's highest heavenly authority, could claim and be intimate with that which was his own: his son Eros, the mortal woman who loved Eros, and their child (Zeus's granddaughter). The Divine could claim the human, which is eternally Feminine and Masculine, that belongs in heaven. And the human could claim the Divine that belongs on earth and is incarnated in all people. It was Psyche's expanded levels of consciousness that raised the levels of consciousness in men. And it was her expanded levels of consciousness that radically changed men as well as women, mortals as well as immortals.

Then Psyche and Eros were united in a new wedding. Apollo sang; and Aphrodite, her wrath and jealousy forgotten, danced at their wedding.

Having changed the reality of what it means to be human, Psyche and Eros were wedded by their free, full erotic love. They did not *get married.* They were not married by a legal or religious authority. The royal authority of human sexual love—their erotic love for each other—wedded them. Because of their new kind of relationship, in which the Masculine cherishes the Feminine and the Feminine transports the Masculine to new levels of meaning and delight, Psyche and Eros were reunited in heaven. In heaven there are no bonds, there is no ownership or belonging. In heaven there is only the freedom to be and the freedom to love. For in heaven all that matters is love.

And the consequence of that freedom was that the more Psyche and Eros loved, the more love they had to give to each other. The measure of their fidelity became the love and support they gave each other, their encouragement of each other's personal development, the compassion they showed each other for their common humanity, and the tenderness with which each protected and guarded the freedom of the other. Eros protected and guarded Psyche from the physical dangers of the world, comforting her and making her laugh. And Psyche protected Eros from meaninglessness by sharing her pleasure and guiding him into ever-expanding visions.

This new kind of wedding (made in heaven) ushered in a new reality on earth. For it was based on the right relationship between woman and man (who form the basic unit of any society). This new reality was the result of the reconciliation and reunion of opposites. Instead of being polarized into separate camps, the two sexes could live in harmony and passionate sexual love. In erotic love the need to control another vanishes. No longer did male and female adults have to come together because of some neglected need (camouflaged as romantic love) or infatuation by the recipients of their own projections or enforced marriage. This new kind of wedding reflects the inner marriage of the Masculine and the Feminine, which could now take place in the heart of each person.

Each person could experience the tremendous good feeling that erotic love created inside of them. Feeling the power of erotic love is what creates evolved women and men. Though lovers might enhance each other's pleasure and enrich each other's lives, they no longer had to be dependent on each other for their good feelings. They did not need to steal energy, power, or good feelings from any other person. Now a real man, one consciously married to his inner woman-self, and a real woman, one consciously married to her inner man-self, married each other.

And Apollo sang! Apollo, representative of the elegance of logos, the rationality of the word, sang. Of all the arts, music is the most rational and the most irrational, the most sensual and the most spiritual. In song, rationality accepts the leadership of the irrational and irrationality accepts the service of the rational. So the marriage of opposites, which took place on all levels of human endeavor, created the new reality and enhanced life.

Psyche and Eros experienced this new reality as truth, the truth that sets people free, the truth that nothing else mattered—only their love. They experienced the new reality as joy—that incredible joy that is generated only by the union of man and woman, the union of the Masculine and the Feminine, the union of differences. And it is this joy that introduces humans to the ultimate joy of being united with the love in the heart of the God/Goddesshead. Thus, they experienced the new reality as fulfillment—that extraordinary kind of fulfillment that includes the fragmentary, the unfinished, the peripheral. And of course, they experienced the new reality as the passion for love (as the passion for being woman and for being man).

The new reality as the passion for love is expressed in the reunion of what has been torn apart, both in our own hearts and in our relationships. And it is expressed in the reconciliation of the split between our heads and hearts. Love reconciles whatever is amiss, unintegrated, unresolved, and in disharmony between people. The love between Psyche and Eros, come together after their separate struggles for individuation, illustrates the passion for reunion and reconciliation, for acceptance and freedom. The way they came together as man and woman translated this passion into everyday, human terms. Psyche shared the power of her well-treasured femininity with Eros, and he shared the power of his well-loved masculinity with her. And thus the power of each was increased and the power of their union doubled.

By overcoming the dark of darkness—its threats and horrors—they reunited the two halves of being human but without destroying the identity of either half. They were able to do this because Psyche loved without being sure of an answering love from Eros or sure of the forgiveness of the Great Goddess.

In the middle of her great disobedience Psyche had suddenly realized that she was accepted, she was loved. This is radical: she was disobeying the Great Goddess and she felt accepted! It was not that she felt a person (such as Eros) or some higher power (such as Aphrodite) accepting her. She was not dependent on any person or any god for her sense of acceptance. She felt acceptance deep inside her self. She was accepted! And the fire of her love burned brighter than ever with an inexhaustible fuel. Her passion for love resulted in her understanding that the love in the very God/Goddess-head was the law of her own human being! It is Divine Love in people that is the power that reconciles and reunites, that accepts and heals. It transcends the power to kill, the power to separate, the power to destroy.

And it is Divine Love that is the power of the truth that set Psyche and Eros free. A collection of prescriptions for living can never set people free. Rules for thinking and feeling and doctrines for believing can only enslave and control. In the new reality people realize that truth can never be expressed in the form of something that can be written down and taken home and memorized. No prescriptions or invitations to join a special faith can guarantee entrance into the new reality. Not even Psyche's tasks are meant to be a law.

The truth that sets us free liberates us from rules and regulations, doctrines and dogma. It liberates us from destructive feelings of unworthiness and guilt. It releases us from a deadly self-rejection. We have inherited a false reality from patriarchy. And this false reality—that an almighty being (an almighty father) has the power of life and death over us, the power over us to grant life everlasting or decree eternal damnation—holds us in the grip of the lies that patriarchy claims are the truth. But we can know that this is an untruth, because it does *not* set us free and make us joyful. Instead of feeling joy we feel shackled and burdened, afraid and unfulfilled.

The way people can identify the truth that sets them free is by the feeling of joy. They want to dance and sing, jump for joy, and hug other people. Their good feelings overflow to all of creation. What is the power of such truth that it can liberate us from guilt and fear, from controlling and being controlled? It is the power of love! The truth that sets us free is rooted in Divine Love and does not desire to control. It lets go while it cherishes; it exonerates while it fosters growth. And such truth takes place here and now; it is in people and it is manifested in imperfect, beautiful human love!

Thus freed to encounter imperfect, beautiful human love, Psyche and Eros experienced the new reality as a passion for joy. Joy is intense, fierce, colorful, and venturesome. Both its heights and its depths are extreme, demanding the utmost that people can bear to experience. A passion for joy does not mean a continuous escape from pain and an incessant pursuit of excitement. Indeed, the passion for joy contains the ability to sustain an awful lot of pain, deprivation, and work. People can disregard travail, tribulations, woe, heartache, and misery when they are focused on the development of their selves and on the people and things they love. The desire to be united with others as they are is a mature desire. Intense feelings of joy are generated when estrangement is overcome, and when a place is found in the soul where hearts and minds can meet in spite of differences, in spite of hurts and deep wounds.

In this life there is no way to avoid differences. And there is no way to avoid the consequences of outrageous fortune: the sorrow of grief, the sorrow of loneliness, the sorrow of dreams unfulfilled. In this world there will always be earthquakes, fires and floods, disease, deprivations, and death. But with the creation of the new reality it is joy that prevails, in spite of sorrow.

Where there is fulfillment there is joy, and where there is joy there is fulfillment (even if only for a second). In the depths of hell Psyche had learned that fulfillment does not depend on completion (much less perfection); it exists in the bits and pieces we as humans are able to manage.

Death is not something external; it is a reality that lives within us—until a power that is stronger and sweeter can expel it and bring a new reality to replace it. Impassioned love is stronger than death. And it is sweeter than ending all pain. It can bear all things. It overcomes separation and alienation. Death may be given power over all things finite, but it has no power over love. Love is eternal—even in the bits and pieces of living.

Though our suffering may be profound, joy is more profound. The end of the way of Psyche is joy because joy cannot be separated from love.

So of course Aphrodite danced at this wedding! Love had triumphed! Of course Her anger and jealousy were gone. Though the course of patriarchy might obscure truth, joy, and love until its power was spent, the Goddess of love and light and laughter had defeated the powers of darkness. Psyche was free of the patriarchal system on earth and in heaven! She was free of any system. And, by the power of her erotic love and the steadfastness of her courage, she had freed Eros and Zeus from the force of patriarchal regression.

Aphrodite, and all heaven with Her, rejoiced that through Psyche—the free, conscious expression of the Feminine—She had restored the psychological and spiritual impact of the truth of erotic love.

When the blessedness of erotic love is restored, the valued Feminine sets the Holy Spirit free to move. And moving, It stimulates our hunger and thirst for love and beauty, for justice and freedom, for abundance and caring, for intellectual activity and spiritual transformation. With a healthy appetite for goodness restored, the Holy Spirit in us and among us fills us with compassion and harmony. Psyche had freed the powers of love and creativity to become the motivating forces in people's lives. The celebration of life became the celebration of love. The erotic love between man and woman affects all humankind, drawing all people together. It cannot help but do this; erotic love is what balances and unites the basic unit of all societies. Erotic love is the greatest manifestation of Divine Love on earth, and it is this manifestation of human love that gets us into heaven.

Psyche's new function was to make so clear the love of the Goddess for all of Her creation that people could rejoice in being human. For the judgment of the Feminine is that people deserve to live! Even the ugly ones, even the evil ones, deserve to live. Even if the criminal has to die, the Goddess can receive him and restore him to life in Her universe. Planted in the good soil of the Feminine, the worst of winter "dies" and comes up as the beautiful, fruit-producing flowers of spring. No matter how ugly people may act, each deserves the love of the Great Goddess. (She loves them just as Psyche loved Eros in spite of his ugliness to her, only more.) And the successful and prosperous, the courageous and strong, the beautiful and wonderful people also deserve the tender care and love of the Great Creating Goddess.

But without consciousness of the irreplaceable value of the Feminine there is no place for people to plant their discarded choices, their leftover energies, their evils and uglies. And there is no power to confirm their goodness. Psyche had to be very clear about her function. *It was not to contend with evil but to convey the love of the Great Goddess.*

And how well she now knew the unrelenting strength of the love that resides in the Feminine. The love of the Goddess is no easy sentimentality! The purpose of conveying such love is to encourage people to grow in the rich soil of the Feminine. Then, rooted and grounded in Her love, they could let their souls dance in the light of Her freedom. (The love of Goddess the Mother in no way negates or lessens the love of God the Father.)

What Psyche and Eros accomplished was much more than the destruction of patriarchy. Their relationship, reestablished in the freedom to be human and the freedom to love, resulted in an ever-increasing and intensifying erotic love, overflowing in good measure to all people. Such love creates the new reality, a reality based upon the holiness of erotic love, the irreplaceable value of the Feminine, the necessity of the Masculine, and the goodness of being human. This new reality is the only foundation upon which a higher civilization can be built.

When men and women are whole and free they are able to construct new, flexible belief systems—belief systems that can hold the energy of erotic love. They can also construct mind-sets that can adapt to the ever-unfolding possibilities that arise in all erotic relationships (sexual or otherwise). As relationships evolve, people's mind-sets about how they can interact need to change.

Out of their love a daughter was born; out of their love a new reality was given. Psyche and Eros named her Pleasure. She was both human and divine.

Out of the union of Psyche and Eros a new being, named Pleasure, is born. She heralds a new possibility full of hope and faith and love, a love which is above all and beyond all and included in all! The sexual transformation of Psyche and Eros, the marriage of the Feminine and the Masculine within each of them, is also the spiritual transfiguration of woman and man. It is the essence of being human, and being human is the highest calling on earth. (Being angelic is not better than being human.) The purpose of the new culture is to enhance life, to stimulate growth, and to enrich each individual.

In the new reality people will once again be aware of the sacredness of life, which inspires awe and wonder. They will once again revere the beauty and mystery of birth. Once again people will consider the power to create—to be productive as mature men and women—greater and more important than the power to destroy. Death must serve life. Life must no longer serve death—or pay for war. As in prepatriarchal times, people will stand in awe before the mystery of the creative force of the Feminine. Only woman has the power to give birth. Man receives his life from woman. And it is from the Feminine Principle dwelling within him that man receives his creative ideas. It is his inner woman who renews his inner man with might, according to the riches of her glory.

But without masculine passionate love, the creative, renewing powers of the Feminine lie dormant. Psyche had needed Eros to shake her out of her second sleep.

In the new reality people will honor human sexuality and rejoice in sexual desire. Both sexes will be valued and loved for the irreplaceable qualities of the Feminine and Masculine Principles dwelling in them. It is the irrational combination of these two forces by the mysterious process of sexual attraction—the wedding of the two halves of being human in holy erotic love—that produces new life, regenerating and empowering individuals through the use of love. By its very nature the new reality will destroy the diabolical system of ranking, dominating, subjugating, and degrading, which tears apart and disempowers through the use of brute force. In the new reality people will honor the value of each person, the goodness of sexual desire, and the holiness of erotic love. When people really desire to celebrate life and love (and know they can!) then they will not tolerate war and terrorism, domination and exploitation, overpopulation and greed.

In the new reality people will consider all things and all places sacred. This will be expressed in the joyous appreciation of everyday experiences: people are glad and excited to be alive. It will be expressed in the appreciation for the wonders of nature and the responsibility that each person takes for the life of this planet. It will be expressed in the appreciation for human creativity and the responsibility that each person takes for the place in which they live. The quest for knowledge (which is no longer considered evil) and the passion for freedom, abundance, and justice for all (which is no longer considered disobedience) will express the new level of consciousness.

In the new reality people will express their "new beings" through the robust, good-natured way they live and work together. A creative playfulness will abound—in work, in art, in music, dance, and song. Freed of fears and guilt, sexual repression and distrust of human nature, people will live in high spirits. And the pleasure of all that the Supreme Being has created will be manifested in each moment and in every place. It will be manifested in every person and between those people who have been willing to face death itself in order to accomplish their tasks and see, if only for a second, the *immensity* of the love in the heart of the God/Goddesshead for Their whole creation. So, by giving birth to Pleasure, Psyche became the mother of a new way—the fulfillment of an ancient way—of being human for us all.

APPENDIX A:
A BRIEF HISTORY
OF PATRIARCHY

It is important to remember that patriarchy is a historical happening; it is not inevitable or natural or ordained by "God." Nor did it create civilization—invent writing and accounting, learn the course of the stars, develop technology, or create art. Patriarchy has a beginning, a middle, and an end.

We know from the trail of conquest that by 4000 B.C. the patriarchal mentality and the nomadic way of life had developed a common value system. Through migrations and conquests across the Eurasian steppe and south into the Arabian and Sinai deserts these nomadic peoples mixed and mingled. Linguistically and ethnically these people are today identified as Semitic in the south and "Indo-European" (Acheans, Aryans, Dorians, Kurgans), Turkish, and Mongol in the north. Though local variations of language and custom remained, a vast geographical area was unified by the love of warfare and its ever-increasing technology; the nomadic, patriarchal life-style; the catholic devaluation of the Feminine in male-centered religious and social values; and the lack of art, creativity, and production of goods.

The mobility of these nomadic tent-dwellers made it relatively easy to amass large numbers of experienced warriors whenever a strong man or chieftain so wished. These barbarians ultimately invaded and conquered all of Old Europe, Anatolia, Syro-Palestine and Mesopotamia, and India and China in the East. They changed the earlier civilized way of life, and they unbalanced the relationship between man and woman, between the human and the Divine, and between the human and nature. In this culture it was unquestioned that man was divinely made superior; it was his god-given duty to name everything and everybody. He was divinely ordained to conquer nature and rule all other people, especially the inferior female sex. It was his right to take whatever he wanted.

These nomadic peoples were uncivilized; they were barbarians. They did not care about anything that could elevate the soul, mind, or body. Their way of life—herding animals upon which they depended for milk, meat, and skins—did not produce wealth. Rather, it produced warfare and the patriarchal mentality. Because shepherded animals eat more grass than can grow in replacement, nomadic peoples must move constantly in search of new grass for their flocks and water for both their people and their animals.

From the beginning, therefore, these people had to use the masculine prowess of their group to fight others and the talents and wealth of their tribe to invent and make ever-more-efficient instruments of killing. Thus man—and anything masculine—became the exalted sex, and warfare became the way of life. Woman—along with anything feminine—was devalued.

The power to kill became the power to live; plundering became the way to gain wealth; the brutality of rape became the way to procure more wives. Killing, plundering, raping, the exaltation of man, and the devaluation of women are the basic values of patriarchy: values that have not changed very much today. Such values result in the degradation of human sexuality, the desecration of the holiness of erotic love, and the devaluation of the human spirit.

These barbarians saw the centers of civilization as little more than large oases to which, like everything else on earth, they had a right. By 2000 B.C., Mesopotamia had felt the devastation of its culture and cities by the Amorites, a Semitic group from the Syrian and Arabian deserts; and the cultures of Old Europe had felt the devastation of its cities and peoples by the Kurgans, nomadic tribes from north of the Black Sea. By 2300 B.C., Anatolia was inundated by a great wave of Indo-Europeans, speaking a Luwain dialect. Their invasion was marked by brutal destruction, killing, and rape. There is every archaeological indication of a massive recession and a decrease in prosperity, art, and technology that lasted for about a century. (And this is the syndrome that followed *all patriarchal invasions of the civilized world.* It makes no difference whether the invasion was by nonviolent infiltration or by brute force, the results are the same. It still manifests itself today: the rise of male domination and rule and the simultaneous oppression of women is followed by *recession, a decrease in prosperity and, often, war.*)

But as a testament to the strength of those first, indigenous peoples of Anatolia, we have the archaeological finds of a whole repertoire of symbolic art that shows that the original culture persisted through those dark ages, withstanding violent political change, brutality, and destruction. The iconography of these peoples—the iconography of the Great Goddess—reappears almost unchanged in the art of 1700 B.C., some six centuries later. And this strength of civilized values (symbolized and motivated by love for the Great Goddess and the sacredness of the Feminine) also manifests itself in the same way in all the other areas of the civilized world.

Civilized, life-respecting, prosperous, and peace-loving societies did indeed exist before they were invaded by patriarchal, barbaric tribes. Our heritage is *not* innately patriarchal. And not even 5000 years of patriarchal domination can completely wipe out the remnants of those first civilizations. Whenever we see the Feminine honored and human sexuality respected; whenever we see beautiful art, music, dance, or drama; whenever we see power as power *for* others (not *over* others), or men and women striving for peace, we are seeing our rightful inheritance. Patriarchy has succeeded only in interrupting that inheritance.

(For more about the history of patriarchy see Gerda Lerner, Riane Eisler, and the following entries in the *Encyclopaedia Britannica:* "Syria"; "Technology in the Ancient World"; "Turkey and Ancient Anatolia"; "Steppes, The History of the Eurasian———.")

APPENDIX B:
DEFINITIONS

The words we have shape the thoughts we think, the emotions we feel, and the values we believe in, whether we are conscious of it or not. They are therefore powerful tools in controlling the belief systems and mind-sets of whole peoples. By claiming the exclusive authority to compose dictionaries and create meanings, patriarchal man gained control of these powerful tools. Most dictionaries reflect the depreciation of the worth of the Feminine and the devalued status of women. They also reflect the inflated worth of the Masculine and the elevated status of men. Definitions of words regarding feminine values and concepts tend to be derogatory, just as definitions of anything masculine tend to be exalted.

Thus we have an inadequate, misleading, and often inaccurate vocabulary to express nonpatriarchal mind-sets and values. Our patriarchal language has made it difficult to describe the strengths and attributes of the Feminine, the experiences of women, and the many levels of female consciousness. Having a language in which the common term for human is "man" renders women invisible, as if they do not exist. With a language that ignores or tokenizes the female half of humanity and defines consciousness itself according to patriarchal beliefs and value systems, it is no wonder many women have a hard time finding consciousness as women.

Likewise we have a meager vocabulary for describing the experience of impassioned love. The patriarchal vocabulary is not only inaccurate, it is perverted. Patriarchy has systematically desecrated the meaning of erotic love. It has so cheapened the meaning of the once-sacred idea of the love between woman and man that today most people think of erotic love only in terms of debased (kinky) sex. This depreciation of erotic love is deliberate. Erotic love is what can cause both man and woman to become conscious, independent persons and frees them from the enthralldom of patriarchy.

Before we can accurately describe the experiences of men and women, therefore, it is necessary to redefine certain words and phrases, to untwist meanings, and to coin new words where needed. (For instance: we have the words "matriarchy" and "patriarchy" to describe a social system that is structured on the basis of domination, wherein one group is ranked over another. But we have no word to describe a social system or a government based on a belief system that includes the worth of both the Masculine and the Feminine Principles, one that values both the sexes equally, one that would reflect the reality of a shared existence. Thinking only in terms of a male-centered hierarchy—the dominant and the dominated—limits our perception of other possibilities. Without words to express different mind-sets, we are bound by the patriarchal habit of ranking.)

In this section I have attempted to explain what I mean by certain words and phrases used in this book. They are not unusual words or complicated phrases; the purpose of explanation is to clarify meaning and to readjust the values associated with certain concepts.

AUTONOMY: The ability to take responsibility for one's own life (self-government). The state of being emancipated from outside authorities (self-authorization). The disregard of all outside authority as final or personal. (Obeying traffic signals has nothing to do with one's personhood. Obeying the Ten Commandments has everything to do with one's personhood.) The freedom to have spiritual and sexual independence (self-empowerment). Freedom from the morals of others (self-sovereignty). Personal liberty (self-direction). The birthright of every human being.

CONSCIOUS and UNCONSCIOUS (adjectives)

CONSCIOUS: Awake, aware, alert, animated. Cognizant, perceptive, responsive, emotional. Sensitive, flexible, tender, thoughtful. Alive. Capable of astute feeling (as in "conscious distinction"), analytical thought (as in "conscious consideration"), and irrational emotion (as in "conscious love"). Deliberate, planned by will, design, or perception (as in "conscious disobedience"). Pertaining to the ability to act or produce an effect. Also the capacity for being acted upon or undergoing an effect (as in "conscious self-development").

Having mental and emotional faculties undulled by collective values, longings, or fears, and emancipated from prescribed belief systems. Possessed of authority. Powerful, comprehensive, magnified.

UNCONSCIOUS: Lacking consciousness. Not cognizant or sentient. Lacking awareness, alertness; not attentive, responsive, or thinking; not feeling; not emotional or sensitive.

Seeing only through the eyes of collective herd values that paint the world in black and white and shades of grey. Blind to the colors of being human and deaf to sounds of love. Incapable of thinking for oneself, incapable of feeling any emotions that are not prescribed. Hearing only the voice of some authority outside of oneself. Deaf to one's inner voice. Not differentiated or individuated.

CONSCIOUS and UNCONSCIOUS (nouns)

CONSCIOUS: The totality of an individual's cognizant, perceptive, imaginative, and emotional states, including the irrational as well as the rational. The awareness of an inward state as well as an outward reality. Critical awareness or concern and interest. The recognition of one's own inner feelings and thoughts. Presence of mind. Recognition of what belongs solely to oneself; individuation. The quality or state of being which is characterized by sensation, emotion, volition, thought, and feeling.

UNCONSCIOUS: That extensive area of the psyche (or mind or soul) that is not in the immediate field of awareness but whose content affects human emotion, thought, and behavior. A conscious person is cognizant of the unconscious.

CONSCIOUSNESS and UNCONSCIOUSNESS

CONSCIOUSNESS: Everything that a sentient human being perceives, knows, thinks, feels, or intuits. The power of self-knowledge and internal perception. The awareness of that which exists without oneself. The capacity to feel deeply and think acutely. Refined sensibility, shown in tenderness or ready sympathy. Any form of intellectual activity that leads to wisdom. The ability to differentiate between one's projections and reality, between the ego and the self.

UNCONSCIOUSNESS: A state that excludes all that a sentient human being can perceive, know, think, or feel. A state of not knowing, but believing one knew; of not seeing, but believing one saw; of not hearing, but believing one heard; of not understanding, but believing one understood. A state of being oblivious to our multisided, multidimensional reality and to the ambiguities of the human heart.

EROTIC LOVE: The kind of strong affection for another that is irrational, unexplainable, unjustifiable. Of divine origin; not manufactured or generated or produced by human effort or will. The kind of emotion that pierces the human heart, causing people to care consciously and passionately about one another. The unexplainable magnetism that draws people together in mutual devotion. More especially it is the deep, irrational affection that unites a man and woman in an enchanted relationship. The power of erotic love opposes death (unconsciousness) and overcomes it.

DIFFERENTIATION: Changing from the general and collective to the unique and individual. The act of defining, fixing, and marking the boundaries of self. The act of determining the essential qualities that define a person as an individual human being who is separate and distinct from all others. The process of becoming an adult person.

FEMININE PRINCIPLE and *MASCULINE PRINCIPLE*

FEMININE PRINCIPLE: The irrational, generative mode of being and doing, thinking and feeling, loving and living. It contains the abilities to conceive and create, to give birth and nourish, to envision and lead, to originate and produce, to feel and evaluate, to illuminate and transform. An essential mode of consciousness that goes beyond reason, logic, or analysis to comprehend reality. It is not exclusive to females, nor does it describe women. It is one of two elementary, primary, and essential forces of being human. Whether people are conscious of it or not, it is operative in both sexes—in women as their primary force of being, and in men as their secondary force of being.

MASCULINE PRINCIPLE: The rational, inseminating (fertilizing) mode of being and doing, feeling and thinking, loving and living. An essential mode of consciousness that uses reason, logic, or analysis (penetration) to comprehend reality. It contains the abilities to cherish and protect, to penetrate and impregnate, to reason and focus attention, to be single-minded and maintain undistracted purpose, to analyze, and to use logic. It is one of two elementary, primary, and essential modes of being human. It is not exclusive to men, nor does it describe men. It is operative in both sexes— in men as their primary mode of being and in women as their secondary mode of being.

(All human beings are born with these two essential principles, just as they are born with two eyes and two ears and a nose on the front of their faces.)

GYLANY: Coined by Riane Eisler in *The Chalice and the Blade.* This word fills a void in our language. It describes a culture or society based on erotic love and the recognition of the irreplaceable worth of the Feminine as well as the Masculine. Eisler defines the word on page 105:

> To describe the real alternative to a system based on the ranking of half of humanity over the other, I propose the new term *gylany.* *Gy* derives from the Greek root word *gyne,* or "woman." *An* derives from *andros,* or "man." The letter *l* between the two has a double meaning. In English, it stands for the *linking* of both halves of humanity, rather than, as in androcracy, their ranking. In Greek, it derives from the verb *lyein* or *lyo,* which in turn has a double meaning: to solve or resolve (as in ana*l*ysis) and to dissolve or set free (as in cata*l*ysis). In this sense, the letter *l* stands for the resolution of our problems through the freeing of both halves of humanity from the stultifying and distorting rigidity or roles imposed by the domination hierarchies inherent in androcratic systems.

There is abundant archaeological evidence that from 9000 B.C. to 3000 B.C. (and much longer on the island of Crete and other relatively protected places) a form of gylany existed in Old Europe, Anatolia, Syro-Palestine and Mesopotamia. It was an age of peace and great prosperity, an age of a great outpouring of art and technology. People cultivated crops of assorted grains and vegetables; they bred sheep, goats, pigs, cows, and donkeys; they kept vineyards and orchards; they mined obsidian, copper, gold, and precious stones; and they sailed the sea in vigorous trade. Since these people worked and *produced their wealth* no one had to steal or plunder or be afraid. *The power to produce was the power to live and live abundantly.* Creating wealth was seen as the power to enhance life and enrich the community. There was freedom for men and women to be sexually and spiritually autonomous. Neither women nor men were considered superior; both the Feminine and the Masculine Principles were highly valued. The sexes brought each other pleasure, and out of that pleasure grew peace and prosperity. Abundant life and exuberant love were celebrated.

Gylanic is the adjective to describe such a society. I plan to use these words as part of my everyday vocabulary, and I hope others will also.

(For studies of gylanic societies see Merlin Stone, Riane Eisler, and Marija Gimbutas.)

HUMAN (adjective): Of or pertaining to people—living, feeling, thinking, being, doing, loving, laughing, crying, spiritual, sexual beings who one day must die. Pertaining to characteristics of women and men that cut across sex, race, gender, and generations: the desire to do what is good, the desire to be good, and the instinct to care for the self and for others.

HUMAN BEING: A being that is composed of body, sex, spirit, and mind. A created, unrepeatable, unique, masculine and feminine being who can think and feel and know she or he is thinking and feeling. A mortal being in whose flesh the Eternal Spirit is incarnated at birth, whether or not this person is later conscious of the fact. It is this unlocatable, undefinable, invisible but observably active spirit that makes a being "human." A being with a tremendous capacity to love and a tremendous capacity for wisdom, for belonging, and for sexual and spiritual autonomy.

INDIVIDUATION: The process of becoming autonomous. The process of bringing into existence one's individuality, separate from all others and separate from the values of the collective unconscious yet capable of and eager for intimate relationships with other individuated people. The process of individualizing all the parts of one's personality so that they can be united into one whole, inseparable self—a self not divisible without the loss of something essential to its life. The process of recognizing pairs of opposites and then accommodating them within one's personality.

The urge towards wholeness drives the process of individuation. The cost of avoiding or denying this urge is the sacrifice of one's individuated, autonomous self and the spontaneous joy of living intimately.

INTIMACY: The passionate and conscious loving connection between two autonomous people. A relationship based on sharing the intrinsic and essential natures of the two people involved. A relationship between two people whose love and care for each other, rather than duty, bind them together. It includes rapport, caring, attention, listening, and, above all, empathy. It may or may not include sexual desire, but the connection is always erotic—the result of the love that draws people together and makes them care about one another.

INTIMATE: Personal and private. Belonging to or characterizing one's deepest sexual and spiritual nature. Whatever is shared by two individuals that pertains to their inmost beings. Whatever is marked by a warm, caring, vital, colorful, robust relationship.

IRRATIONAL and RATIONAL

IRRATIONAL: Whatever involves visions, dreams, hopes, and expectations that are beyond what is reasonable. Pertaining to or possessing the faculties of intuition, feeling, instinct, and faith, or knowledge attained by such faculties. Whatever is not governed by reason is irrational.

An irrational person is one who is capable of thinking in ways that are beyond the ordinary process of reason. An irrational mind is one that is open to nonrational reality, one that is susceptible to the influences of human tragedy and comedy, of human greatness and failure, of separateness in unity. An irrational mind is open to the inspiration of poetry, the holy, the inaudible music of the universe, and (above all) the mystery of love.

RATIONAL: Capable of reasoning; pertaining to or attained by reason. Whatever or whoever conforms to reason.

A rational mind is one that is capable of the ordinary process of "directed thinking"; it is open to but limited by the influences of reason. A rational person is capable of using reason, and a reasonable person uses reason as a habit. The rational is opposed to the fanatical, the misguided, the obstinate, the unreasonable, the sensational, and the erratical. It is not opposed to the irrational!

IRRATIONALITY and RATIONALITY

IRRATIONALITY: A way of arriving at solutions to problems and explaining reality that is not bound by the reasonable. A system of thinking that uses acumen, wit, intuition, instinct, and faith in order to go beyond rationality, analytical ability, logic, and reason. A way of apprehending truth by imaginative thought, insight, perception, intellect, paradox, and hope. The ability to dream the impossible dream and conceive a vision of what is yet to be. A way of communicating through words (and images) that evoke rather than explain the reality they express.

Contrary to patriarchal teaching, irrationality is not the same as craziness, delusion, folly, senselessness, eccentricity, or insanity. Rather, it is a state of mind or spirit that is capable of being astute, aware, sensitive, discerning, intellectual, sagacious, shrewd, understanding, and humorous. Moreover, it is the courage to be and do whatever it takes to accomplish the vision and fulfill the dream.

Irrationality has the ability to reach into the unconscious and bring into consciousness the spontaneous ability to be human—to laugh and to cry, to sing and to lament, to love and to desire solitude. It has the ability to strengthen with might a person's inner resolve.

Irrationality does not preclude a person from using reason or logic.

RATIONALITY: The reliance on reason alone for the establishment of truth and the accomplishment of what is reasonable. A way of arriving at solutions to problems and explaining reality that is based on logic, analytical ability, and reason. A system of thinking that excludes the irrational and relies on logic and the establishment of proof. The ability to focus attention on whether things or ideas are true or false. A way of apprehending reality that is based on the idea that reason is a source of knowledge superior to and independent of revelation, intuition, and sense perception. The belief that ideas, truth, and knowledge already exist and are attainable through reason rather than experience.

Rationality is opposed to empiricism. What a person experiences, such as anger or love, is not valid unless it agrees with what is considered rational (reasonable). What a person hears, sees, touches, smells, or intuits is subordinate to the authority of reason. Rationality is a state of mind controlled by the laws of logic and concerned with influencing the outer world.

NOTE BENE: Both rationality and irrationality form ways of apprehending truth. They are not mutually exclusive; rather they complement and counterbalance each other. Irrationality produces the revolutionary idea. Rationality allows reason to bring the idea into being. (This has resulted in the explosion of knowledge in modern times.) An irrational image conveys to one's consciousness the personally felt significance of what is perceived, whether in the outside world or in the soul. Both ways of apprehending truth are necessary. Loss of contact with irrationality results in the loss of meaning in one's life, and rationality has no power to make up for this loss.

MASCULINE PRINCIPLE: See *FEMININE PRINCIPLE and MASCULINE PRINCIPLE.*

THE OTHER and THE TOTAL OTHER

THE OTHER: One of two. That which is different from one's self but whose differences are needed in order to complete one's personality. A person's primary *other* is a person of the opposite sex. Woman is man's *other*, as he is hers. The differences between the sexes—their *otherness*—is the outward and physical manifestation of the two essential, fundamental principles of being human: the Feminine Principle (which is the *other* of the Masculine Principle) and the Masculine Principle (which is the *other* of the Feminine Principle). Neither men nor women can become fully human without the conscious incorporation of the *other* (principle) into the very fabric of their primary modes of being, so that whatever is *other* becomes part of them.

(In patriarchal societies man and woman are broken up as a pair of opposites. They are polarized into opposing factions, rather than united as a pair by erotic love. The result of this polarization is not the autonomy of either sex, but a mutual dependence in which each partner must give up consciousness of her or his own *other* sexuality—her or his own essential secondary mode of being. Man can identify only with what patriarchy considers masculine, and woman only with what the system considers feminine.)

THE TOTAL OTHER: Something or someone who is totally different. The Divine is the *total other* of the human. Yet the human needs the Divine in order to become fully human, and the Divine needs the human in order to express Itself.

OTHERNESS: Experiencing oneself as different from another person of the opposite sex, as well as experiencing the sexuality of that person as radically different from one's own self. The experience of the irrational union of what cannot be united rationally—two distinct and eternally different but equal human beings. The experience of the fitting together of man and woman through sharing their pleasure. The encounter between conscious Feminine and conscious Masculine elicits *otherness.*

The energy generated by sexual *otherness* symbolizes the energy generated by all the pairs of *others* (opposites) which must be woven into an individual's deepest inner self. The recognition of the worth of the Feminine, therefore, is crucial. Suppression of the Feminine, one half of being human, means the suppression of the natural and fundamental experience of *otherness* in our daily lives. The experience of *otherness* disappears if there are not two equal others!

PATRIARCHY: (Also see Preview.) The system of rule (or government) and the structure of society based on the moral and legal subordination of most men by a few men and all women by all men. This subordination by the domineering few is economical, political, emotional, intellectual, spiritual, and sexual.

Such a society deprives women (and lesser classes of men) of the same power the dominating men have. Women do not have the power to rule. They do not have the power to decide how men (or women) shall act. Any rights or resources women may have derive from the men who let them have them. Patriarchal rule means that at any time men have the power to rescind whatever rights women may have gained. In patriarchal value systems the very idea of "woman" is considered marginal or disappears entirely in the assumption that "man" or "mankind" represents all of humanity.

The institutionalization of the moral and legal subjugation of women is the patriarchal form of marriage—or its modern equivalent, the live-in relationship. Patriarchal marriage is based on the superiority of man and his rights, the inferiority of woman, and woman's obedience to man. A woman must think her man's thoughts, uphold his values, and feel his feelings. She has no right to think, feel, or evaluate for herself.

The basis for relationships in patriarchy is the domination of most of society by a few domineering men, and patriarchal marriage is the model for these relationships. The domineering male gives economic support, protection, and social acceptance of some kind (when he wants to) in exchange for the surrender of the autonomy of his subordinates. Only a privileged man has the right to live the life he is given. Woman does not have a right to live her own life. Nor do lesser classes of men. Living their lives means living for others.

Because anti-feminine sexism is structured into Western (patriarchal) culture—into the language we speak, the movies we watch, the books we read, the hymns we sing, the creeds we recite, the jokes we laugh at—both men and women are trapped in a system that defies political change, religious reforms, or sexual revolutions. Equality in the schools, in the work place, in government, and in the professions does not rid men (or women) of the patriarchal mentality. Wherever women are treated as subordinated, second-class citizens—in the home or in society—patriarchy exists. And whenever men and women are trapped in the dark anti-feminine, anti-sexual mentality of patriarchy, its rebirth is guaranteed. (There is also a growing anti-male sexism among militant feminists which is as distasteful as patriarchy's anti-feminine sexism and which does nothing to extricate women [or men] from the patriarchal system.)

It is important to remember that patriarchy is a historical happening; it is not inevitable or natural or ordained by "God." Nor did it create civilization—invent writing and accounting, learn the course of the stars, develop technology, or create art. Patriarchy has a beginning, a middle, and an end. (See Appendix A, "A Brief History of Patriarchy.")

RATIONAL: See *IRRATIONAL and RATIONAL.*

RAVISH: To fill with strong emotion, especially delight. To enrapture, captivate, charm, enchant, entrance, overjoy, transport. To penetrate a woman (though not necessarily bodily) with passionate, sexual, masculine love for the Feminine. Or, to transport a man by means of the passionate, sexual love of the Feminine for the Masculine.

Antonym: RAPE: To brutalize, molest, harm, exploit. To corrupt, disgrace, debase, degrade, pervert. To crush, damn, desecrate. The immoral carnal penetration of a woman against her will by brute force. Rape is a violation, not only of the body but also of the Spirit, for Spirit is incarnated in a woman's body. Rape is a crime, therefore, against the Holy Spirit, and is unforgivable.

SEX and GENDER

SEX: The biological manifestation and identification of the two halves of being human. Contrary to patriarchal teachings the female is the first sex. Woman comes first; she is not made out of man. The male is the second sex. The male body and male brain develop out of the female's through the secretion of testosterone (see the video tape, "The Sexual Brain"). Sex is also the biological differential by which all organisms are identified. There are only two sexes: female and male.

GENDER: Linguistically and culturally there are three genders: female, male, and neuter. These classifications have nothing to do with sexual characteristics.

Also the classification of the characteristics and behavior of men and women according to socioeconomic and cultural demands. *Gender* is not a definition of either sex. Nor is it a synonym for sex. It is a definition of the roles the sexes must play, roles which their particular societies have defined as right and proper. Often the attitudes and behavior of men and women reflect not the characteristics of their sex but rather the characteristics of gender roles which have been imposed upon them.

SEXUALITY: The sexual nature and capacity of women and men, which they experience and express mentally and spiritually as well as physically. The capacity to embrace fully one's primary sexual nature as well as to integrate one's secondary (or opposite) sexual nature. The capacity to enjoy the opposite sex and one's own sex.

Though human sexual capacity is influenced by a person's individual as well as familial genetic makeup, the psychological effects of early conditioning have more of an influence on the adult's sexual nature. The dark anti-sexual views of Western (patriarchal) society have made it difficult for men and women to enjoy fully their sexual natures: the human experience and expression of the spirit with the body.

Sexuality includes the enjoyment of life moment by moment, and it includes sharing that enjoyment with one's *other.* The enjoyment of sexuality can range from the inhalation of air to sustained orgasmic intensity. It includes the sexual pleasure of loving plants, animals, children, and other adults in a nongenital way. It includes the physical, orgasmic experience of knowing the Divine Being directly. It also includes sex for fun—alone or between two or more adults. It *excludes* sexual duty in marriage, obsequious behavior, pornography, and obsession with cultural idols. The conscious expression of one's sexual nature is above and beyond one's gender roles.

SPIRIT: The irrational principle—the essence, source, and reason—of life and energy. The essence of personality, the reason life exists. Mysterious in nature and ascribable to a divine origin. The animating principle of all people. Spirit is incarnated in the sexual body, though it is different from the body and from the sex of a person. But it is expressed in and through human sexuality. It is characterized by intelligence, emotion, conscious individuality, will, and passion.

SPIRITUALITY: The spiritual nature of women and men. (It would be more accurate to say "spiritkind" than "mankind" when speaking of people.) A person's experience and expression of the irrational, immaterial principle of life in and through the body. Sensitivity to spiritual values. That side of one's personality which keenly appreciates beauty, loveliness, refinement, excellence—whatever exalts the mind and soul and body.

The personal ability to find the irrational or spiritual meaning of everyday life. The ability to understand the spiritual meaning of events and relationships. The ability to express love and joy and to give and receive pleasure. The ability to share whatever one has with another.

Spirituality is that disposition of *the mind* which is characterized by firmness and assertiveness, enterprise and determination, humor and aptitude. That disposition of *the heart* which is characterized by deep feeling, resilience, stamina, resourcefulness, bravery, and endurance. That disposition of *the soul* which is characterized by erotic love, intimacy, autonomy, initiative, spunk, drive, and vigor. An individual's spiritual nature—the personal disposition of mind, heart, and soul—is expressed through the body, through a person's sexuality. "Spirituality" is a source of delight!

THE TOTAL OTHER: See *THE OTHER and THE TOTAL OTHER.*

VULNERABLE: Open and receptive; expectant; yielding. Brave enough to receive the unknown (to be penetrated by the Holy Spirit), to become emotionally involved with others, and to be exposed. Able to open the self to view and allow the self to be seen disarmed and defenseless. Subject to attack; capable of being wounded.

Contrary to popular notions, "vulnerable" does not mean feeble, impotent, dependent, helpless, powerless, weak; or anxious, insecure, impaired, nervous, or uncertain. It means strong, powerful, courageous, courteous, spiritual, sexual, independent (a dependent person is not able to be vulnerable), happy, secure, certain, and capable of being hurt but not destroyed!

RECOMMENDED
FURTHER READING

Encyclopaedia Britannica. 15th ed. 1988. "Syria," "Technology in the Ancient World," "Turkey and Ancient Anatolia," "Steppes, The History of the Eurasian——."

Eisler, Riane. *The Chalice and the Blade*. San Francisco: Harper and Row, Publishers, Inc., 1987.

Fiorenzo, Elisabeth Schüssler. *In Memory of Her: A Feminist Theological Reconstruction*. New York: The Crossroad Publishing Co., 1983.

Forward, Susan, and Joan Torres. *Men Who Hate Women and the Women Who Love Them*. Toronto: Bantam Books, 1986.

Gimbutas, Marija. *The Goddesses and Gods of Old Europe: Myths and Cult Images*. Rev. ed. London: Thames and Hudson Ltd., 1974. Berkeley: University of California, 1982.

Kramer, Samuel Noah. *History Begins at Sumer*. 3rd rev. ed. Falcon's Wing Press, 1956. Philadelphia: The University of Pennsylvania Press, 1981.

Lerner, Gerda. *The Creation of Patriarchy*. New York: Oxford University Press, 1986.

Lesko, Barbara S., ed. *Women's Earliest Records from Ancient Egypt and Western Asia*. Proceedings of a Conference on Women in the Ancient Near East. 5–7 Nov. 1987. Atlanta: Scholars Press, 1989.

Nissen, Hans. J., *The Early History of the Ancient Near East 9000–2000 B.C.* Trans. Elizabeth Lutzeier and Kenneth J. Northcott. Chicago: University of Chicago Press, 1988.

Schaef, Anne Wilson. *Women's Reality*. New York: Harper and Row, Publishers, Inc., 1981.

Stone, Merlin. *Ancient Mirrors of Womanhood: A Treasury of Goddess and Heroine Lore from Around the World*. New Sibylline Books, Inc., 1979. Boston: Beacon Press, 1984.

————. *When God Was a Woman*. London: Virago Ltd., 1976. New York: Harvest/ Harcourt Brace Jovanovich, Publishers, 1978.

Time-Life Books, eds. *The Age of God-Kings. TimeFrame 3000–1500 B.C.* Alexandria: Time-Life Books, 1987.

Walker, Barbara G. *The Crone: Women of Age, Wisdom, and Power.* San Francisco: Harper and Row, Publishers, Inc., 1985.

BIBLIOGRAPHY

Aeschylus, Euripides, Sophocles, Aristophanes. *Seven Famous Greek Plays*. Whitney J. Oates and Eugene O'Neill, Jr., eds. New York: Random House–Vintage Books, 1938.

Berdyaev, Nicolas. *The Destiny of Man*. Trans. Natalie Duddington. London: Geoffrey Bles Ltd., 1955. New York: Torchbook–Harper and Row Publishers, Inc., 1960.

———. *Slavery and Freedom*. Trans. R. M. French. New York: Charles Scribner's Sons, 1944.

Blake, William. "Songs of Innocence," "Songs of Experience," "There Is No Natural Religion," "All Religions Are One," "The Prophetic Books." *The Portable Blake*. New York: The Viking Press, 1946. England: Penguin Books, 1956.

Bonhoeffer, Dietrich. *The Communion of Saints*. Trans. R. Gregor Smith. München: Christian Kaiser Verlag, 1960. New York: Harper and Row Publishers, Inc., 1963.

———. *The Cost of Discipleship*. Rev. ed. München: Chr. Kaiser Verlag, 1937. New York: The Macmillan Co., 1963.

Buber, Martin. *I and Thou*. New York: Charles Scribner's Sons, 1958.

Campbell, Joseph. *The Flight of the Wild Gander: Explorations in the Mythological Dimension*. New York: The Viking Press, 1969.

———. *The Hero with a Thousand Faces*. 2nd ed. New York: Bollingen Foundation, Inc., 1949. Princeton: Princeton University Press, 1968.

———. *The Masks of God: Creative Mythology*. New York: The Viking Press, 1968.

———. *The Masks of God: Occidental Mythology*. New York: The Viking Press, 1964.

———. *The Masks of God: Primitive Mythology*. New York: The Viking Press, 1959.

———, ed. *Myths, Dreams, and Religion*. Series of lectures sponsored by the Society for the Arts, Religion and Contemporary Culture. New York: E. P. Dutton, 1970.

Campbell, Joseph, and Bill Moyers. *The Power of Myth*. New York: Doubleday, 1988.

Castillejo, Irene Claremont de. *Knowing Woman*. G. P. Putnam's Sons, 1973. New York: Harper Colophon Books–Harper and Row, Publishers, Inc. 1974.

Chardin, Pierre Teilhard de. *Letters from a Traveller*. Trans. René Hague, Violet Hammersley, Barbara Wall, Noel Lindsay. Bernard Grasset, 1956. London: William Collins Sons and Co., Ltd., 1962.

———. *The Phenomenon of Man*. Trans. Bernard Wall. Paris: Editions du Senil, 1955. London: Wm. Collins Sons and Co., Ltd., 1959. New York: Harper Torchbook–Harper and Row, Publishers, Inc., 1961.

Chopin, Kate. *The Awakening*. 1899. Bantam Classic, 1981.

Corriere, Richard, and Patrick M. McGrady, Jr. *Life Zones*. New York: William Morrow and Co., Inc., 1986.

Danielsson, Bengt. *Love in the South Seas*. Trans. F. H. Lyon. Honolulu: Mutual Publishing Paperback Series–Tales of the Pacific, 1986.

Dante. *The Divine Comedy*. New York: Vintage Books–Random House, 1950.

Dass, Baba Ram. *Remember Be Here Now*. San Cristobal: Lama Foundation, 1971.

Dodds, E. R. *The Greeks and the Irrational*. Berkeley: University of California Press, 1951.

Dostoyevsky, Fyodor. *The Brothers Karamazov*. Trans. Constance Garnett. New York: The Modern Library–Random House, Inc., n.d.

Eliot, T. S. *The Cocktail Party*. New York: Harcourt, Brace and Co., 1950.

———. "Murder in the Cathedral." *The Complete Plays of T. S. Eliot*. New York: Harcourt, Brace and World, Inc., 1935.

———. *Collected Poems 1909–1962*. New York: Harcourt, Brace and World, Inc., 1934.

Erikson, Erik H. *Dimensions of a New Identity: The 1973 Jefferson Lectures on the Humanities*. New York: W. W. Norton and Co., Inc., 1974.

Fraser, Antonia. *Mary Queen of Scots*. England: Weidenfeld and Nicolson, 1969. New York: Dell Publishing Co., Inc., 1971.

Fromm, Erich. *The Art of Loving*. New York: Harper and Row, 1956. New York: Harper Colophon Books–Harper and Row Publishers, Inc., 1962.

———. *Escape from Freedom*. New York: Holt, Rinehart and Winston, 1941.

———. *The Forgotten Language*. New York: Grove Press, Inc., 1951.

———. *Man for Himself*. New York: Holt, Rinehart and Winston, 1947.

Gibran, Kahlil. *The Prophet*. 1923. New York: Alfred A. Knopf, Inc. 1971.

———. *Spirits Rebellious*. Trans. H. M. Nahmad. New York: Alfred A. Knopf, Inc., 1948.

Graves, Robert. *The Golden Ass: A New Translation by Robert Graves from Apuleius*. New York: Farrar, Straus and Giroux, 1951.

————. *The Greek Myths.* 2 vols. Rev. ed. Middlesex: Penguin Books Ltd., 1955.

————. *The White Goddess.* Amended and enlarged, 1966. New York: Farrar, Straus and Giroux, 1948.

Hamilton, Edith. *The Echo of Greece.* New York: W. W. Norton and Co., Inc., 1957.

————. *The Greek Way.* New York: W. W. Norton and Co., Inc., 1930.

Harding, M. Esther. *The Way of All Women.* G. P. Putnam's Sons, 1970. New York: Harper Colophon Books—Harper and Row, Publishers, Inc., 1975.

Hemingway, Ernest. *Across the River and into the Trees.* New York: Charles Scribner's Sons, 1950.

————. *For Whom the Bell Tolls.* New York: Charles Scribner's Sons, 1940.

————. *A Moveable Feast.* New York: Charles Scribner's Sons, 1964.

————. *The Old Man and the Sea.* New York: Charles Scribner's Sons, 1952.

————. *To Have and Have Not.* New York: Charles Scribner's Sons, 1937.

————. *The Sun Also Rises.* New York: Charles Scribner's Sons, 1926.

————. *Winner Take Nothing.* New York: Charles Scribner's Sons, 1933.

Hibben, Frank C. Lectures. *Classical Archaeology.* University of New Mexico. Albuquerque, 1952.

————. Lectures. *Anthropology I.* University of New Mexico. Albuquerque, 1952.

————. Lectures. *European Prehistory.* University of New Mexico. Albuquerque, 1953.

Homer. *The Iliad.* Trans. Richmond Lattimore. Chicago: University of Chicago Press, 1951.

————. *The Odyssey.* Trans. Richmond Lattimore. New York: Harper and Row, Publishers, Inc., 1975.

Hyde, Lilian S. *Favorite Greek Myths.* Boston: D. C. Heath and Co., 1904.

Jacobsen, Thorkild. *The Treasures of Darkness: A History of Mesopotamian Religion.* New Haven: Yale University Press, 1976.

Jaynes, Julian. *The Origin of Consciousness in the Breakdown of the Bicameral Mind.* Boston: Houghton Mifflin Co., 1976.

Johnson, Robert A. *He.* Prussia: Religious Publishing Co., 1974. New York: Perennial Library edition—Harper and Row, Publishers, Inc., 1977.

————. *She.* Prussia: Religious Publishing Co., 1976. New York: Perennial Library edition—Harper and Row Publishers, Inc., 1977.

————. *We.* New York: Harper and Row, Publishers, Inc., 1983.

Jones, Ernest. *The Life and Work of Sigmund Freud.* Basic Books Publishing Co., Inc., 1961. Garden City, NY: Anchor Books—Doubleday and Co., Inc., 1963.

Jung, Carl G., et al. *Man and His Symbols.* London: Aldus Books, Ltd., 1964. New York: Dell Publishing Co., 1968.

Kaam, Adrian van. *Dynamics of Spiritual Self Direction.* Denville, NJ: Dimension Books, 1976.

Kazantzakis, Nikos. *The Last Temptation of Christ.* Trans. P. A. Bien. New York: Simon and Schuster, 1960.

———. *Zorba, The Greek.* Trans. Carl Wildman. London: Faber and Faber, 1961.

Keats, John. "To Autumn," "Ode on a Grecian Urn," "Ode on Indolence," "Ode to a Nightingale." *The Complete Poetry and Selected Prose of John Keats.* Ed. Harold Edgar Briggs. New York: The Modern Library–Random House, 1951.

Kelsey, Morton T. *Healing and Christianity.* New York: Harper and Row, Publishers, Inc., 1973.

———. *The Other Side of Silence.* New York: Paulist Press, 1976.

Kierkegaard, Søren. *Works of Love.* Trans. Howard and Edna Hong. New York: Harper and Brothers, Publishers, 1962.

King, Martin Luther Jr. *Strength to Love.* New York: Harper and Row, 1963. New York: Pocket Books, 1964.

Kott, Jan. *The Eating of the Gods.* Trans. Boleslaw Taborski and Edward Czerwinski. New York: Random House, Inc., 1973. New York: Vintage Books–Random House, Inc., 1974.

Kramer, Samuel Noah. *History Begins at Sumer.* 3rd rev.ed. Falcon's Wing Press, 1956. Philadelphia: The University of Pennsylvania Press, 1981.

———. *The Sumerians: Their History, Culture, and Character.* Chicago: The University of Chicago Press, 1963.

Laing, R. D. *The Facts of Life.* New York: Pantheon Books–Random House, 1976.

Lewis, C. S. *A Grief Observed.* England: Faber and Faber Ltd. New York: The Seabury Press, 1961.

———. *The Problem of Pain.* New York: The Macmillan Co., 1962.

———. *The Screwtape Letters.* Rev. ed. New York: The Macmillan Co., 1957.

———. *The World's Last Night and Other Essays.* New York: Harcourt, Brace and Co., 1952–60.

Lindbergh, Anne Morrow. *Gift from the Sea.* New York: Pantheon Books–Random House, 1955.

Luke, Helen M. *Dark Wood to White Rose: A Study of Meanings in Dante's Divine Comedy.* Pecos, NM: Dove Publication, 1975.

———. *The Inner Story: Myth and Symbol in the Bible and Literature.* New York: The Crossroad Publishing Co., 1982.

———. *Woman, Earth and Spirit: The Feminine in Symbol and Myth.* New York: The Crossroad Publishing Co., 1981.

Lund, R. D. *Development and Plasticity of the Brain.* New York: Oxford University Press, 1978.

Luthman, Shirley Gehrke. *Energy and Personal Power.* San Rafael: Mehetabul and Co., 1982.

Mann, Thomas. *Doctor Faustus.* Trans. H. T. Lowe-Porter. Stockholm: Bermann-Fischer Verlag A.B., 1947. New York: Vintage Books–Random House, 1971.

Maslow, Abraham H. *Toward a Psychology of Being.* New York: Van Nostrand Reinhold Co., 1968.

May, Rollo. *The Courage to Create.* New York: W. W. Norton and Co., Inc., 1975.

———. *Love and Will.* New York: W. W. Norton and Co., Inc., 1969.

———. *Man's Search for Himself.* New York: W. W. Norton and Co., Inc., 1953. New York: Signet–The New American Library, Inc., 1967.

———. *The Meaning of Anxiety.* New York: Ronald Press Co., 1950.

———. *Power and Innocence.* New York: W. W. Norton and Co., Inc., 1972.

McCombe, Elizabeth. Lectures. *Bible CPII.* The Masters School. Dobbs Ferry, NY, 1949–50.

Mead, Margaret. *Male and Female.* New York: William Morrow and Co., Inc., 1949. New York: Morrow Quill Paperbacks, 1976.

Nilsson, Martin P. *Greek Folk Religion.* New York: Columbia University Press, 1940. Pennsylvania Paperback, 1972.

———. *Greek Piety.* Trans. Herbert Jennings Rose. New York: W. W. Norton and Co., Inc., 1969.

Noble, Vicki. *Motherpeace: A Way to the Goddess through Myth, Art, and Tarot.* San Francisco: Harper and Row, Publishers, Inc., 1983.

O'Neill, Nena, and George O'Neill. *Open Marriage.* New York: M. Evans and Co., Inc., 1972.

———. *Shifting Gears.* New York: M. Evans and Co., Inc., 1974.

Pagels, Elaine. *The Gnostic Gospels.* New York: Random House, Inc., 1979. New York: Vintage Books–Random House, Inc., 1981.

Paul, Jordan, and Margaret Paul. *Do I Have to Give Up Me to Be Loved By You?* Minneapolis: CompCare Publications, 1983.

Plato. *The Republic.* Trans. B. Jowett. New York: Modern Library–Random House, 1987.

Post, Laurens van der. *A Story Like the Wind.* Hogarth Press, 1972. England: Penguin Books, 1974.

Rehfuss, Amy. Lectures. *Bible I.* The Masters School. Dobbs Ferry, NY, 1947–48.

———. Lectures. *Bible CPI.* The Masters School. Dobbs Ferry, NY, 1948–49.

Rogers, Carl R. *On Becoming a Person.* Boston: Sentry–Houghton Mifflin Co., 1961.

Rogers, Carl R., and Barry Stevens. *Person To Person: The Problem of Being Human.* Lafayette, CA: Real People Press, 1967.

Rubin, Theodore I., and Eleanor Rubin. *Compassion and Self-Hate.* New York: David McKay Co., Inc., 1975.

Saggs, H. W. F. *The Encounter with the Divine in Mesopotamia and Israel.* London: The Athlone Press–University of London, 1978.

Sanford, Agnes. *Creation Waits.* Plainfield: Logos International, n.d.

———. *Sealed Orders.* Plainfield: Logos International, 1972.

Sanford, John A. *Dreams: God's Forgotten Language.* Zürich: Rascher Verlag. New York: J. B. Lippincott Co., 1968.

———. *Dreams and Healing.* New York: Paulist Press, 1978.

———. *Healing and Wholeness.* New York: Paulist Press, 1977.

———. *The Kingdom Within.* New York: Paulist Press, 1970.

Seton, Lloyd. *The Archaeology of Mesopotamia.* 1978. Rev. ed. New York: Thames and Hudson, Inc., 1984.

The Sexual Brain. Videocassette. Princeton, N.J.: Films for the Humanities and Sciences, 1988. 28 min.

Shakespeare, William. *The Complete Works of William Shakespeare.* Ed. William Aldis Wright. Garden City, NY: Doubleday and Co., Inc., 1936.

Shaw, Bernard. "Candida," "Saint Joan." *Seven Plays.* New York: Dodd, Mead, and Co., 1951.

Stapleton, Ruth Carter. *The Gift of Inner Healing.* Waco, TX: Word Books, Publisher, 1976.

Stone, Irving. *Love Is Eternal.* Garden City, NY: Doubleday and Co., Inc., 1954.

———. *The Passions of the Mind.* Garden City, NY: Doubleday and Co., Inc., 1971.

———. *Those Who Love: A Biographical Novel of Abigail and John Adams.* Garden City, NY: Doubleday and Co., Inc., 1965.

Strayer, Maude-Elizabeth. Lectures. *Bible IV.* The Masters School. Dobbs Ferry, NY, 1950–51.

Tanner, Nancy Makepeace. *On Becoming Human.* New York: University of Cambridge–Press Syndicate, 1981.

Temple, William. *Readings in St. John's Gospel.* Rev. ed. London: Macmillan and Co., Ltd., 1939.

Tillich, Paul. *The Courage to Be.* New Haven: Yale University Press, 1952.

———. *The Eternal Now.* New York: Charles Scribner's Sons, 1956.

———. *Morality and Beyond.* New York: Harper and Row Publishers, Inc., 1963.

———. *The New Being.* New York: Charles Scribner's Sons, 1955.

———. *Reason and Revelation, Being and God.* 3 vols. Chicago: The University of Chicago Press, 1951.

———. *The Shaking of the Foundations.* New York: Charles Scribner's Sons, 1948.

Tournier, Paul. *The Gift of Feelings.* Trans. Edwin Hudson. Neuchâtel: Delachaux et Niestlé, 1979. Atlanta: John Knox Press, 1981.

————. *Guilt and Grace: A Psychological Study.* Trans. Arthur W. Heathcote. New York: Harper and Row Publishers, Inc., 1962.

————. *The Meaning of Persons.* Trans. Edwin Hudson. New York: Harper and Row, Publishers, Inc., 1957.

————. *Secrets.* Trans. Joe Embry. Geneva: Éditions Labor et Fides, 1963. Richmond: John Knox Press, 1964.

————. *The Strong and the Weak.* Trans. Edwin Hudson. Neuchâtel: Delachaux et Niestlé, 1948. Philadelphia: The Westminster Press, 1963.

Ulanov, Ann Belford. *The Feminine in Jungian Psychology and in Christian Theology.* Evanston: Northwestern University Press, 1971.

Underhill, Evelyn. *Concerning the Inner Life with the House of the Soul.* London: Methuen and Co., Ltd, 1947.

————. *Mysticism: A Study in the Nature and Development of Man's Spiritual Consciousness.* Rev. ed. New York: E. P. Dutton and Co., Inc., 1930.

Wilde, Oscar. *De Profundis.* New York: Vintage Books–Random House, 1964.

Wolkstein, Diane, and Samuel Noah Kramer. *Inanna, Queen of Heaven and Earth: Her Stories and Hymns from Sumer.* New York: Harper and Row, Publishers, Inc., 1983.

Woodman, Marion. *Addiction to Perfection.* Toronto: Inner City Books, 1982.

INDEX

Spirit:
    bonding with body and mind, 108
    defined, 363
    experiencing the, 104, 108
    in patriarchy, as male only, 259-260
    reclaiming, 258, 271-279
    separation from body, 103-104, 107, 110
    as source of erotic love, 267
Spiritual power, 256
Spirituality, defined, 363
Stress levels, and gender roles, 217-218
Subordination of women:
    as result of patriarchal system, 47-50
    of sexuality, 73-75
Sun rams, as male consciousness, 224
Support groups, limited value of, 196
Symbols, role of, 1

Tasks, Psyche's four:
    descent into hell, 3, 21-22, 174
    filling the crystal vessel, 3, 19-22, 173-174, 255-289
    gathering the golden fleece, 3, 19-20, 173, 223-254
    role of, 178-183
    sorting the seeds, 3, 19, 172-173, 185-222
Thanatos, god of death, 64, 85, 91
Time, regaining sense of, 283
Total other, defined, 359

Unconscious:
    defined, 351, 352
    denial of, 191
    forgetfulness as symbol of, 259
    and remembering, 256-257
    sorting seeds of, 198
Unconsciousness:
    containing irrationality, 260
    defined, 352
    forgetfulness as symbol for, 259

Violence:
    not present in male sexuality, 159
    and patriarchal values, 4-5, 72
    powerlessness as source of, 226, 229-230
Vulnerable, defined, 364

Wants, distinguished from needs, 144
War, and masculine power, 72
Wedding, of Psyche and Eros, 336-337
Whore, as patriarchal icon, 31, 34, 40, 267

MARY HUGH SCOTT

Mary Hugh Scott writes about the problems of being human—the hopes and fears of men and women face-to-face with the changing reality of a world on the brink of a new century.

Mary Hugh has acquired a unique ability to see reality as it is—not as it is taught by anyone claiming to have a monopoly on truth and/or reality. Spiced with humor and imagination and leavened with love, *THE PASSION OF BEING WOMAN* explores a revolutionary solution that will take women and men beyond the impasse of both the women's and men's movements.

Mary Hugh Scott lives in Aspen, Colorado with her husband, Doctor Russell Scott, and their grandson, Andrew. She is a graduate of the Masters School, Dobbs Ferry, New York.

Order Form

How to order additional copies of THE PASSION OF BEING WOMAN:

Please send me _____ copy(ies) of THE PASSION OF BEING WOMAN at $12.95 each:

Book total ($12.95 x number of copies)	$ _____
Postage & Handling ($2.00 for the first book, $.50 for each additional book to the same address)	$ _____
Applicable state sales tax	$ _____
TOTAL (Amount of check enclosed)	$ _____

Colorado residents please add appropriate sales tax. Please allow 6 weeks for delivery. Prices are subject to change without notice.

Please print or type the information below:

Name _____

Address _____

City _____

State _____ Zip _____

Phone _____ (For order clarification only)

☐ Please send me your latest catalog.

> Send this order form and your check to:
> MacMurray & Beck Communications
> P.O. Box 4257
> Aspen, CO 81612